IMAGES
of America

EXPLORING THE ST. JOHNS RIVER

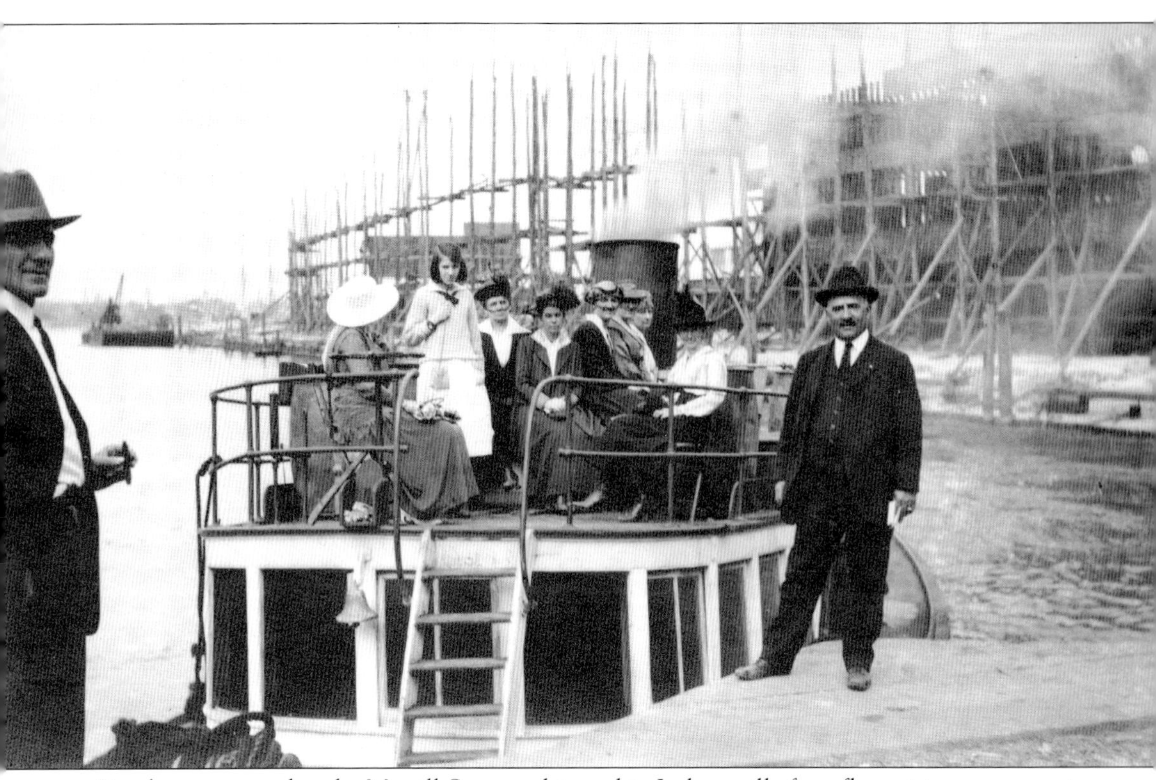

People are pictured at the Merrill-Stevens shipyard in Jacksonville for a flag raising ceremony in 1918. The shipyard was on the St. Johns River near the present-day area of TIAA Bank Field. (State Archives of Florida.)

On the Cover: A boat travels under the Main Street Bridge on the St. Johns River in the 1960s.

IMAGES
of America

EXPLORING THE ST. JOHNS RIVER

Andrew R. Nicholas

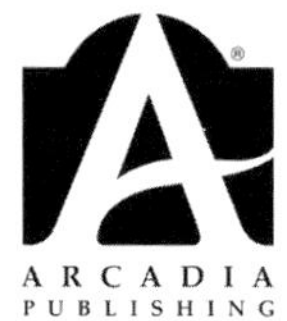

ARCADIA
PUBLISHING

ISBN 978-1-4671-0932-1

Published by Arcadia Publishing
Charleston, South Carolina

Printed in the United States of America

Library of Congress Control Number: 2022948152

For all general information, please contact Arcadia Publishing:
Telephone 843-853-2070
Fax 843-853-0044
E-mail sales@arcadiapublishing.com
For customer service and orders:
Toll-Free 1-888-313-2665

Visit us on the Internet at www.arcadiapublishing.com

To the St. Johns River.

Contents

ACKNOWLEDGMENTS

I want to thank the following people and organizations for helping me to create this publication: Jacksonville Historical Society, University of North Florida, University of South Florida, Clay County Historical Archives, West Volusia Historical Society, Stetson University, Florida Historical Society, David Taylor, Carlton Higginbotham, Rhonda Lovett, Marlene Sparks, Alice Kiger, Jennifer Lanam, Greg Pflug, Thomas Lynch, Brad Shubert, Ty Bednarski, Sarah A. Nicholas, and my mother, Lisa Moody.

INTRODUCTION

The St. Johns River is the longest river in Florida. It flows north beginning in the Blue Cypress Conservation Area and the surrounding marshes of Indian River County. The river begins in central Florida at the Upper Basin or Upper St. Johns River, where it mostly consists of marshes. Its average width in the Upper Basin is around 200 feet. As the river flows north, it gradually widens and flows into several large, interconnected lakes: Lakes Washington, Winder, Poinsett, Harney, Jesup, and Monroe. The lakes region of the river is called the Middle Basin. Flowing north out of Lake Monroe, the river reaches the second largest lake in Florida, Lake George. This area consists of the manatee-loved Blue Springs, Ocala National Forest, and Hontoon Island. North of Lake George is the Ocklawaha River, the principal tributary of the St. Johns. After the Ocklawaha River and Dunn's Creek flow into the St. Johns, it continues to widen, flowing north towards Palatka. The section from Palatka to the Atlantic is called the Lower Basin, or Lower St. Johns River. The Lower Basin is where the river is at its widest, excluding the lakes, reaching an average width of over two miles.

The human history of the St. Johns River began with the Native Americans. The Timucua were the main group that inhabited the region of the river. When Europeans first reached the area in the 16th century, they encountered the Timucua. Gradually, the Timucua declined as Europeans settled. The Seminole were another group that settled on the St. Johns River. They used the name Welaka to refer to the St. Johns, and for the narrow part of the river at Palatka, they called it Pilo-taikaita. A similar part of the river where it narrows north of Palatka was called Wacca Pilatka, which means "cow's crossing" or "Cow Ford."

The colonial era of the St. Johns River consisted of defense and offense among the three main European powers of Spain, France, and Great Britain. France named the river the May River and established Fort Caroline somewhere near St. Johns Bluff. The short-lived French presence in Florida was replaced with Spain, which cemented itself with missions, forts, and place names that still exist. One such mission was the San Juan del Puerto at the mouth of the St. Johns River, which is long gone except for the legacy of naming the entire river after it. The British presence on the St. Johns also left a legacy of place names, such as Fort George and Lake George. The United States acquired Florida from Spain in 1822 and with it a peninsula full of history and the unique St. Johns River. Americans began settling on the St. Johns by establishing such places as Mayport, Jacksonville, Orange Park, Green Cove Springs, Palatka, and Sanford.

The St. Johns River flows north, but the flow of this work begins at the Atlantic, traveling west toward Jacksonville and then south all the way to central Florida. The final chapter ends at Blue Cypress Lake, the headwaters of the St. Johns. Edward A. Mueller wrote *Along the St. Johns and Ocklawaha Rivers* in 1999 as part of the Images of America series. I tried to the best of my abilities to not duplicate photographs that he used. Mueller's book focuses more on steamships, and it is suggested that the reader also purchase his work to learn more about the region, including the Ocklawaha River.

For my research into the history of the St. Johns River, I read several books, articles, and online posts from verified historians on the subject. *Jacksonville: Riverport-Seaport* by George E. Buker was used as a reference for the Lower Basin of the St. Johns River. Prof. Daniel Shafer went to extraordinary lengths in writing about creeks, tributaries, and historical areas of the St. Johns. Most of the information on the historical settlements on the creeks and tributaries in this book is from the works of Shafer.

Brendan Rivers's article "A Century of Altering the St. Johns River has Left Jacksonville More Vulnerable to Flooding" was used for research on how the river has changed in Jacksonville, including interesting numbers such as depth level and width. Other material used in this publication is from the Florida Fish and Wildlife Conservation Commission, the St. Johns River Water Management District, and St. Johns Riverkeeper.

One

Enter the St. Johns River

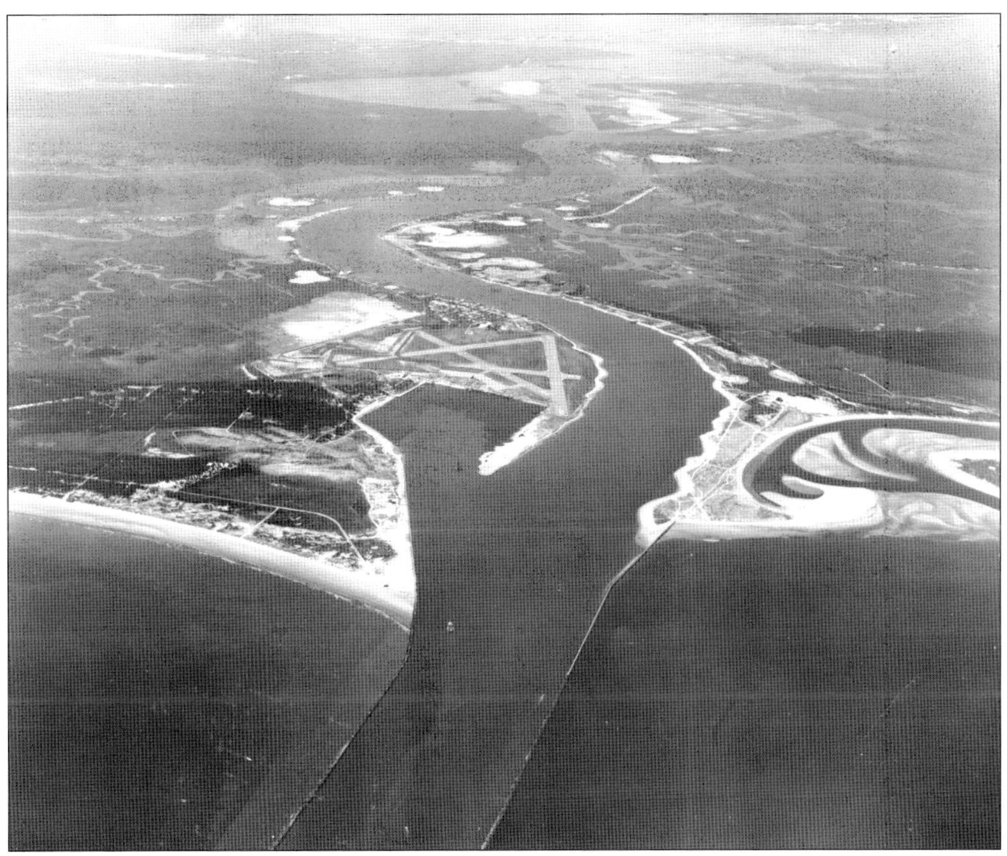

The St. Johns River is over 300 miles long and is the longest river in Florida. Its headwaters are at Blue Cypress Lake in central Florida. The river is unique in that it flows north from Blue Cypress Lake all the way out to the Atlantic Ocean east of Jacksonville. This aerial view shows the mouth of the river in 1951. (Jacksonville Historical Society.)

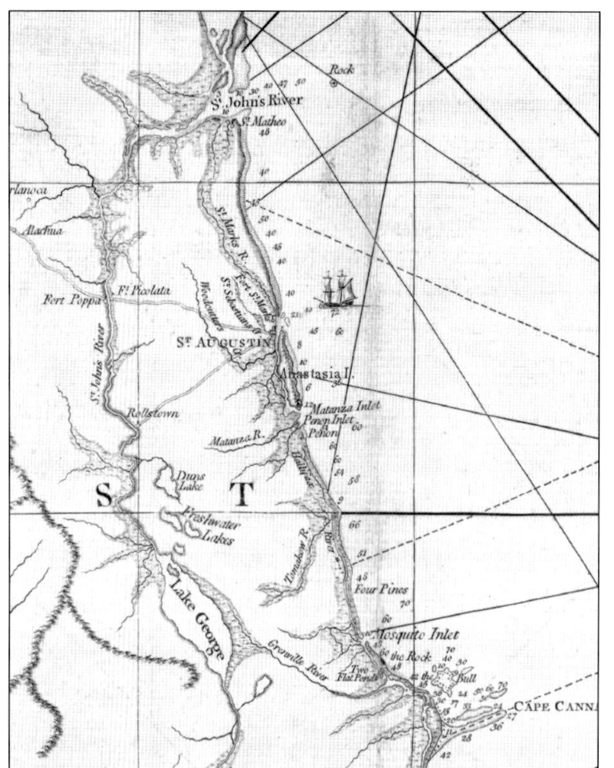

This is a portion of a map from 1775 by Thomas Jefferys. The Lower St. Johns River can be seen from the Atlantic south to Lake George. The Spanish forts of Fort Picolata and Fort Poppa on the river can be seen north of the small British settlement of Rollestown. At this time, St. Augustine was the only major settlement in north Florida. (Library of Congress.)

In 1562, Frenchman Jean Ribault led an expedition to the New World to establish a French colony. Ribault left France on February 18 and arrived at the mouth of the St. Johns River three months later. Because he found the river in May, Ribault called it the River May. This detail from LeMoyne's 1590 map shows a variety of rivers, including the May, near center. The May is presumed to be the St. Johns. (Library of Congress.)

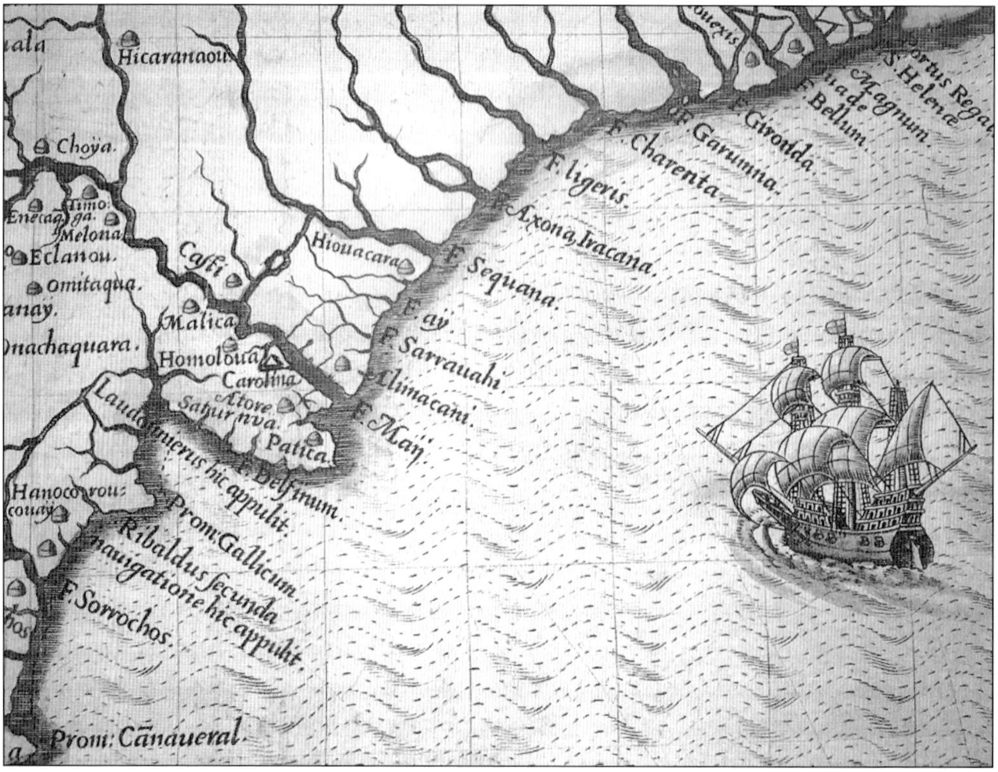

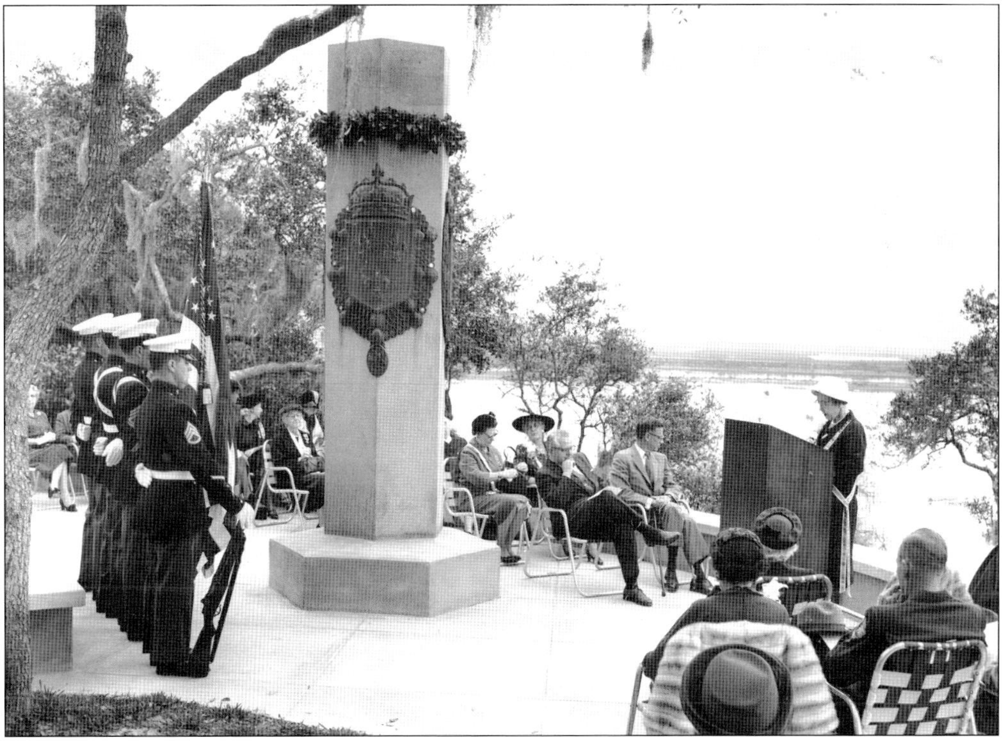

Ribault erected a stone monument at an unknown location near the mouth of the St. Johns River and claimed the land for France. His second in command, René Goulaine de Laudonnière, later visited this area in 1564. Athore, son of the Timucuan king Saturiwa, showed Laudonnière Ribault's stone monument, which was still standing. Unfortunately, Ribault's original stone monument has been lost to history. In 1924, a replica was erected near present-day Naval Air Station (NAS) Mayport. It was moved to its present location on St. Johns Bluff near the river in 1958. This photograph shows the Ribault Monument on St. Johns Bluff in 1958. (Jacksonville Historical Society.)

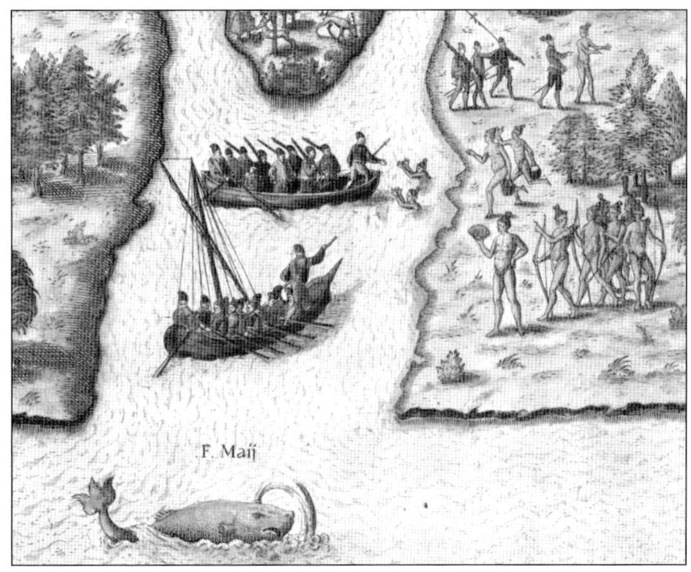

Jacquese Le Moyne was an artist who accompanied Rene Goulaine de Laudonnière on his 1564 expedition to the area. Le Moyne painted what he saw on the expedition, including the Timucuans and the River May. Belgian artist Theodor de Bry made copies of Le Moyne's work from the 1564 expedition in the form of engravings. This engraving, printed in 1591, shows the French traveling the River May in 1564, encountering the Timucua. (Library of Congress.)

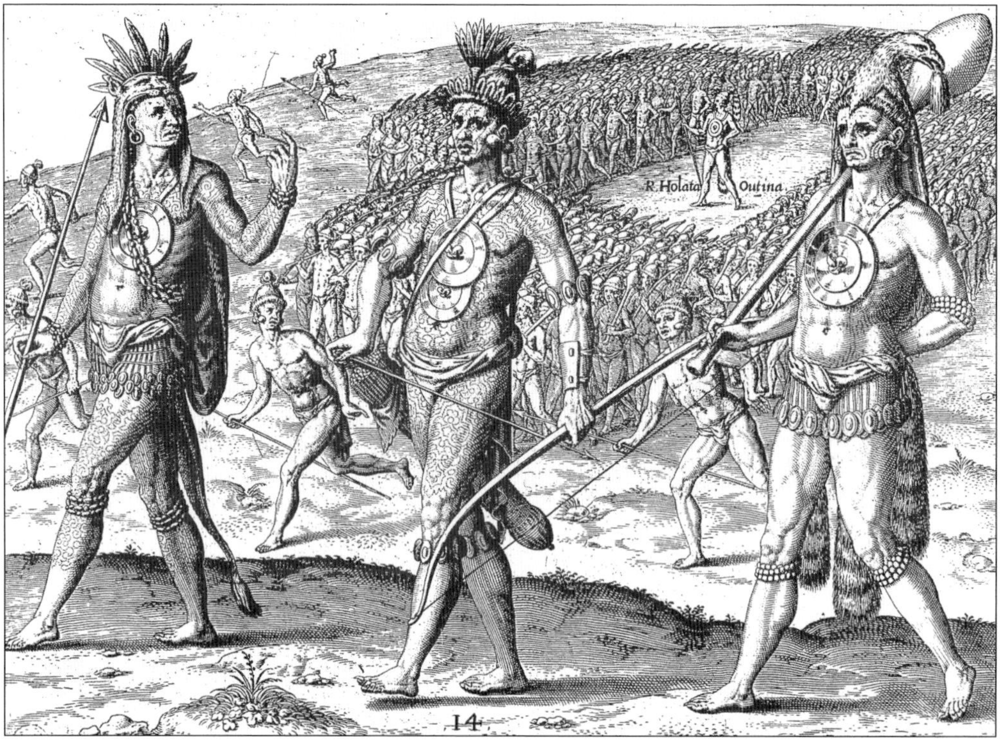

The Timucua lived in north Florida and southeastern Georgia. They spoke dialects of the same language but lived in separate chiefdoms. They used agriculture, but also hunted and fished. When Europeans first arrived in Florida, the number of Timucua was estimated to be 200,000. They were the first Native Americans that early European explorers encountered when they came to Florida in the 16th century. This sketch by De Bry shows Timucua preparing for war near the St. Johns River. Ribault and Laudonnière had encountered the Saturiwa chiefdom, which was near the mouth of the river. The Timucua gradually declined by the early 1700s. After Spain ceded Florida to Great Britain in 1763, they transferred the last remaining Timucua to Cuba. (Library of Congress.)

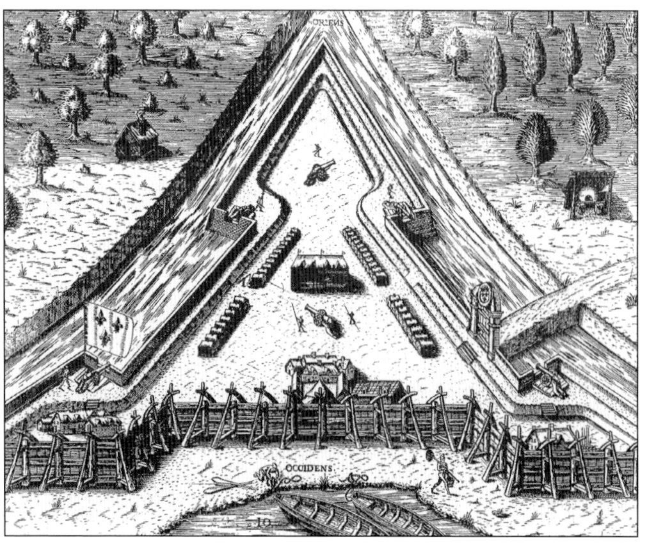

René Goulaine de Laudonnière led a new expedition with around 200 settlers in 1564, landing in the area where Ribault had been in 1562. On June 22, Laudonnière established Fort Caroline, named after King Charles IX of France. The Spanish at Saint Augustine marched overland, destroyed the fort, and killed the majority of the settlers. The original location of Fort Caroline has never been found. After the Spanish destroyed the fort, they renamed the river San Mateo. (Library of Congress.)

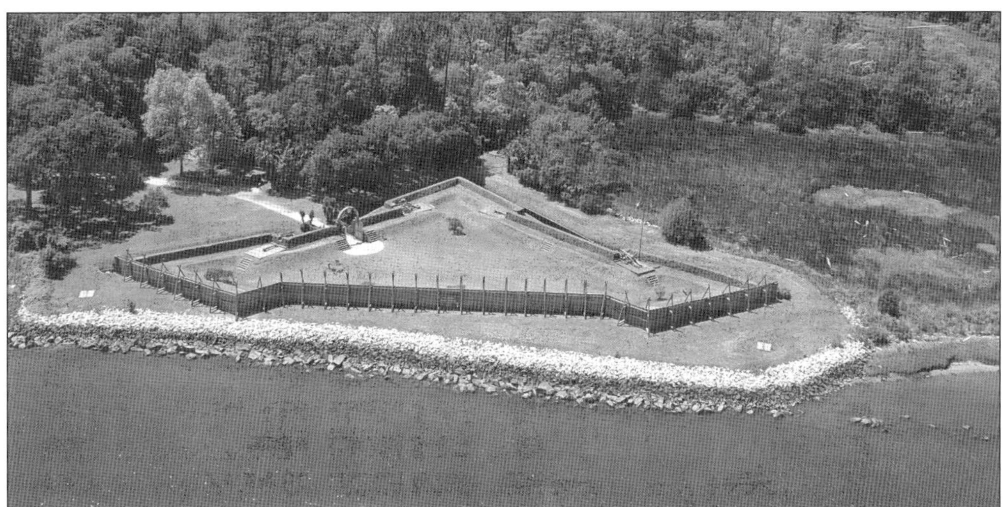

In 1964, the National Park Service created a replica of the original Fort Caroline at Fort Caroline National Memorial, believed to be the general area where the original fort was located. The replica fort did not last long before Hurricane Dora destroyed it later that year. A second replica was built in the same area and continues to stand today. This aerial photograph was taken in 1991. (University of North Florida.)

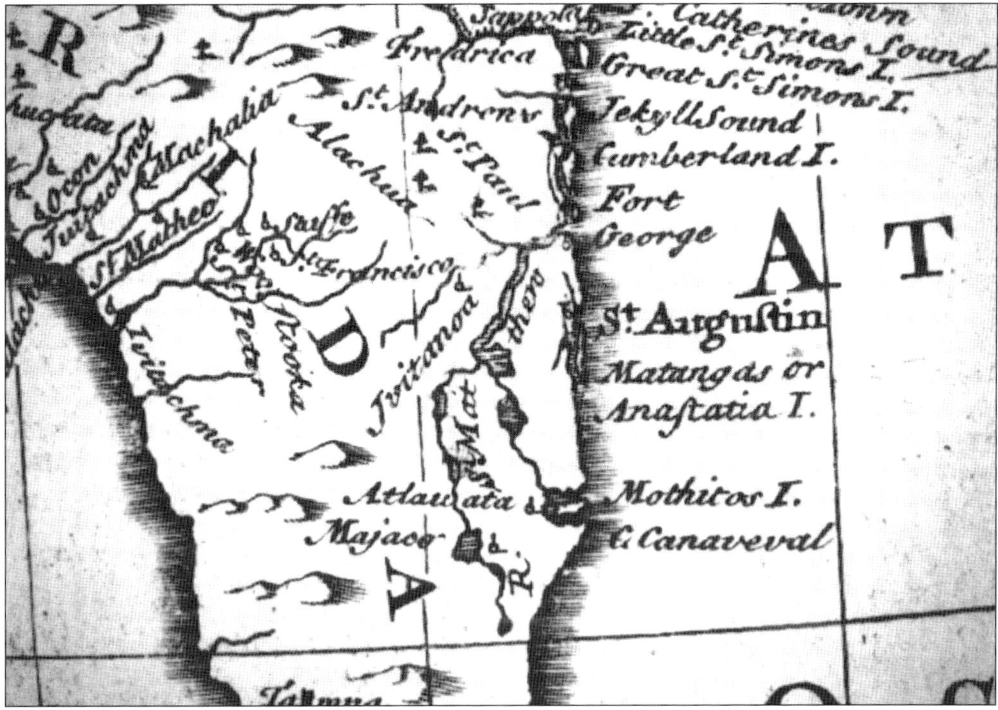

In 1736, James Oglethorpe, the founder of Georgia, established a fort on Fort George Island called Fort Saint George. It was on a hill overlooking Talbot Island by the Fort George River. The purpose of the fort was to guard Georgia's southern frontier against the Spanish in Florida. Although the location of Fort Saint George is lost to history, the name ended up becoming the name of the island. This detail of a 1752 map of Florida shows Fort George near the mouth of the St. Johns River, which is labelled R. Mateo. (Library of Congress.)

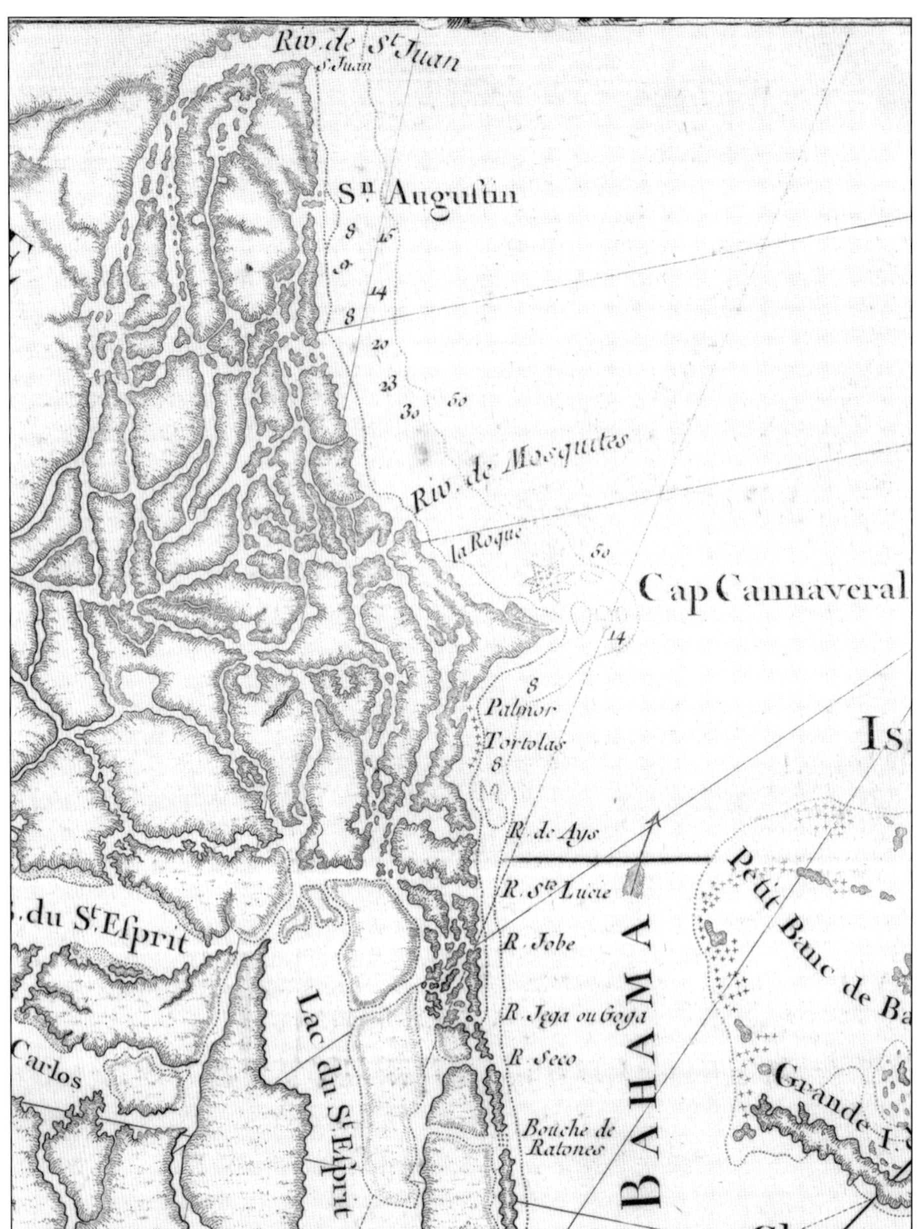

A Franciscan Spanish mission called San Juan del Puerto was founded near the mouth of the St. Johns River on Fort George Island around 1587. Like other Spanish missions, it was established to convert the Timucua to Catholicism, pacify them, and integrate European culture into their society. Francisco Pareja was a prominent Franciscan who stayed at San Juan del Puerto. He is best known for writing down the Timucua language and creating religious texts in both Spanish and Timucua. The mission was abandoned around 1736 due to raids from Native Americans and English colonists. The structures are long gone, and archaeologists have found only a scant amount of artifacts. However, the writings of Pareja and Franciscan friars show the importance of the mission. Its Spanish name, San Juan, or Saint John in English, later became the name of the St. Johns River. This detail of a 1765 map by Jacques Nicolas Bellin, although inaccurate, shows the northeast coast of Florida with the St. Johns River as Rio de St Juan. (Library of Congress.)

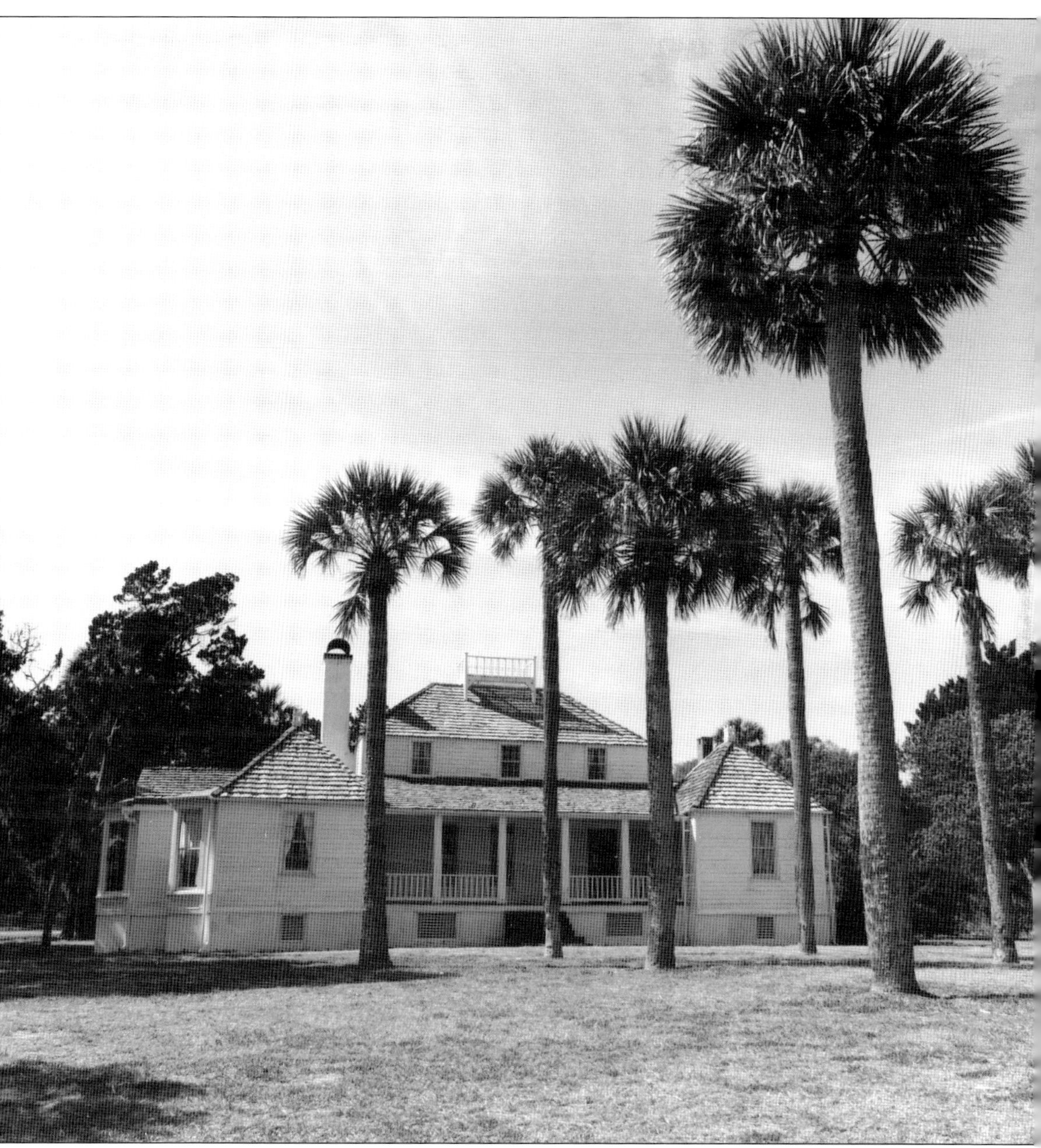

Zephaniah Kingsley was born on December 4, 1765, in Bristol, England. He became successful in the slave trade and shipping industry. In 1803, Kingsley acquired the Laurel Grove plantation in present-day Orange Park, where he relocated his slaves from South Carolina. In 1806, he bought a 13-year-old slave girl named Anna Madgigne Jai in Havana, Cuba, where he married her in an African ceremony. They later started a family together. Returning to Florida, Kingsley relied on Anna to run his Laurel Grove plantation. Kingsley and Anna settled on Fort George Island in 1814 and acquired a plantation later called the Kingsley Plantation. This photograph shows the plantation in 1991. It is on the northern end of Fort George Island overlooking the Fort George River. (University of North Florida.)

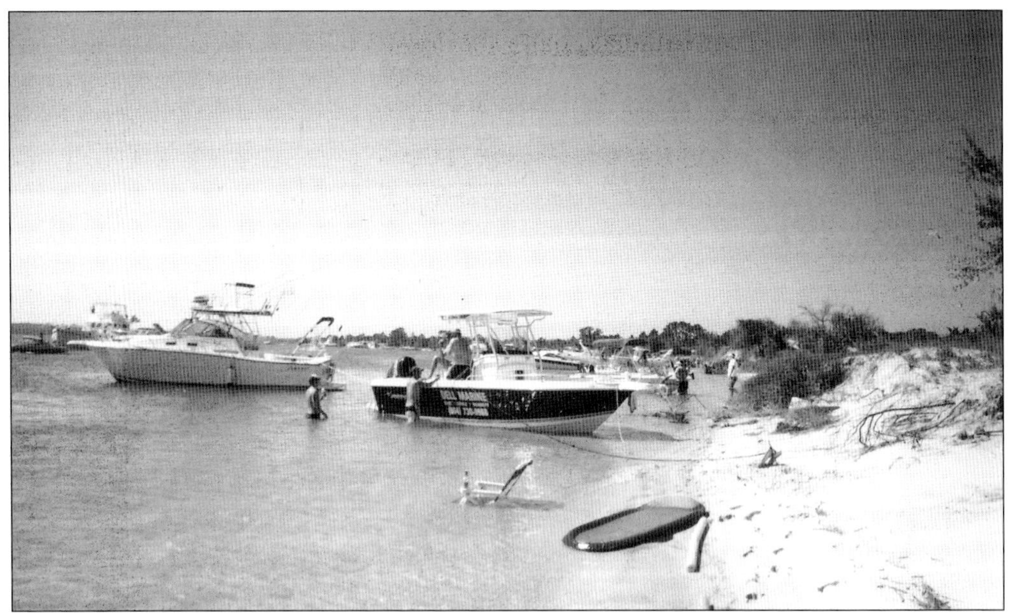

Fort George Island is a common destination for boaters to beach or anchor on the sandbars for recreation. The St. Johns River flows by the southern end of the island, making it easily accerssible for boaters. The river also flows on the left side of the island where it becomes Clapboard Creek. This photograph shows boaters at Fort George Island in 2004. The boat at center has an advertisement for Dell Marine, a local boat dealership and service center. (Andrew R. Nicholas.)

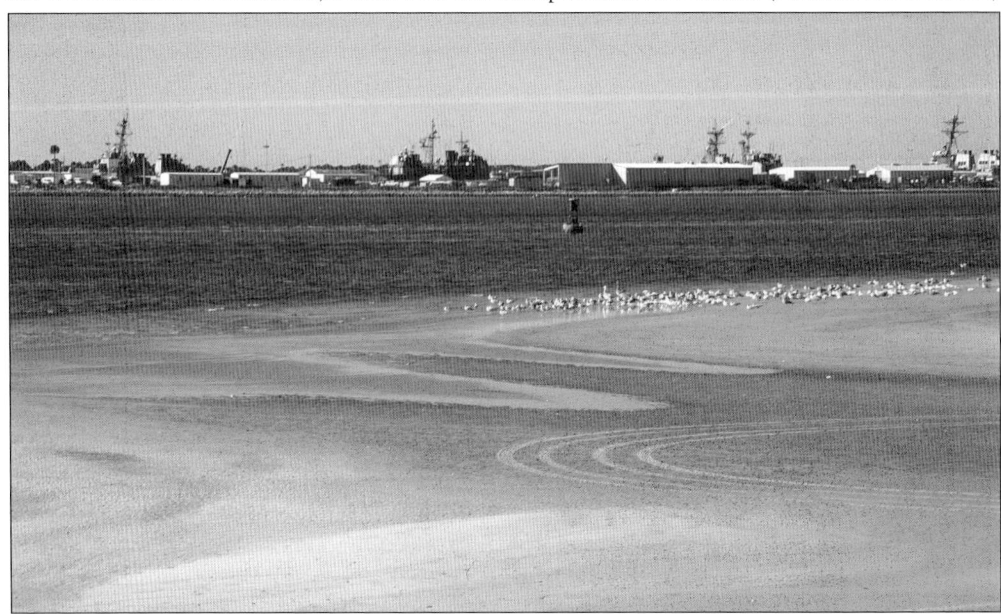

The Huguenots were French Protestants in the 16th and 17th centuries. They were persecuted because they were Protestants in a Catholic country. Jean Ribault was one Huguenot who ventured to the New World for religious freedom. Huguenot Memorial Park is at the mouth of the St. Johns River on the peninsula by the north jetties. The name is fitting, because Ribault would have sailed past this area in the 16th century. This photograph was taken in 2003 at Huguenot Memorial Park looking toward the St. Johns River and NAS Mayport. (University of North Florida.)

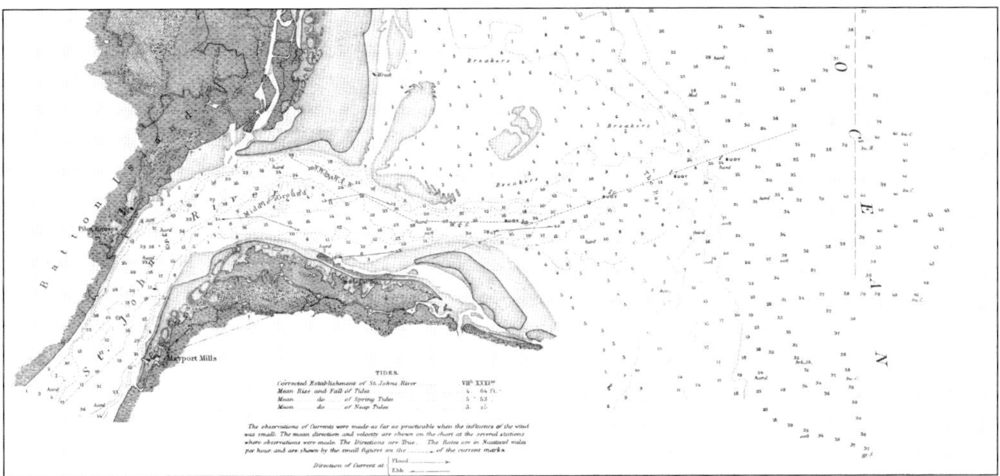

The St. Johns River before the 20th century was much different from today's river. The mouth of the river had a sandbar called the St. Johns River bar, which made river transportation difficult at times. The sandbar was also notable for always changing locations. Boaters today have no difficulty leaving and entering the river because of the solutions enacted by the US Army Corps of Engineers. This map from 1853 shows the mouth of the St. Johns with sandbars. (State Archives of Florida.)

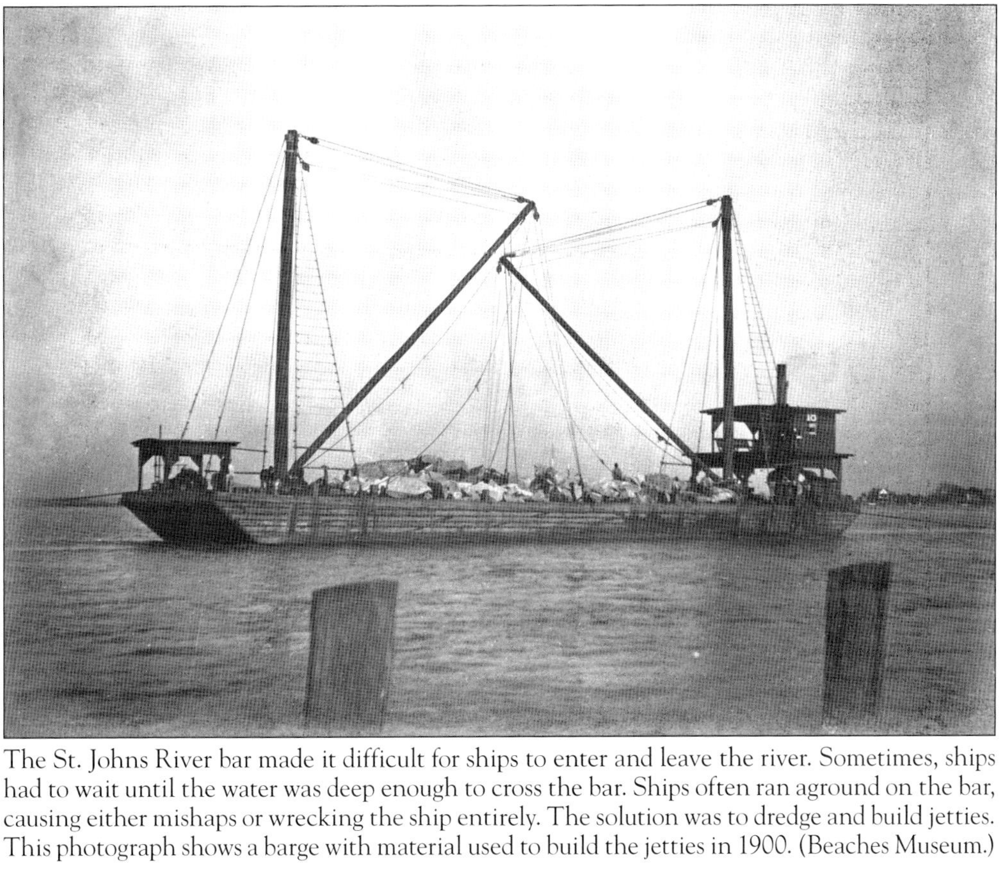

The St. Johns River bar made it difficult for ships to enter and leave the river. Sometimes, ships had to wait until the water was deep enough to cross the bar. Ships often ran aground on the bar, causing either mishaps or wrecking the ship entirely. The solution was to dredge and build jetties. This photograph shows a barge with material used to build the jetties in 1900. (Beaches Museum.)

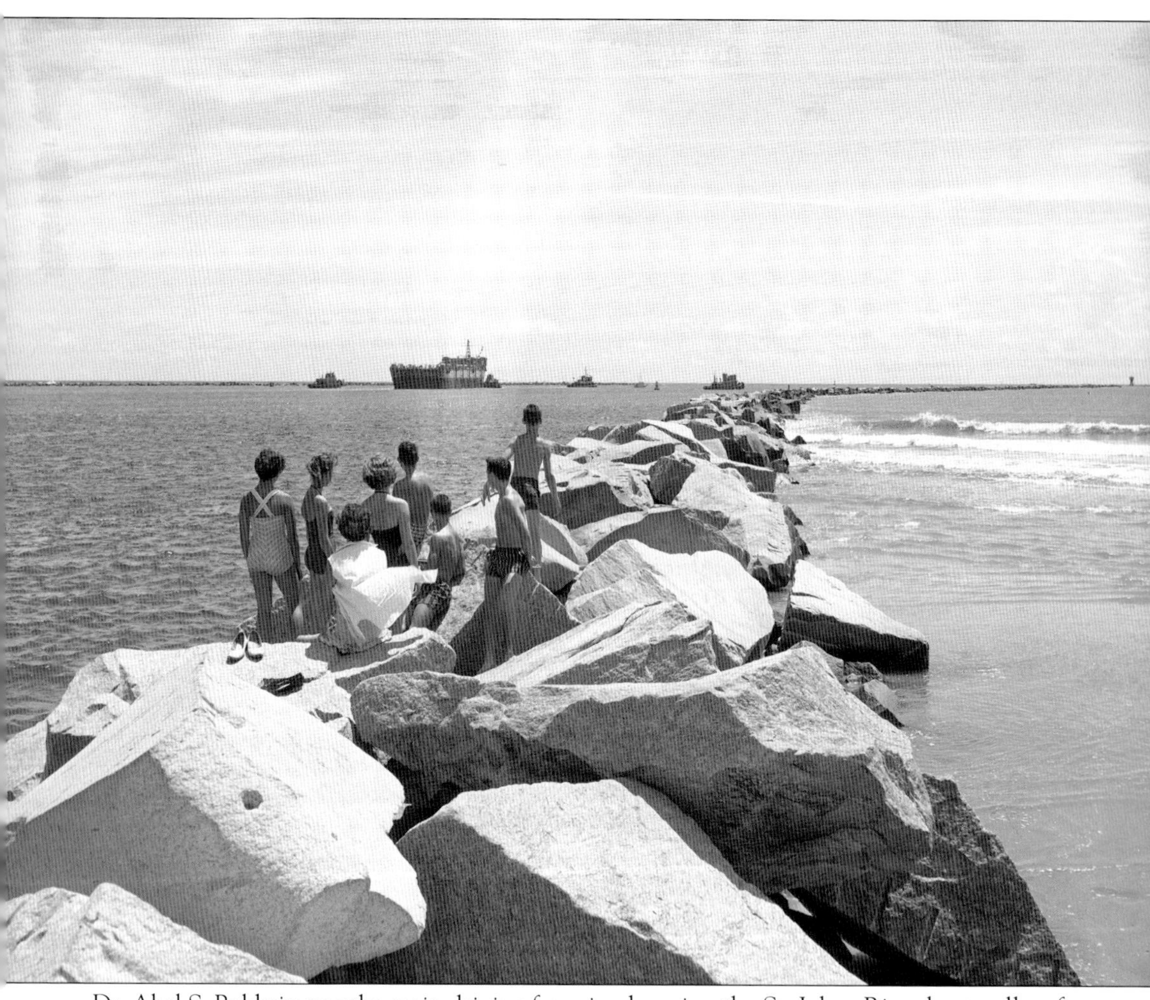

Dr. Abel S. Baldwin was the main driving force in changing the St. Johns River bar to allow for easier transportation on the river. Gen. Quincy Adams Gilmore of the Corps of Engineers was in charge of surveying and creating the changes to the river. In 1878, Baldwin brought in Capt. James B. Eads, who had worked on the mouth of the Mississippi River. Eads recommended that two converging jetties be built to create a deeper channel out to sea. The Corps of Engineers created two jetties with the northern extending out three miles into the Atlantic and the southern extending two and a half miles. By 1895, there was 15 feet of water over the bar and an 18-foot channel to Jacksonville. This photograph from 1957 shows people on the southern jetties looking out at tugboats and a ship entering the river. The success of the jetties and dredging of the river caused unexpected erosion upriver. The banks of St. Johns Bluff and Dames Point eroded considerably. The original location of Fort Caroline is presumed to have been lost to the river from the erosion. (State Archives of Florida.)

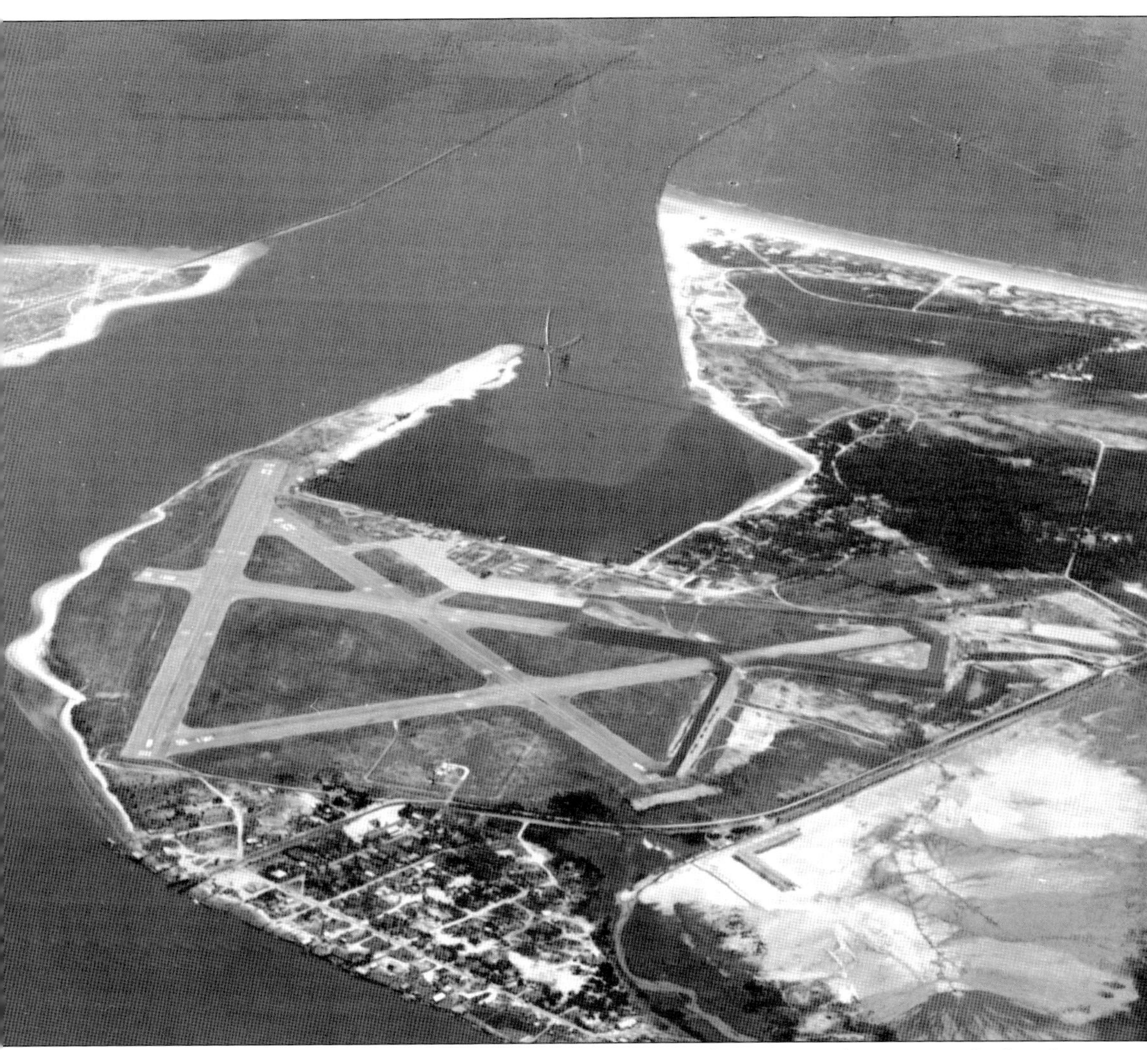

Under the Hepburn Act of 1938, a board headed by Rear Adm. A.J. Hepburn was tasked with finding a location for a naval air base in the southeastern United States. The board recommended establishing a base at Jacksonville that had to have specific facilities, such as for two carrier groups and three patrol squadrons. In April 1939, the US Navy Department chose a site near the south jetties to develop an aircraft carrier basin. Ribault Bay, the squared-off area of water seen here, was chosen to be the location for the basin. It was dredged to 29 feet and was used by patrol craft, target, and rescue boats during World War II. In 1944, an air facility was commissioned as a naval auxiliary air station. After the war, the naval and air station areas of the base were decommissioned. The Coast Guard used the base for several years until budget cuts forced it to vacate in 1947. In June 1948, the base was reactivated as a naval outlying landing field under Naval Air Station Jacksonville. This photograph from the late 1940s shows airfields at the Mayport base with an almost empty basin. (Jacksonville Historical Society.)

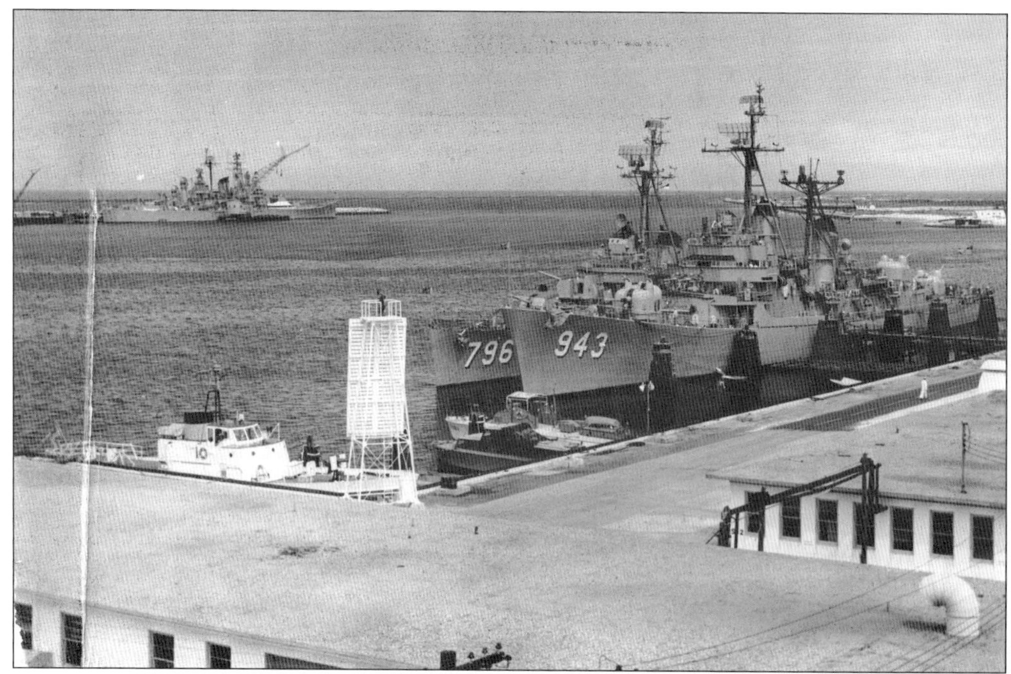

In 1952, the USS *Tarawa* (CVS 40) became the first capital ship to use Mayport's carrier basin. In 1953, the Corps of Engineers began to re-dredge the basin to over 40 feet to allow Midway-class carriers to enter. In 1955, the base became US Naval Auxiliary Air Station Mayport, with more facilities and upgraded runways. This photograph from 1959 shows three ships in the carrier basin of NAS Mayport. (State Archives of Florida.)

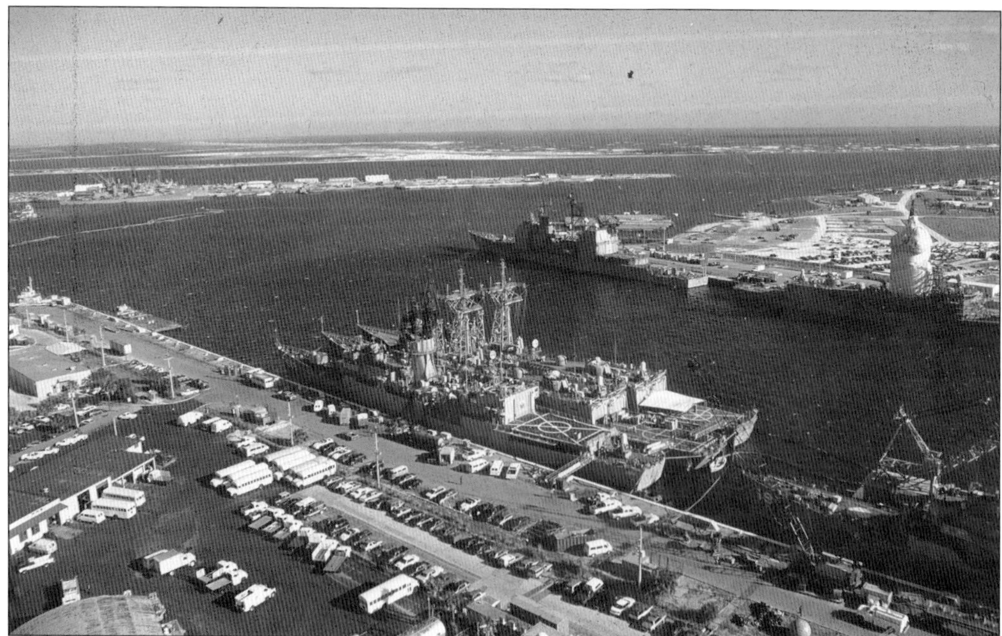

NAS Mayport has been the homeport of several aircraft carriers including the USS *Forrestal* (CV-59), USS *Saratoga* (CV-60), and USS *John F. Kennedy* (CV-67). This photograph shows an aerial view of NAS Mayport in 1990. (University of North Florida.)

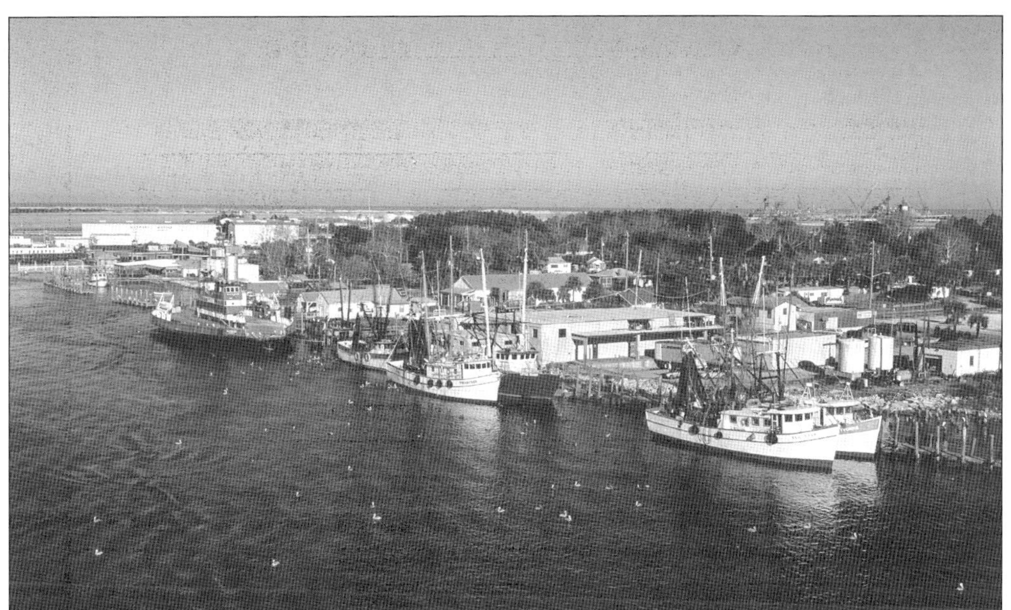

Mayport is a fishing and shrimping community near the mouth of the St. Johns River. The name is derived from the original French name of the St. Johns. In the 1840s, Mayport Mills was established here to process lumber. The fishing and shrimping community of today emerged by the end of the 19th century. In 1900, the Florida East Coast Railway reached Mayport, further contributing to the growth of the area. This photograph shows several shrimp boats docked at Mayport in 1990. NAS Mayport can be seen in the distance. (University of North Florida.)

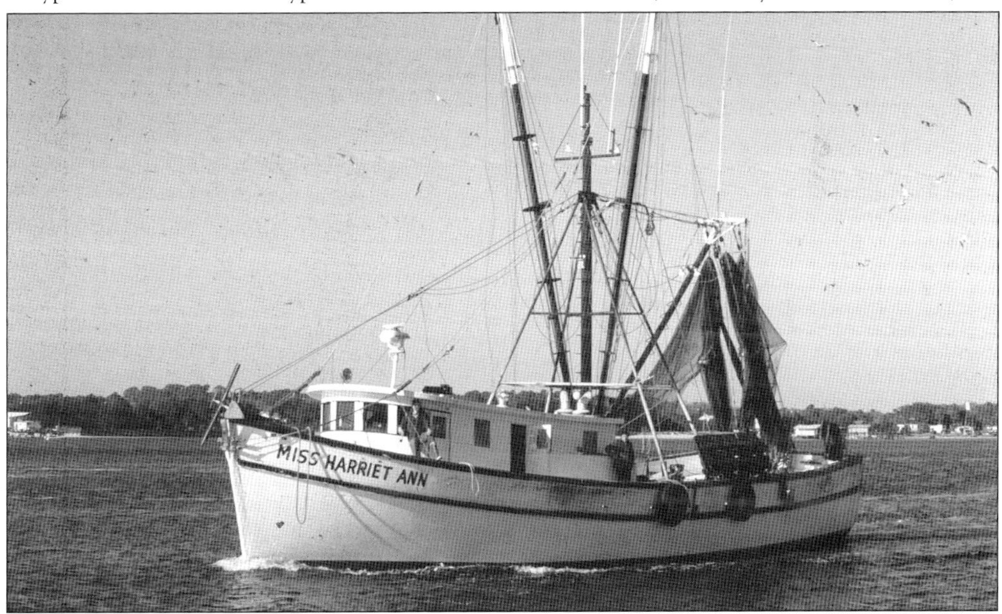

Shrimp are an important part of the Mayport community. The name "Mayport Shrimp" is applied to the shrimp of the region and can be found at many restaurants in north Florida. The Jacksonville Suns minor league baseball team was renamed the Jacksonville Jumbo Shrimp in 2016 due to the influence of shrimp on the St. Johns River. This photograph from 1977 shows the shrimp boat *Miss Harriet Ann* on the river at Mayport. (University of North Florida.)

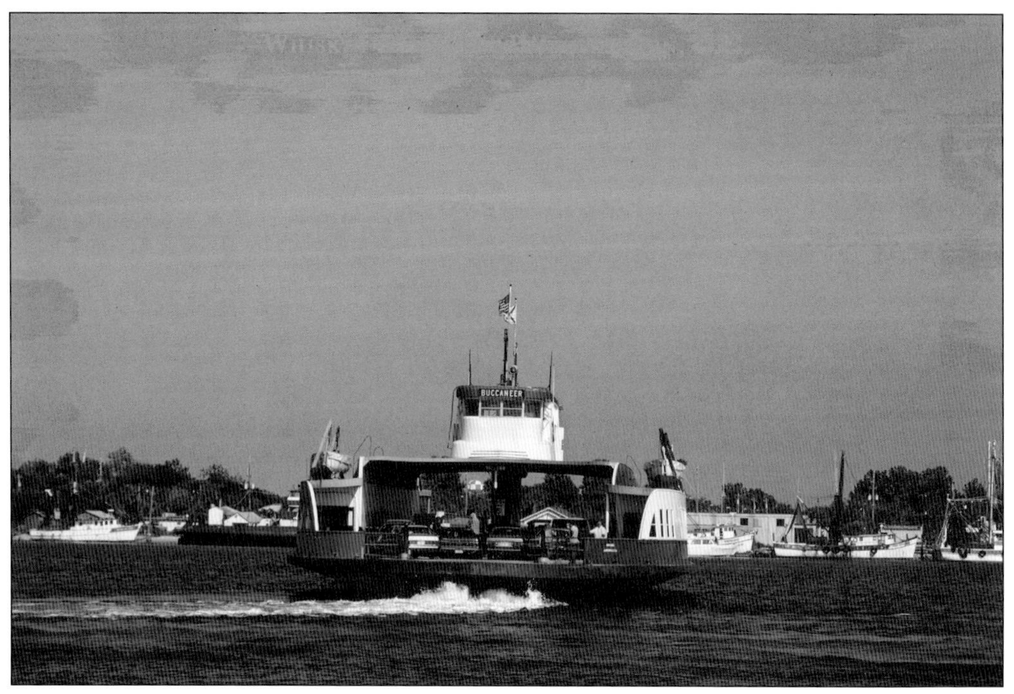

In 1948, the Mayport Ferry began operations, ferrying vehicles across the St. Johns River from Mayport to Fort George Island. This photograph shows the *Buccaneer* with a load of automobiles and passengers traveling across the St. Johns to Mayport in 1986. (University of North Florida.)

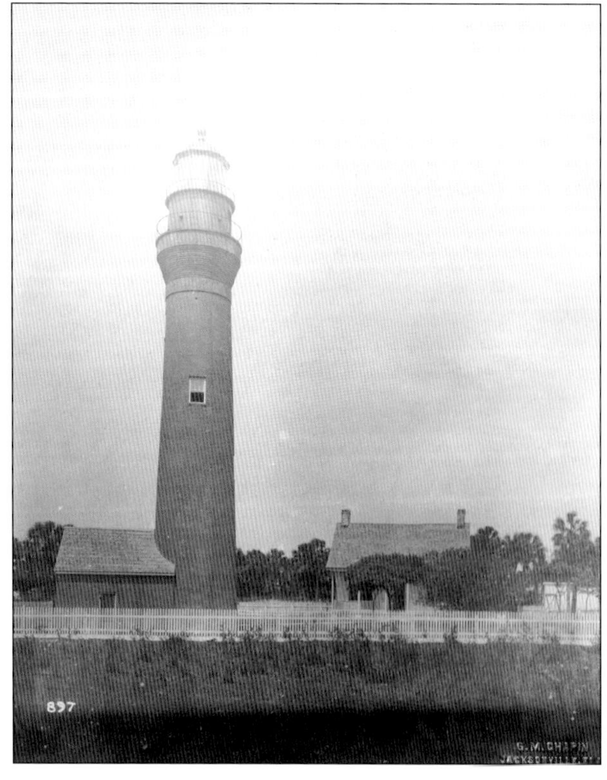

The first lighthouse at Mayport was built in 1830, but the Atlantic Ocean destroyed it. The second lighthouse was built in 1835, but erosion gradually made it inoperable after 20 years. A stronger and taller lighthouse was built in 1858. This third lighthouse was called the St. Johns River Light. It was decommissioned in 1929 and replaced by a lightship about eight miles off the river mouth. In the 1940s, the US Navy acquired the land around the St. Johns River Light that would later become NAS Mayport. In 1954, the St. Johns Light was built to replace the lightship. The old St. Johns River Light, seen in this photograph, still stands strong at Mayport despite being decommissioned in 1929. (Jacksonville Historical Society.)

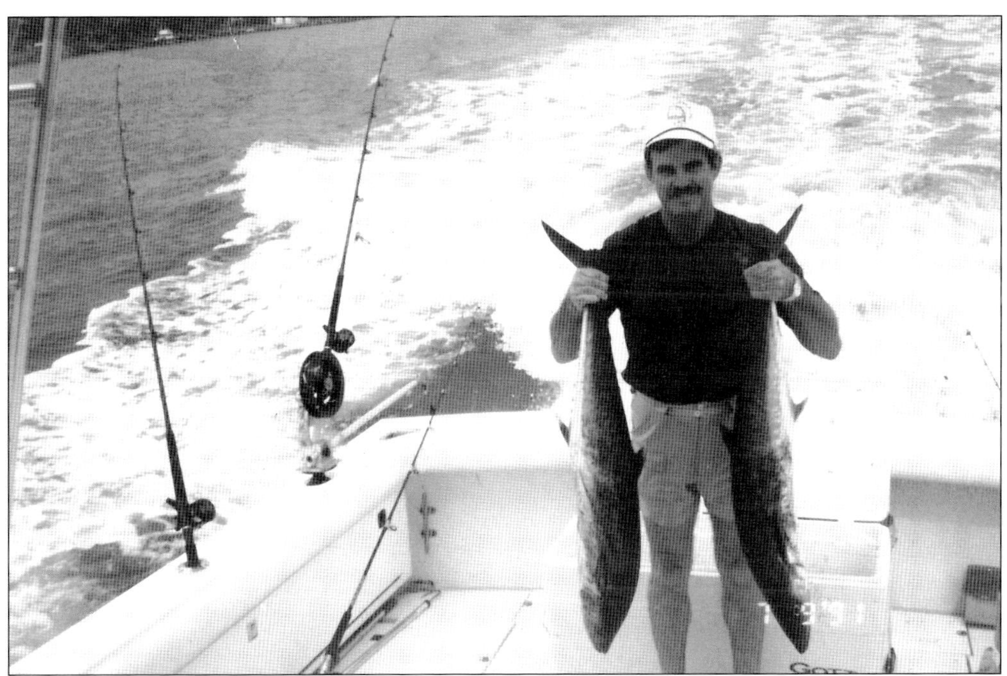

In 1980, the Kingfish Tournament was created by Walt Murr, Pete Loftin, and Bob Gipson because Jacksonville lacked a fishing tournament comparable to those in south Florida. The tournament was first held at Beach Marina on the Intracoastal Waterway. Boaters took the St. Johns River out into the Atlantic to catch kingfish. In 1996, the tournament was relocated to Sisters Creek on the St. Johns. This photograph shows Maxey Moody III returning with two kingfish in 1991. (Andrew R. Nicholas.)

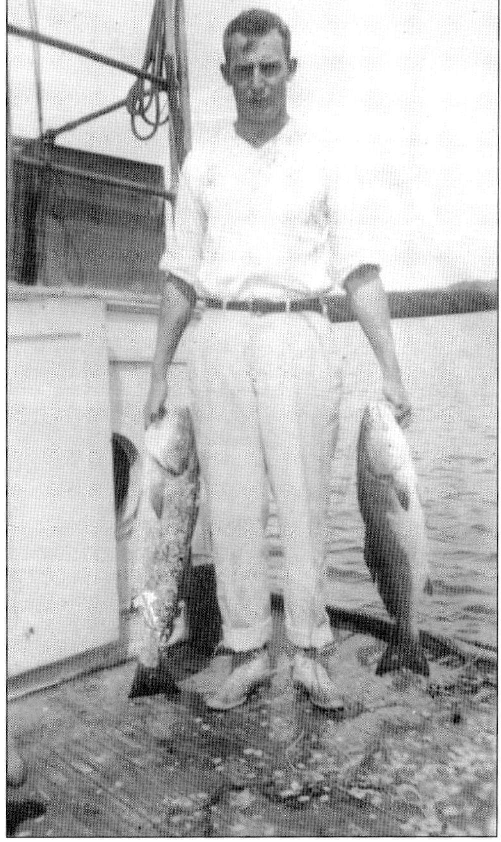

Sisters Creek was first known as Two Sisters Creek in Spanish Florida. The name comes from two similar hardwood hammocks on the sides of the creek. This photograph shows a man holding fish caught on Sisters Creek on September 21, 1913. (Jacksonville Historical Society.)

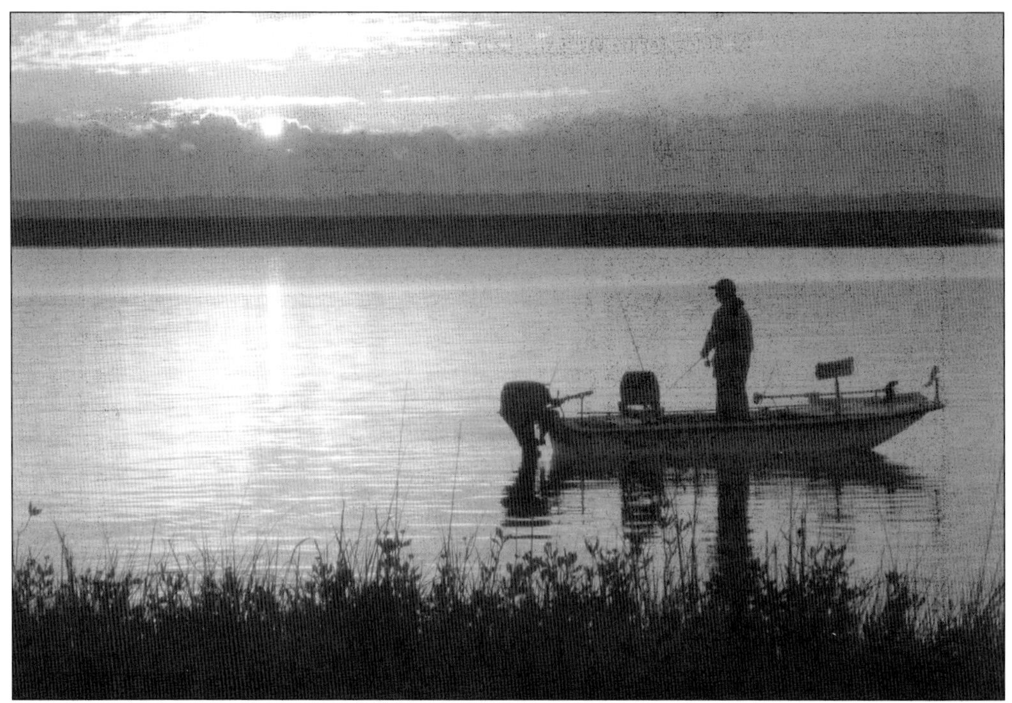

Clapboard Creek is a large series of creeks going through Timucuan Ecological and Historic Preserve. This photograph shows a man fishing in a Carolina Skiff on Clapboard Creek in 2021. (David Taylor.)

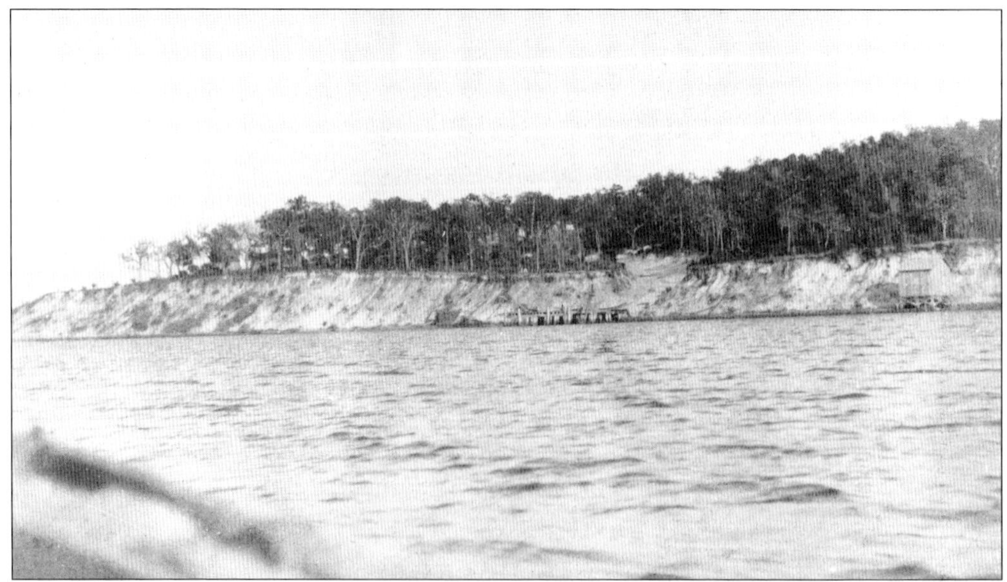

A bluff is a steep shoreline formed in sediment like sand or gravel that overlooks a body of water. St. Johns Bluff is one example of a bluff on the St. Johns River. During the Civil War, Confederates established an artillery battery on the bluff to attack incoming Union ships. Confederate forces abandoned the bluff by October 3, 1862. After Union forces seized the battery at St. Johns Bluff, they went to nearby Yellow Bluff Fort. This photograph taken from the river shows St. Johns Bluff around 1900. (State Archives of Florida.)

Two

Blount Island to Exchange Club Island

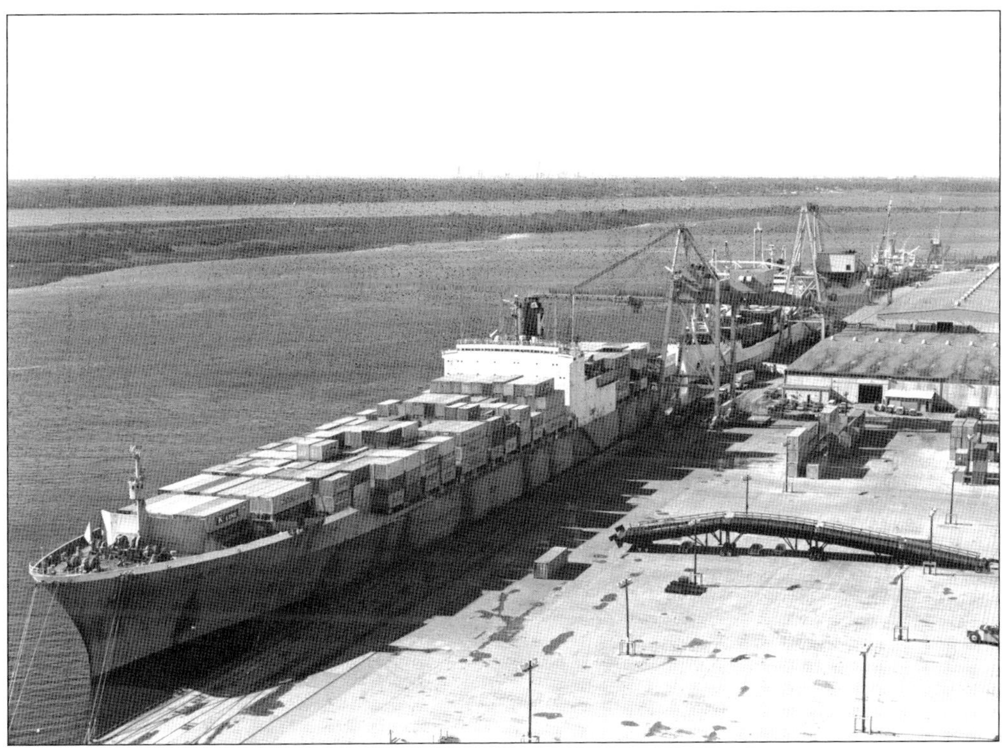

On June 15, 1822, a petition was sent to Secretary of State John Quincy Adams to designate Jacksonville as a customs port of entry. The petition was denied, but it is this document that is used to date the name of the city on the St. Johns River. Today, Jacksonville is a major transportation and shipping hub due to its strategic location on the river. This photograph shows container ships at the Port of Jacksonville, or JAXPORT, on Blount Island in 1976. (JAXPORT.)

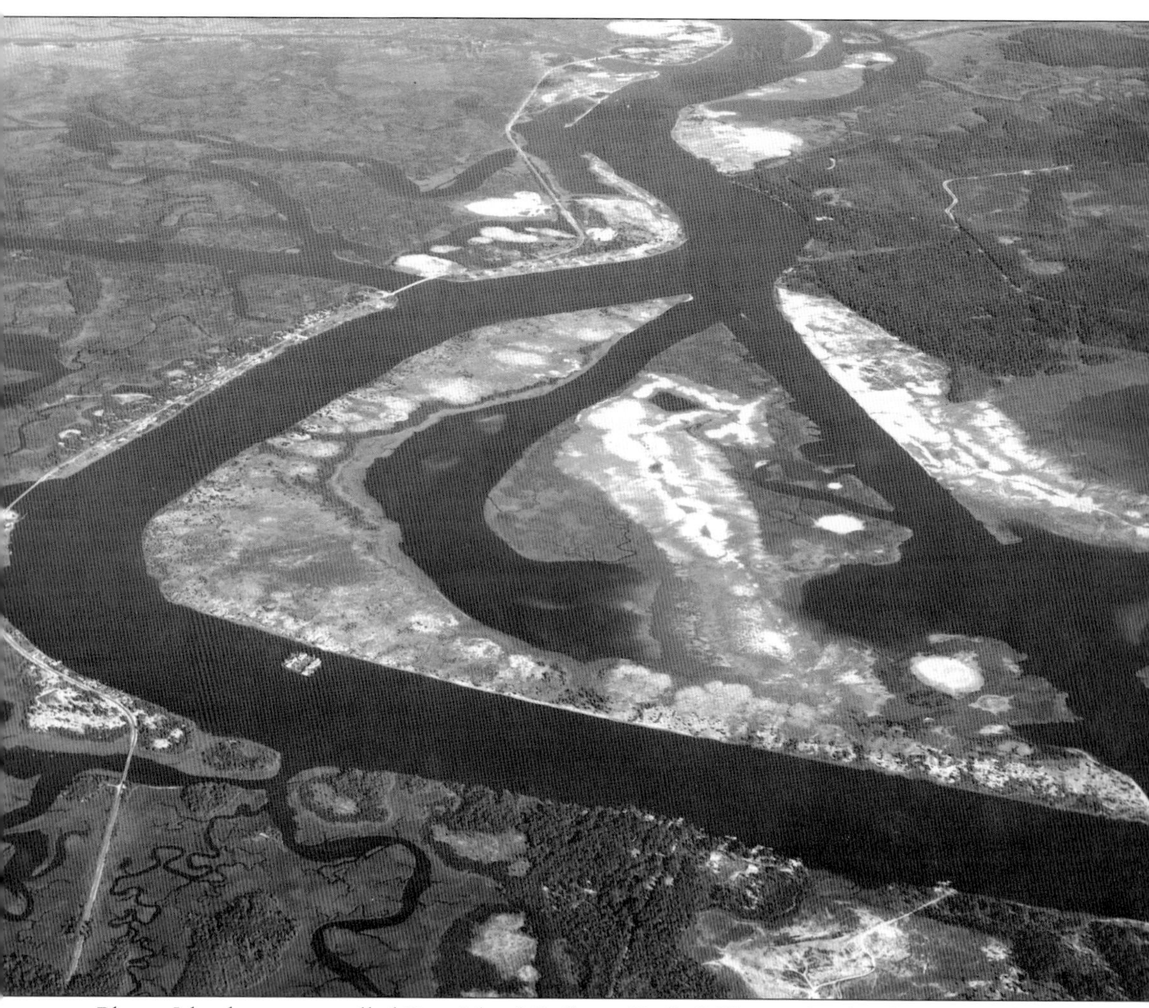

Blount Island was once called Goat Island. Rollians "Rollie" Christopher lived on Goat Island for many years with his goats, claiming squatter's rights. In the 1950s, the Duval County Commission and Florida Ship Canal Authority struggled to acquire the island due to Christopher's refusal to leave. After a prolonged battle, the island was secured by the Duval County Commission and renamed Blount Island after J. Henry Blount, who had assisted with the process. This aerial photograph of the island was taken in the 1960s. (JAXPORT.)

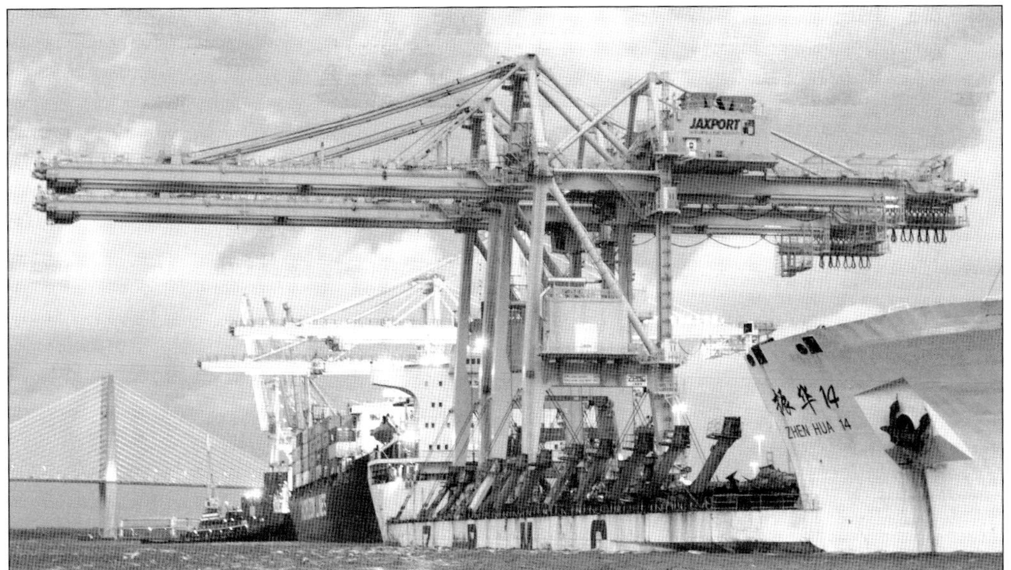

In August 2008, two cranes were destroyed when they fell over during a storm. JAXPORT ordered two brand new cranes already assembled from the Chinese company ZPMC. The cranes were transported on a specially designed ship. In June 2011, the ship left China and went on a long journey westward through the Indian Ocean, around the Horn of Africa, and arrived in Panama to drop off four cranes. This photograph from September 2011 shows the ship arriving at JAXPORT with the two cranes. (JAXPORT.)

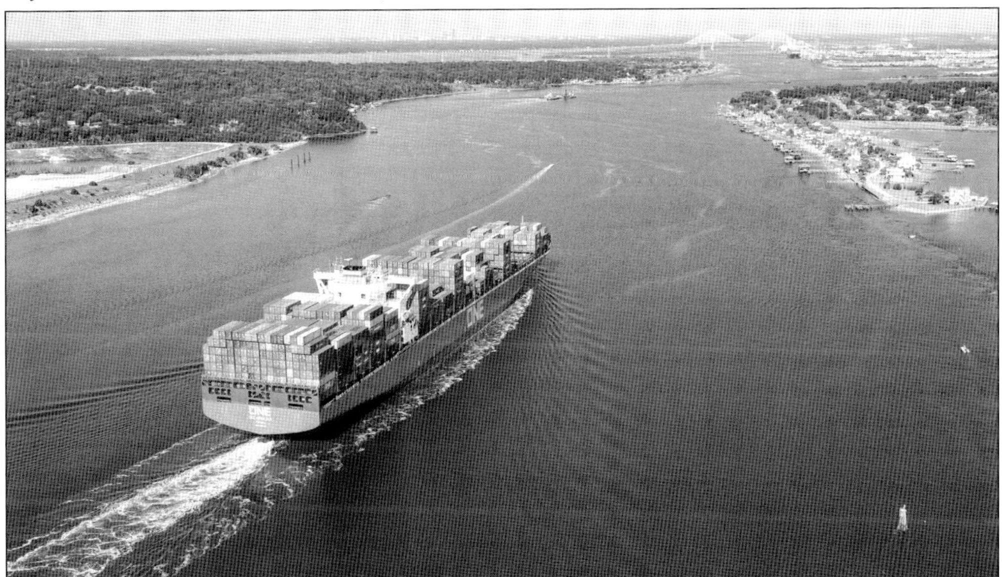

This photograph from 2020 shows a container ship owned by the Japanese shipping company Ocean Network Express Holdings approaching Blount Island with a full load. A constant influx of container ships to Blount Island means an inevitable need to deepen the channel to allow larger ships into the port. The St. Johns River in this area was around 18 feet deep in 1898. The maximum width of the river was around 100 feet, but now is between 400 and 1,000 feet in the shipping channel. In 2021 the channel was 40 feet deep, and in May 2022 it was dredged to 47 feet. A turning basin was also dredged to allow larger ships to turn around at Blount Island. (JAXPORT.)

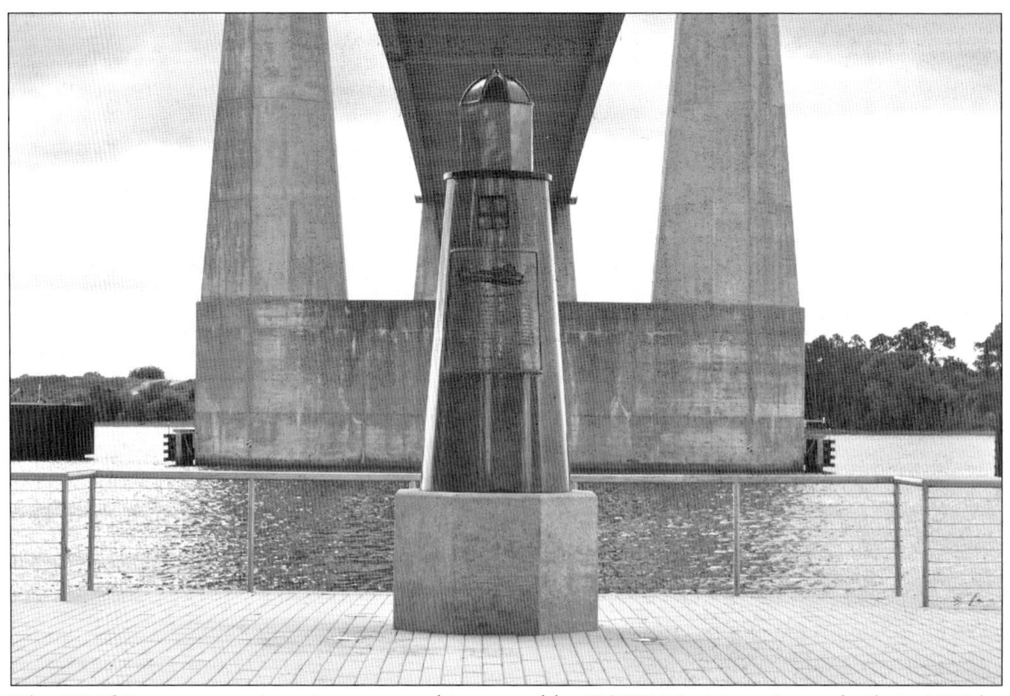

The SS *El Faro* was an American cargo ship owned by TOTE Maritime. It was built in 1975 by Sun Shipbuilding & Drydock Company. On September 29, 2015, the *El Faro* departed JAXPORT for Puerto Rico with a load of shipping containers, trailers, cars, and a crew of 33. At the time of departure, Tropical Storm Joaquin was southeast of Florida, near the route *El Faro* was traveling. The tropical storm turned into a category three hurricane. On October 1, the *El Faro* lost propulsion and began to list 15 degrees when it was near the eye of the hurricane in the Bahamas. The *El Faro* was declared missing the next day and a large search operation was conducted by the US military to locate it. On October 31, the underwater wreckage of the *El Faro* was located. The park underneath the Dames Point Bridge was renamed El Faro Memorial Park in 2016. A memorial statue was erected at the park in honor of the 33 crewmen who lost their lives. (Andrew R. Nicholas.)

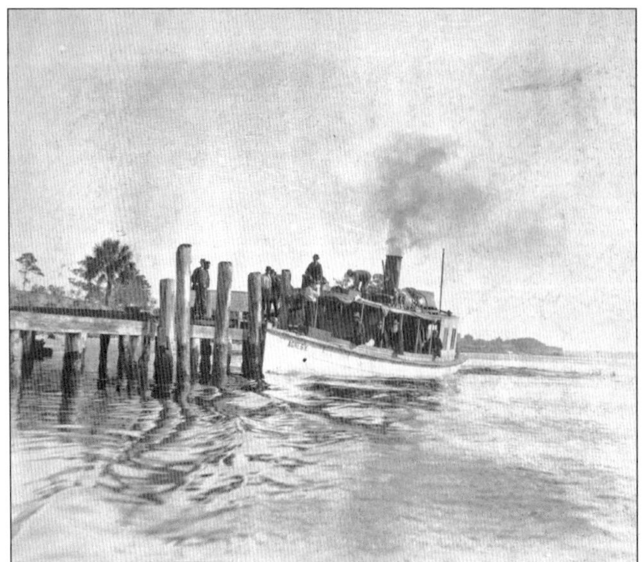

New Berlin was a village on the St. Johns River near Dames Point. It was founded in 1860 when Dr. Henry Von Balsan acquired 50 acres of land at Yellow Bluff. The name was chosen by Dr. Balsan because he was born in Berlin, Germany, in 1798. The creation of JAXPORT at Blount Island destroyed the fishing industry of New Berlin. New Berlin still has a small community with a road bearing the name New Berlin Road leading to it. This photograph shows the steamer *Agnes K* at a dock on the St. Johns in New Berlin in 1900. (State Archives of Florida.)

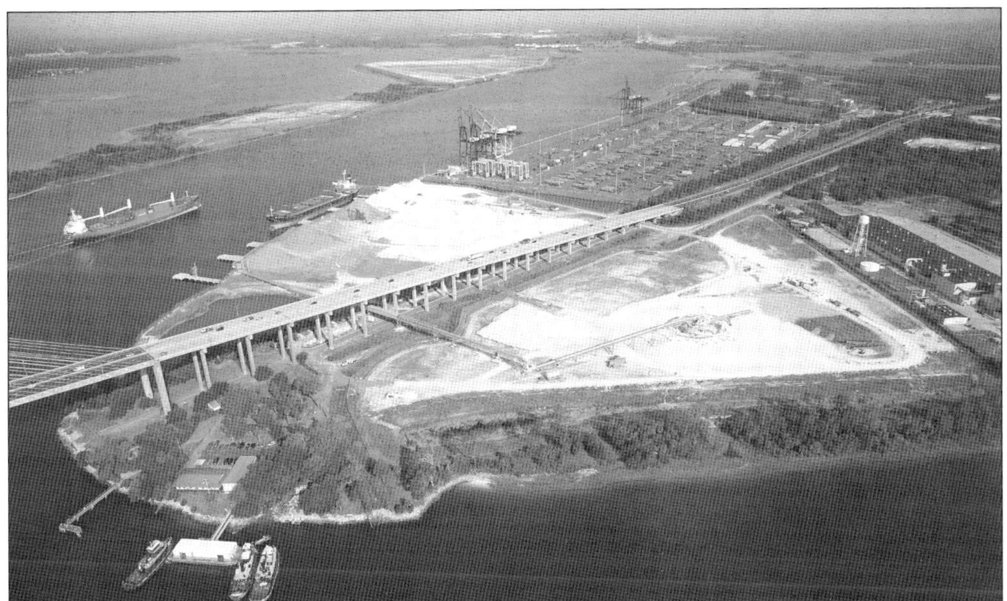

In 1780, Capt. Charles Dames acquired 300 acres of land where he established a shipbuilding industry. Dames also cleared land, planted crops, and built structures on the land. After the Revolutionary War, Dames decided to relocate to the Bahamas, where many British loyalists had also gone. His name continued to be used to refer to the land near Blount Island. This photograph shows Dames Point with JAXPORT facilities on the left side of the point next to Martin Marietta, a supplier of aggregates and heavy building materials. The northern end of the Dames Point Bridge is at the center of Dames Point. (JAXPORT.)

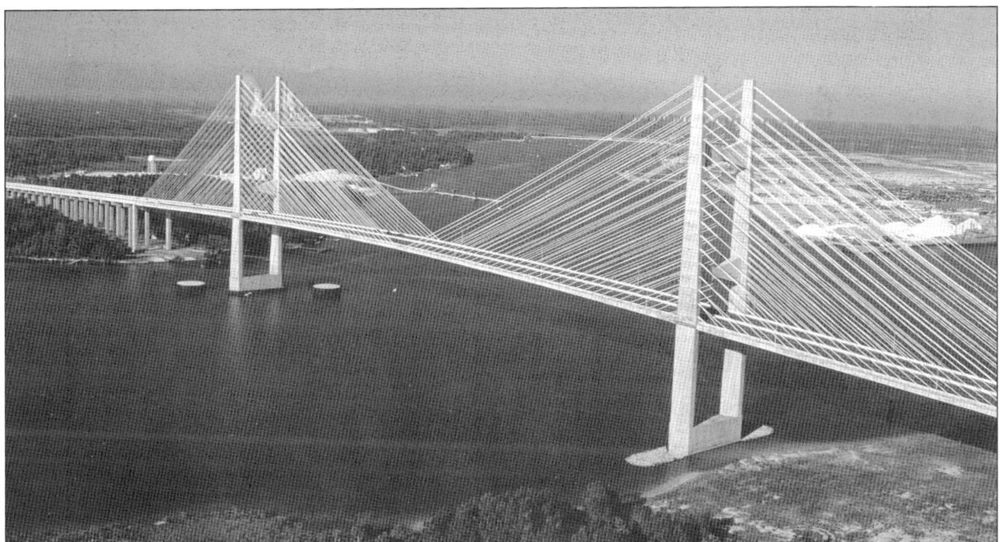

The Napoleon Bonaparte Broward Bridge, commonly called the "Dames Point Bridge," began construction in 1985 and opened in 1989 connecting the Southside to the Northside. It is a cable-stayed bridge with 21 miles of cable. The total length is 10,646 feet, and it goes over the St. Johns River and Mill Cove. The vertical clearance of the Dames Point Bridge is 174 feet, making large container ships and cruise ships able to cross safely underneath. This photograph of the bridge was taken in 1990. (University of North Florida.)

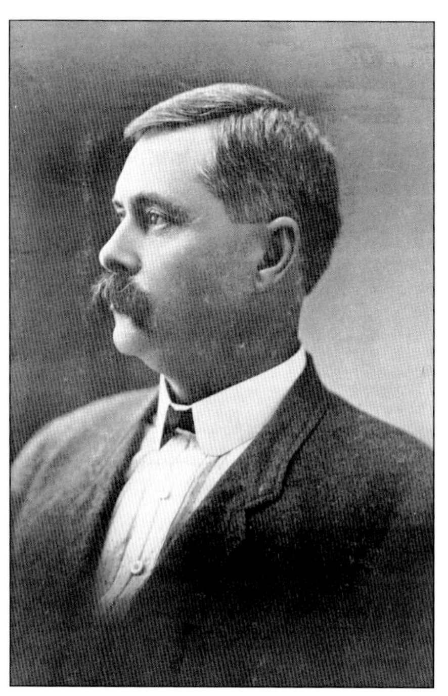

Napoleon Bonaparte Broward was born on April 19, 1857, in Duval County. He grew up near the St. Johns River and worked various jobs on a steamboat. In 1876, Broward moved to New England, where he became a ship's mate. After working on ships for two years, he returned to Jacksonville to work on tugboats on the St. Johns. In 1883, he began piloting ships over the difficult St. Johns River bar. In 1905, Broward became governor of Florida, serving until 1909. This photograph of him was taken around 1905. (Library of Congress.)

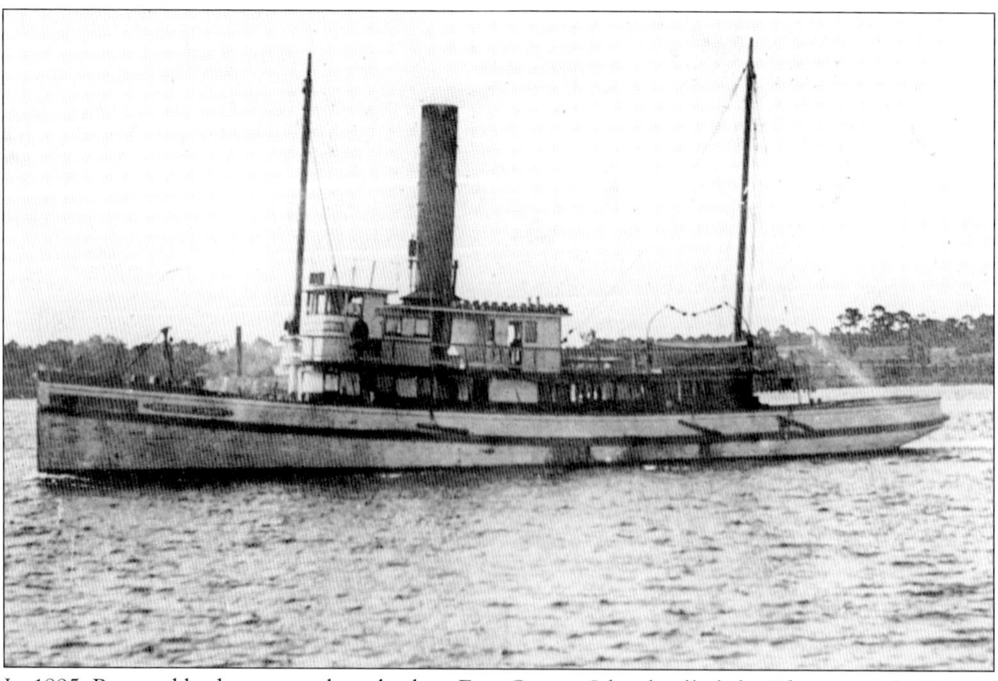

In 1895, Broward had a new tugboat built at Fort George Island called the *Three Friends*. During its construction, tensions in Cuba worsened, with the Cuban War of Independence beginning in the same year. Broward was approached by a member of the Cuban community in Jacksonville about shipping ammunition and Cuban expatriates to Cuba. In 1896, he decided to use the *Three Friends* to ship ammunition, supplies, and Cuban expatriates to Cuba to assist in the fight against Spain. The *Three Friends* operated out of the St. Johns River. This photograph shows it in the 1890s. (State Archives of Florida.)

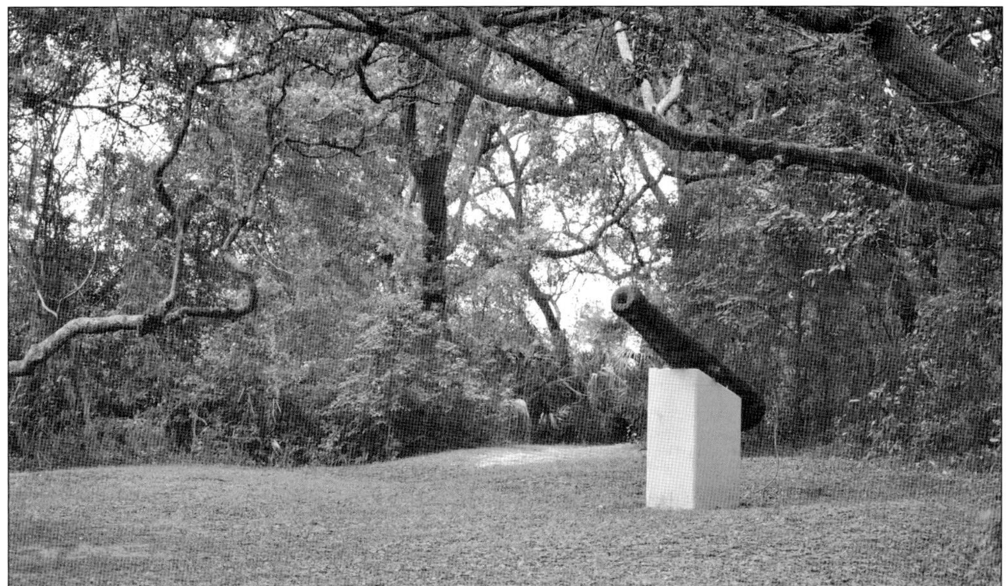

Yellow Bluff Fort was established by Confederate forces in 1862 on Yellow Bluff by Dames Point. The fort was part of the defense of Jacksonville and the St. Johns River along with a similar fort downstream on St. Johns Bluff. Yellow Bluff Fort was made of earthworks and was more like a camp than a typical fort with structures. This photograph shows a Civil War canon replica among the dense forest at Yellow Bluff Fort Historical Park in 2022. (Andrew R. Nicholas.)

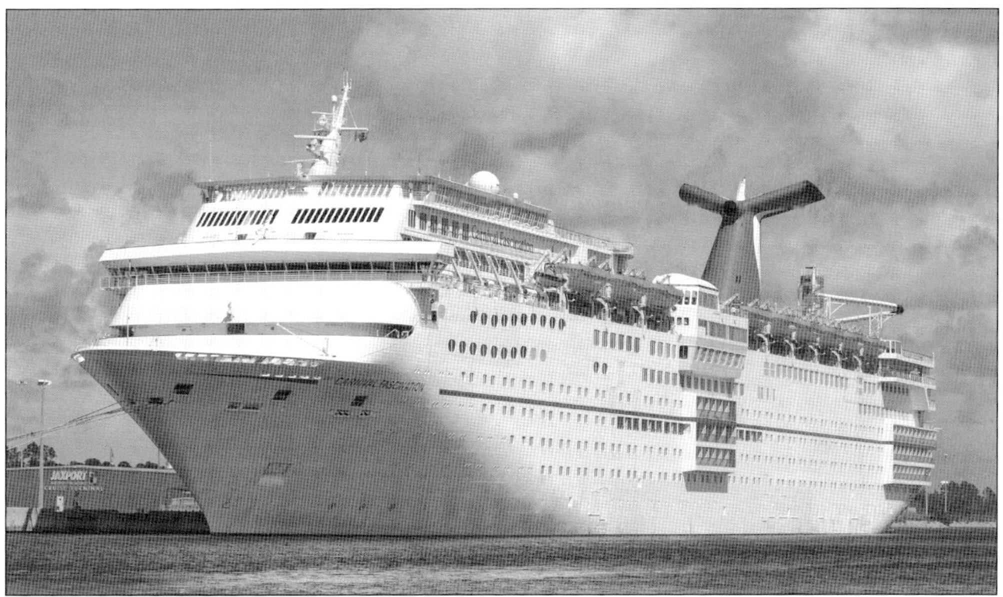

The JAXPORT Cruise Terminal was built in 2003 on the western side of Dames Point, making Jacksonville a destination for cruise ships. Carnival Cruise Lines began operations out of Jacksonville in February 2004, when the *Miracle* departed from the cruise terminal. Cruise ships departing from Jacksonville only sail to the Bahamas. In October 2004, the Carnival ship *Celebration* offered year-round cruises from Jacksonville to the Bahamas. The *Celebration* sailed for four years to 2008, when it was replaced with the *Fascination*. This photograph shows the *Fascination* docked at the cruise terminal in 2012. (JAXPORT.)

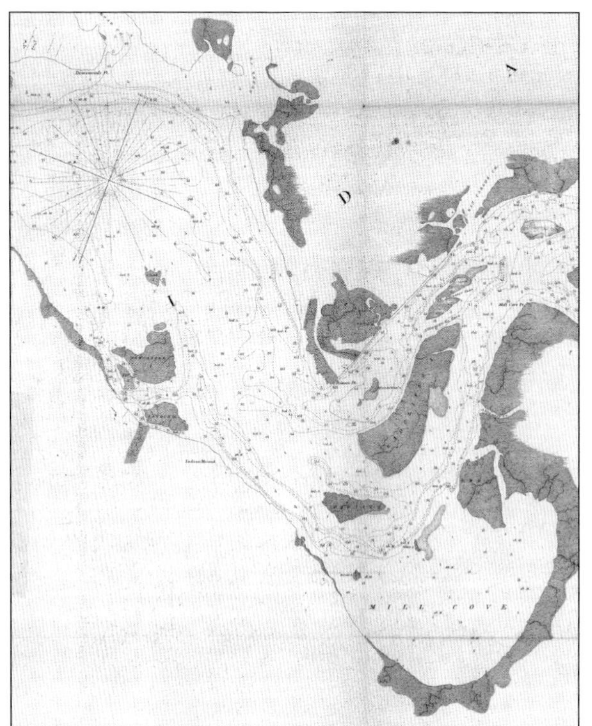

Mill Cove is the portion of the St. Johns River that flows along Arlington and becomes a cove in the Fort Caroline neighborhood. Mill Cove was once a thriving bay for fishermen to catch mullet, shad, and tarpon. Unfortunately, the Corps of Engineers dredged that part of the river in the 1950s, forever altering Mill Cove to a shallow cove of mud. The dredging was done to create a straighter shipping channel. This portion of a coast survey from 1856 shows what the Mill Cove area once looked like. (State Archives of Florida.)

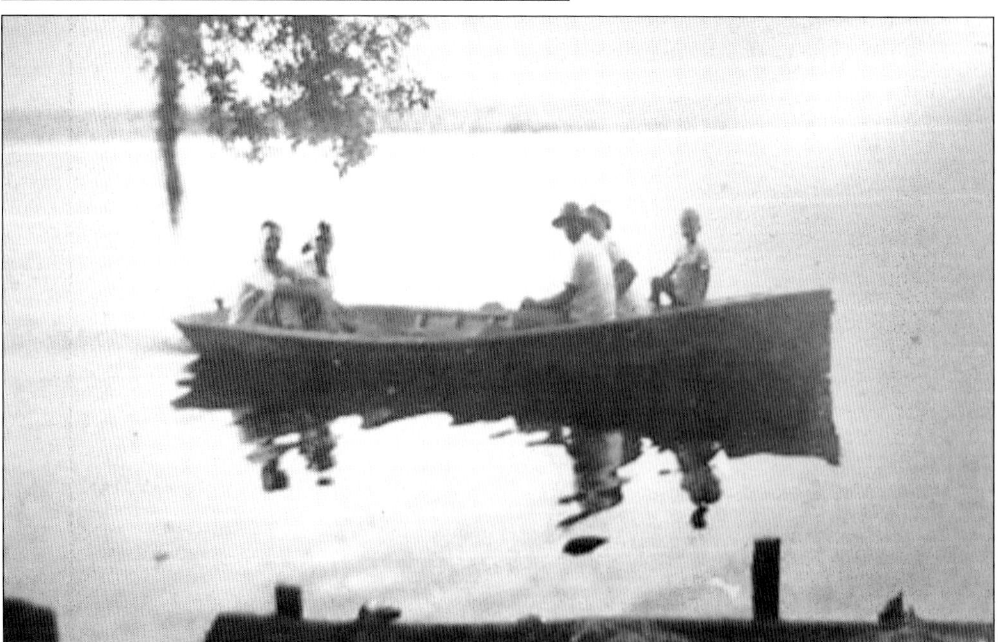

Mill Cove is now filled with mostly mud and marsh grass. The docks of homeowners had to be extended to reach the receding water. At low tide, it is virtually impossible to operate a boat in Mill Cove. In the early 2000s, the Corps of Engineers dredged an 80-foot-wide channel from Reddie Point to the eastern entrance of the cove, deepening it to six feet. The project did little to curb the effects of the dredging from the 1950s. This photograph shows several people on a canoe in Mill Cove in the 1940s, in better days. (Carlton Higginbotham.)

Dunn Creek is a tributary of the St. Johns River flowing north through Oceanway. This photograph shows a Heckscher Drive bridge going over Dunn Creek in 1986. (State Archives of Florida.)

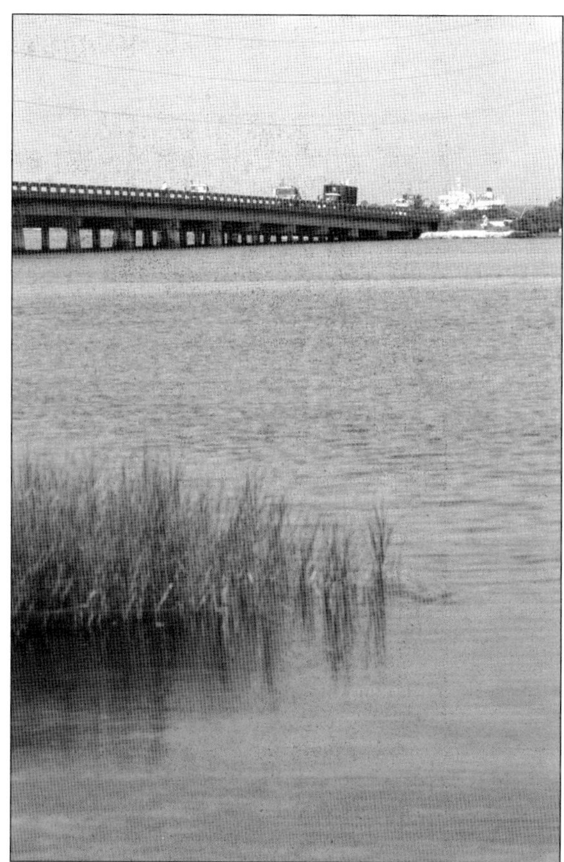

The Broward River is a tributary of the St. Johns. It flows north and then west going under Main Street and Interstate 95. This photograph shows a Heckscher Drive bridge going over the Broward in 1986. (State Archives of Florida.)

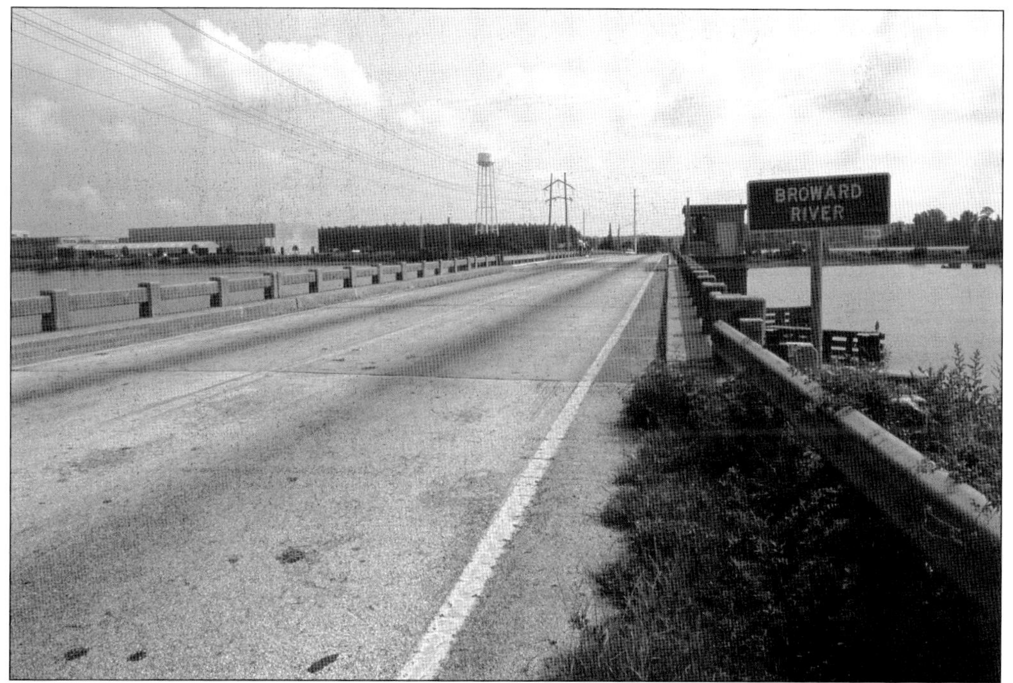

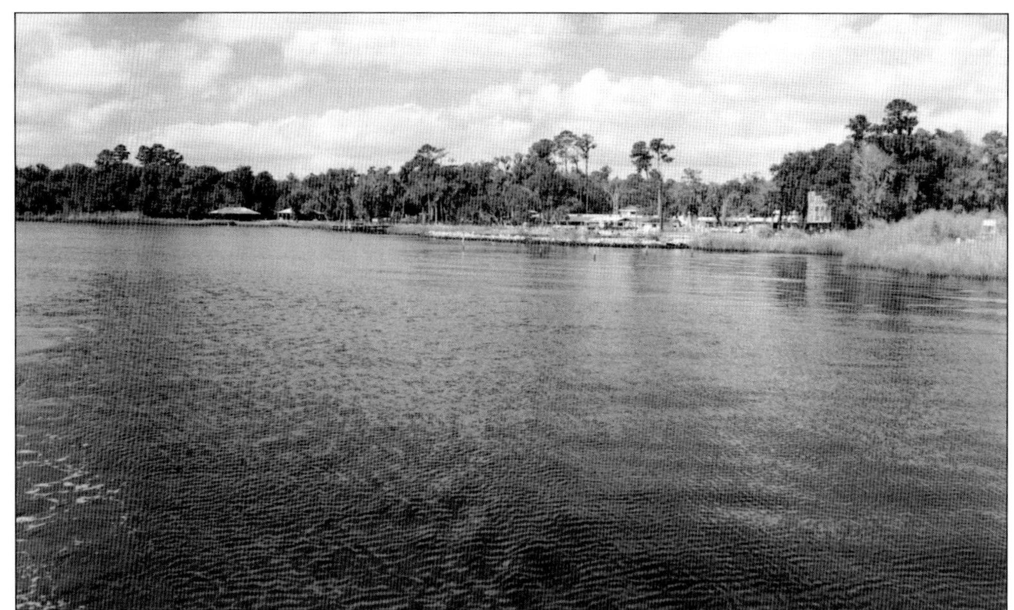

The Jacksonville Municipal Zoo opened on May 12, 1914, at its first location in Springfield. In 1925, the zoo relocated to its present-day location on the Trout River. In 2003, the zoo was renamed the Jacksonville Zoo and Gardens. The portion of State Road 105 from Interstate 95 to Interstate 295 was renamed Zoo Parkway. This photograph of the zoo was taken from the Trout River in 1968. (State Archives of Florida.)

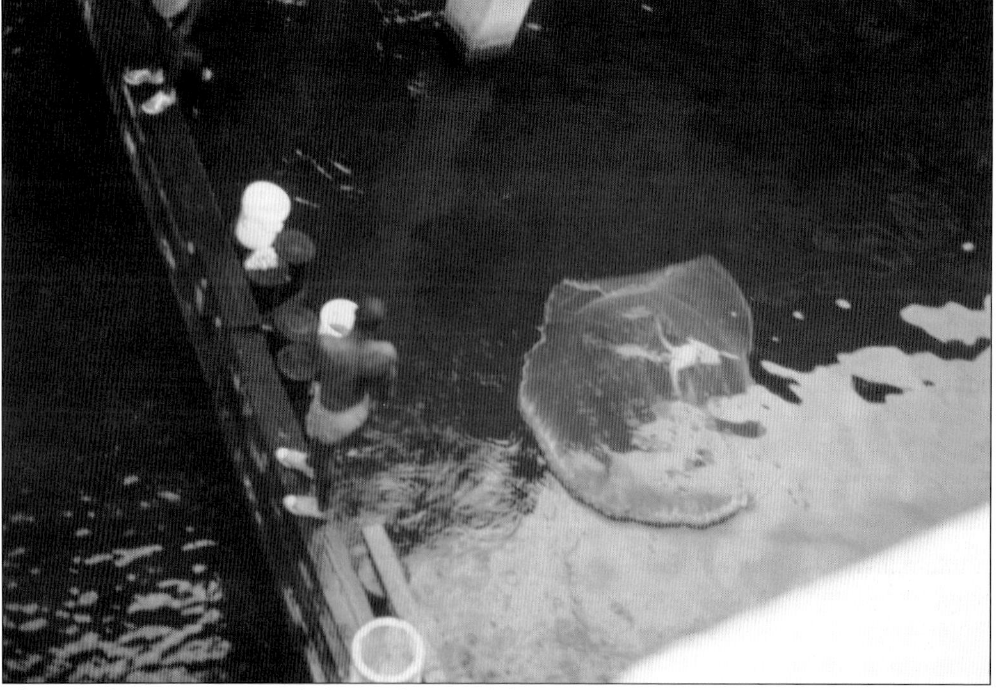

The Ribault River is a 6.4-mile-long tributary of the Trout River. It flows southwest, going under Lem Turner Road, Moncrief Road, and New Kings Road. This photograph from 1984 shows a man using a cast net to fish in the Ribault. (State Archives of Florida.)

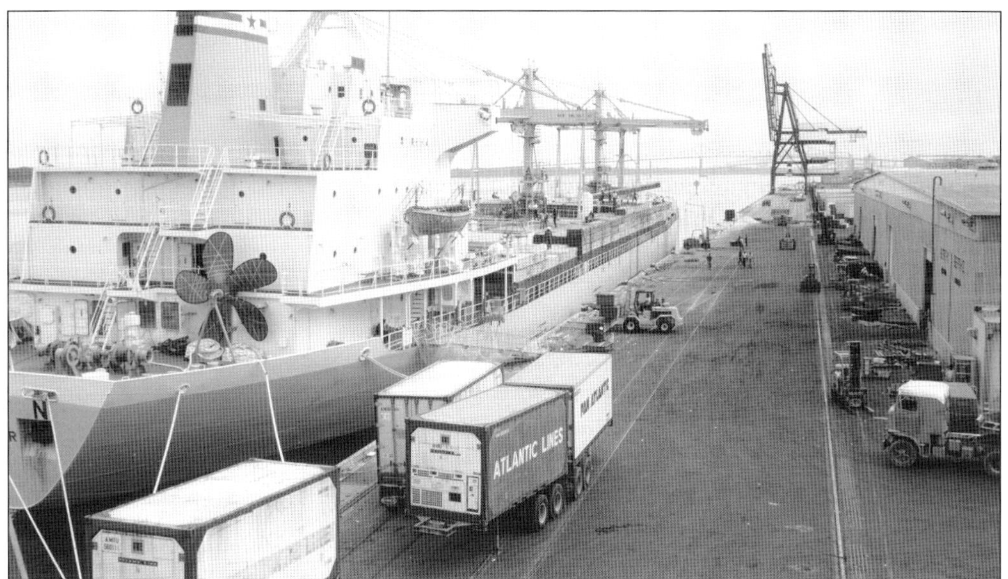

In 1873, Talleyrand Avenue was created by Jacob S. Parker to connect the Panama Park neighborhood to Jacksonville. The name comes from Charles Maurice de Talleyrand-Perigord, a French diplomat who negotiated the Louisiana Purchase. The area of Talleyrand Avenue became more industrialized after the Great Fire of 1901. Talleyrand grew to become a port with manufacturing plants along the St. Johns River by the 1930s. At one time, Talleyrand emitted an odor from paper mills in the area, which was called "the smell of money." By the 1990s, Talleyrand had managed to subdue its decades-long odor, but at the same time, it became less dependent on shipping due to the growth of JAXPORT at Blount Island. This photograph shows the Talleyrand marine terminal in 1970. (JAXPORT.)

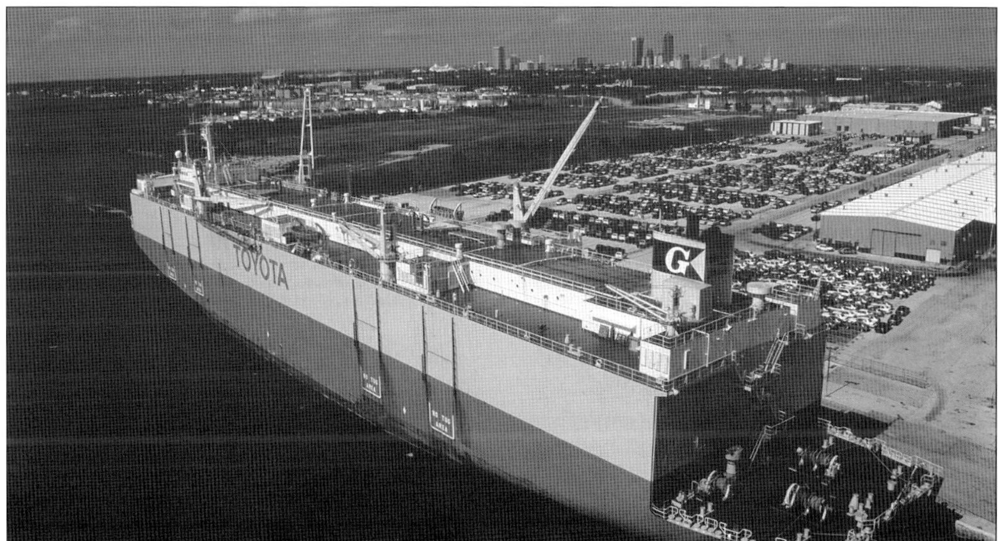

In 1968, Jim Moran of JM Family Enterprises established Southeast Toyota Distributors after entering into an agreement with Toyota to distribute vehicles in Jacksonville. The company's main vehicle processing facility is at Talleyrand. Plans are underway as of 2022 for Southeast Toyota Distributors to relocate from Talleyrand to Blount Island. This photograph shows the facility in Talleyrand in 2021. (Southeast Toyota.)

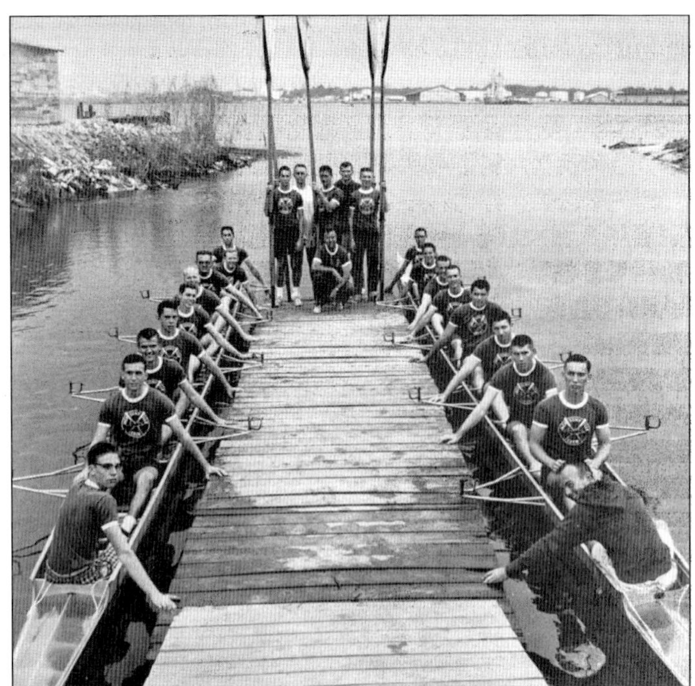

In 1956, coach "Tiger" Tim Taylor started a rowing program at Jacksonville University (JU). Taylor was a graduate of the US Military Academy and had served in the Navy but had never actually rowed before. Through his connections with his alma mater, he managed to get the equipment needed to start the program. In spring of 1956, the JU rowers earned their first win against American University. This photograph of the crew on the St. Johns River was taken around 1958. Talleyrand can be seen in the distance. (Jacksonville University.)

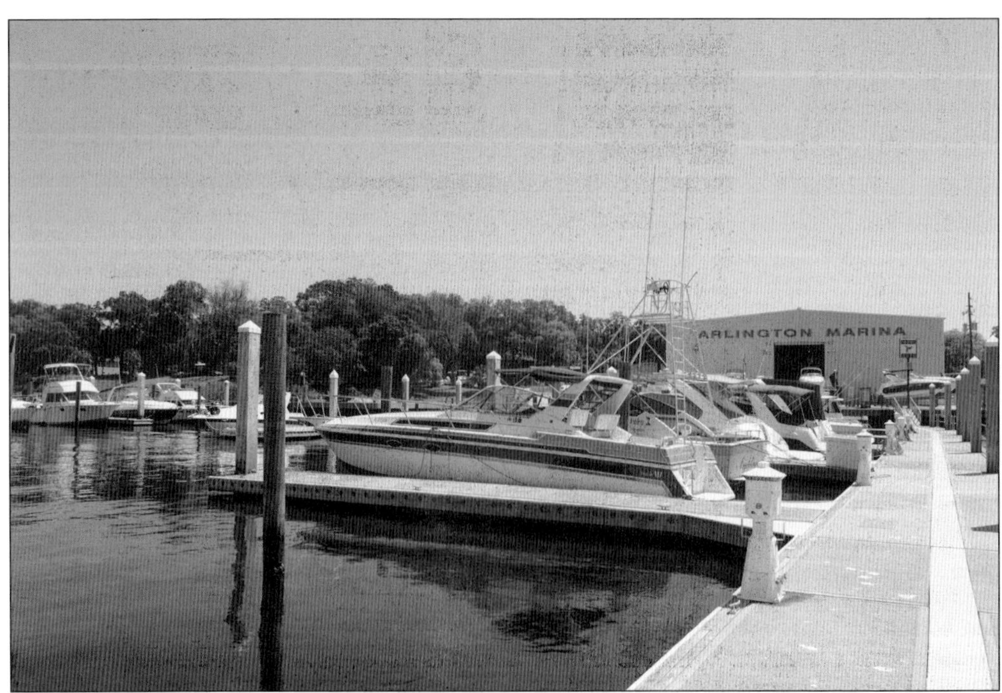

Arlington Marina was built in the early 1990s as a dry-dock marina on the St. Johns River in Arlington. This photograph shows the marina from the St. Johns in 2011. (Andrew R. Nicholas.)

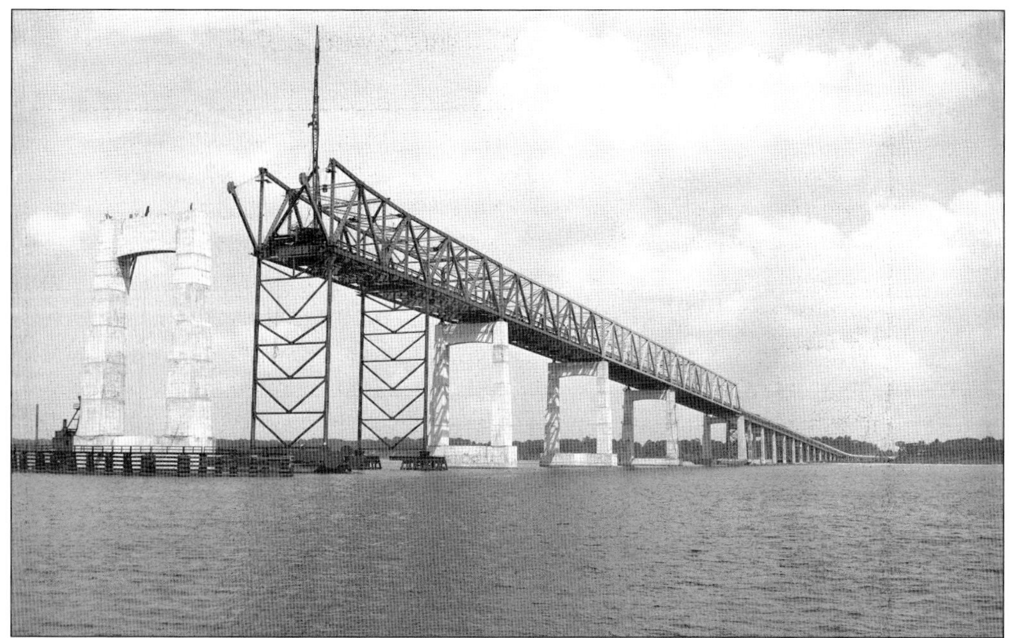

In 1952, construction began on a bridge connecting Arlington to East Jacksonville. Funds for the bridge were secured through bonds and tolls that remained in force until 1989. At the time of construction, there were only two bridges crossing the St. Johns River in Jacksonville. The Mathews Bridge opened in 1953 and was named after John E. Mathews. This photograph shows the Mathews Bridge under construction in 1952. (State Archives of Florida.)

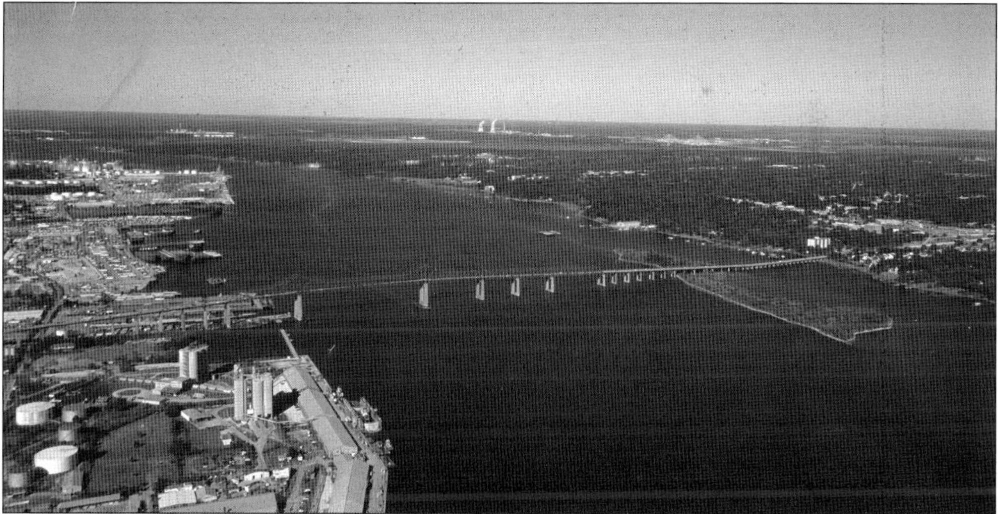

Exchange Club Island is a 34-acre uninhabited island under the Mathews Bridge. It was formed from the dredging of the St. Johns River during construction of the bridge. It was first called Mud Island since the dredging had dug up so much mud. In 1956, the island was renamed and was made into a public park in 1960. Unfortunately, it did not last long, as vandalism made the park unusable. Since the 1960s, the island has been a favorite destination for boaters, which is the only way to access it. In recent years, it has made some progress with the addition of docks. This photograph shows the Mathews Bridge going over the St. Johns River and Exchange Club Island in 1991. In the distance is the Dames Point Bridge. (University of North Florida.)

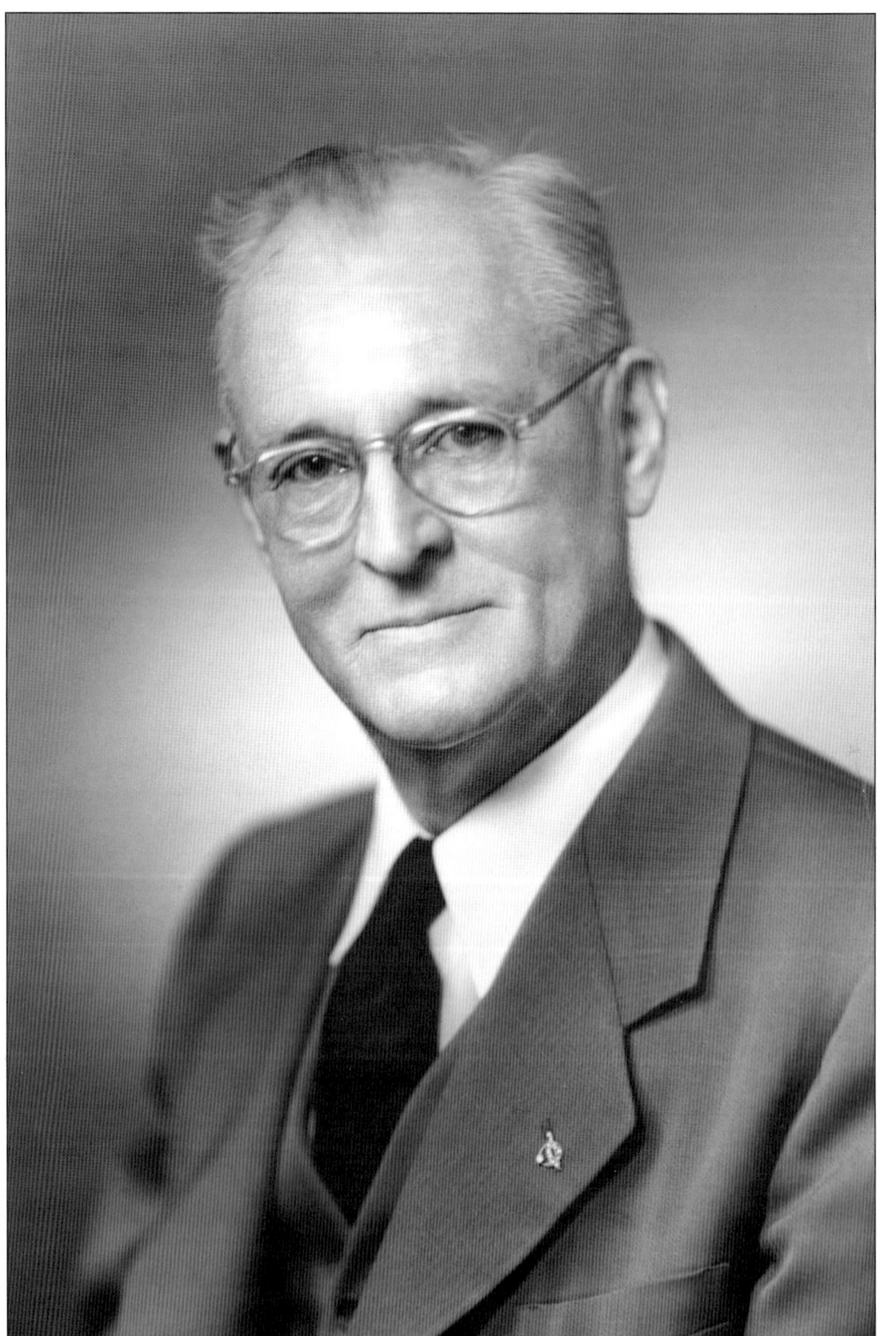

John Elie Mathews was born on July 19, 1892, in Tattnall County, Georgia. He moved to Jacksonville in 1916, where he opened a law practice. Mathews served in the Florida House of Representatives from 1928 to 1932 and was elected to the Florida Senate in 1942. In 1951, Justice Alto Adams resigned from the Florida Supreme Court to run an unsuccessful campaign for governor of Florida. Gov. Fuller Warren selected Mathews to replace Adams as a justice in 1951, serving until his death in 1955. The Mathews Bridge was named after Mathews due to his support for it. (State Archives of Florida.)

Three

The River City

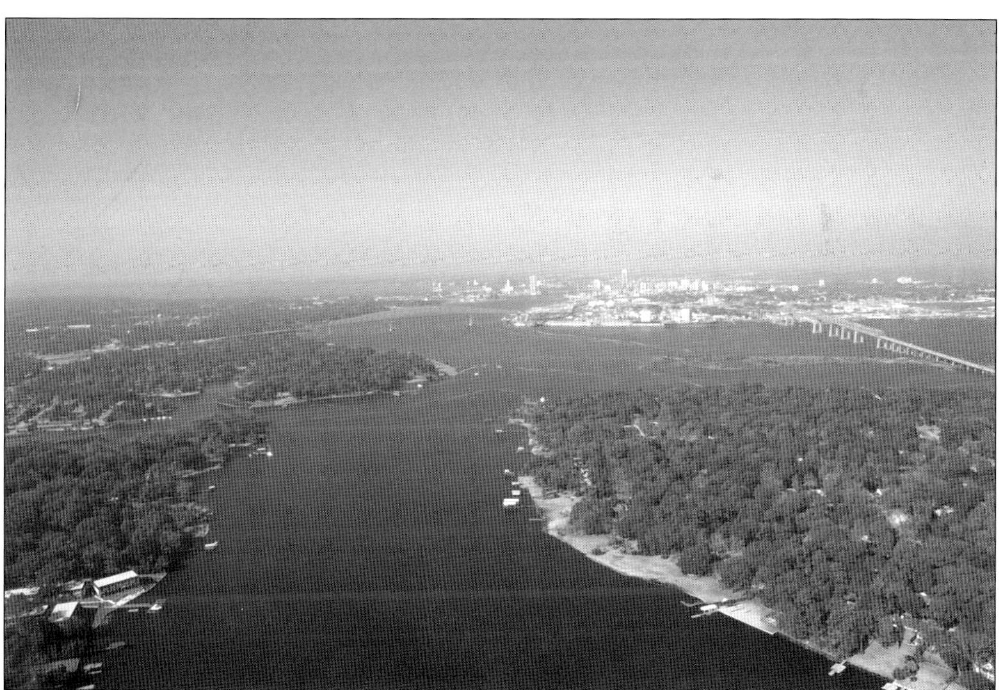

The Arlington River is a tributary of the St. Johns River beginning near Empire Point and Exchange Club Island. Pottsburg Creek and Silversmith Creek flow out of the end of the Arlington. This photograph shows the mouth of the Arlington River in the 1970s. Empire Point is at left center. The Hart Bridge and downtown Jacksonville can be seen in the distance. Little Pottsburg Creek is to the left of Empire Point. (University of North Florida.)

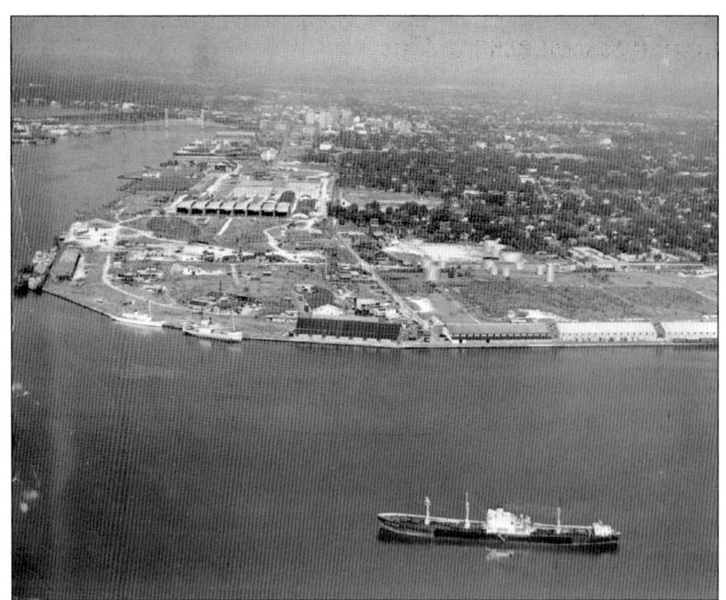

Commodore Point is the last point on the St. Johns River traveling south on the river into downtown Jacksonville. Commodore Point had a bustling maritime and manufacturing industry comparable to nearby Talleyrand. This photograph from 1951 shows the point with several ships docked on the river. Downtown Jacksonville is in the distance. (Jacksonville Historical Society.)

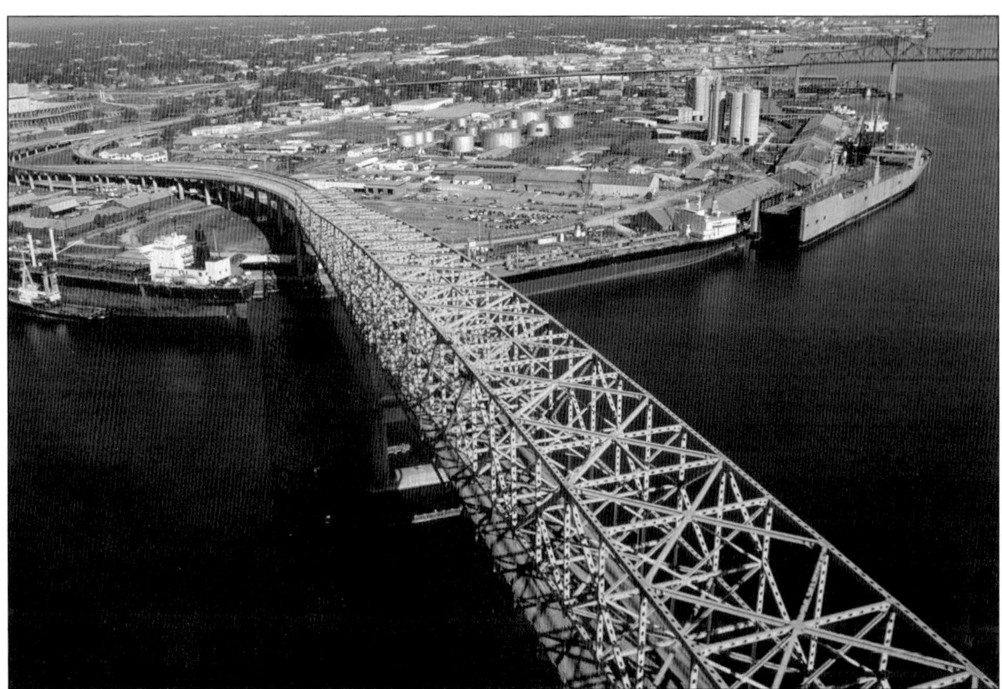

This aerial photograph of the Isaiah D. Hart Bridge going over Commodore Point is from the early 1990s. To the right of the bridge is Fincantieri Marine Repair. The cylindrical buildings in the background near the river are cement storage tanks for Lafarge North America. To the left of the bridge is Manson Construction, a Seattle-based marine business. (University of North Florida.)

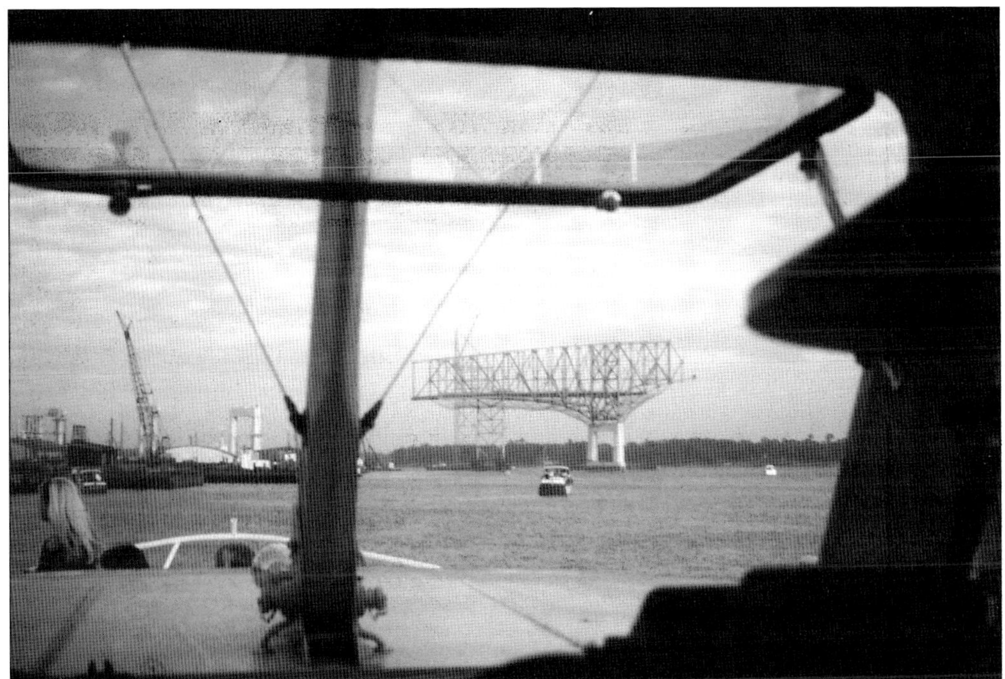

The Hart Bridge connects the Southside to downtown Jacksonville over the St. Johns River. The bridge was opened in 1967 and was built with bonds to be paid off with tolls. The tolls ended in 1989. The highest clearance of the bridge is 141 feet. It is named after the founder of Jacksonville. This photograph from 1966 shows the Hart Bridge under construction from Max Moody Jr.'s boat traveling east on the St. Johns near the Jacksonville Shipyards. (Andrew R. Nicholas.)

Pottsburg Creek is a 16-mile waterway that flows through the Southside and empties into the St. Johns River at Arlington. The name comes from a London merchant named Samuel Potts who had acquired a 10,000 acre tract of land in 1769. Potts established Pottsburg Plantation on the present-day high bluff of Clifton. He cultivated his plantation until 1784, when Florida was ceded back to Spain from Great Britain. This photograph shows Pottsburg Creek in 2022. (Andrew R. Nicholas.)

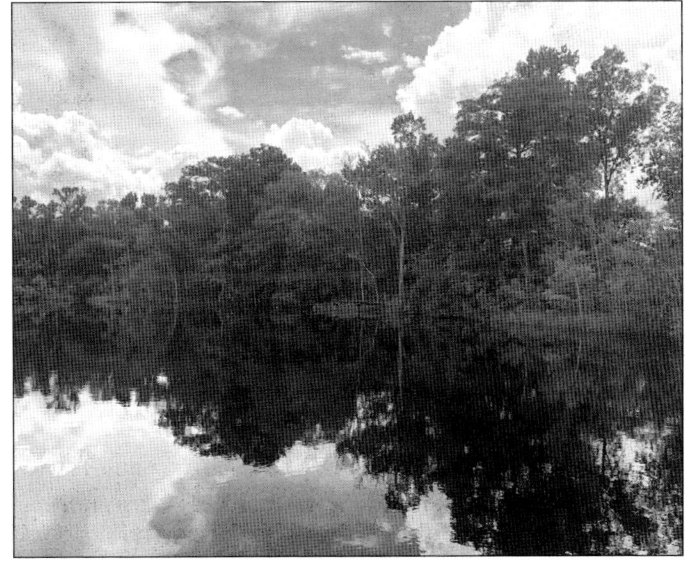

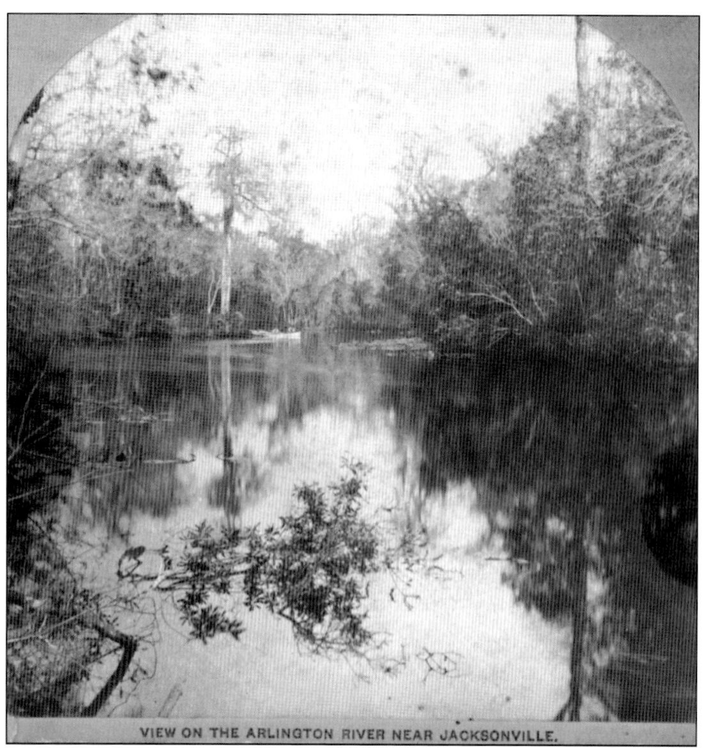

The Arlington River flows east past Empire Point and around Oak Haven. The river flows into Pottsburg Creek near Atlantic Boulevard and continues south, where it ends in the Secret Cove neighborhood. This stereograph image shows the Arlington River in 1875. (New York Public Library.)

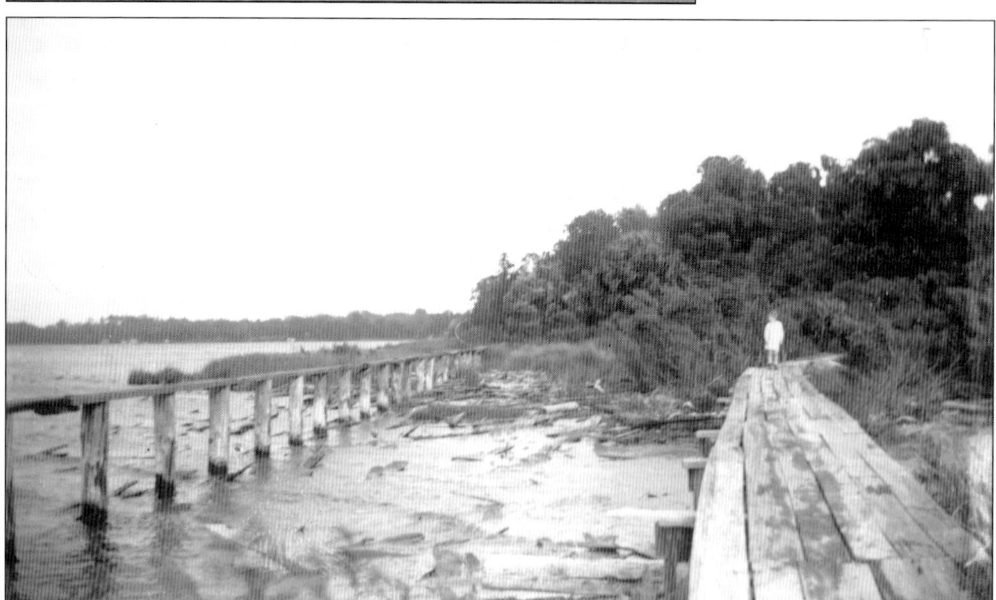

In 1808, Reuben Hogans acquired a Spanish land grant of 385 acres from Miller Creek east to the Arlington River. His property was transferred to Francis Richard in the 1820s and then to John Sammis, who sold off parts of the property for three mills called the Highlands, Clifton, and Empire. The mills were burned down during the Civil War, but the Empire Mill was later rebuilt to become Florida's first circular steam sawmill. It was at the mouth of Pottsburg Creek. The name was later used for the neighborhood of Empire Point as well as the point on the St. Johns River. This photograph shows a boy on a dock at Empire Point in 1902. (Jacksonville Historical Society.)

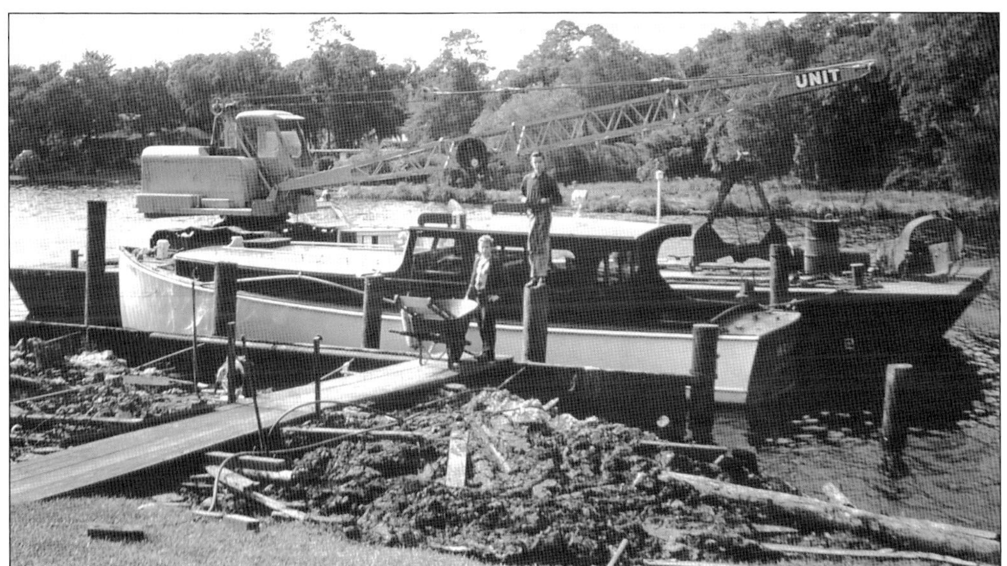

Miller Creek in the St. Nicholas neighborhood is named after Englishman David Solomon Hill Miller, who settled there in 1799. He married Anna Hogans Bagley, a widow and owner of a Spanish land grant of 300 acres west of the creek. Miller served Spain as captain of the Rural Militia of the St. Johns River, San Nicholas District. This photograph by Maxey Moody Jr. shows a barge with a crane and a boat on Miller Creek in 1957. The crane was dredging the dock area. Maxey Moody III is standing on a piling, with his brother Boyd Moody near the wheelbarrow. (Andrew R. Nicholas.)

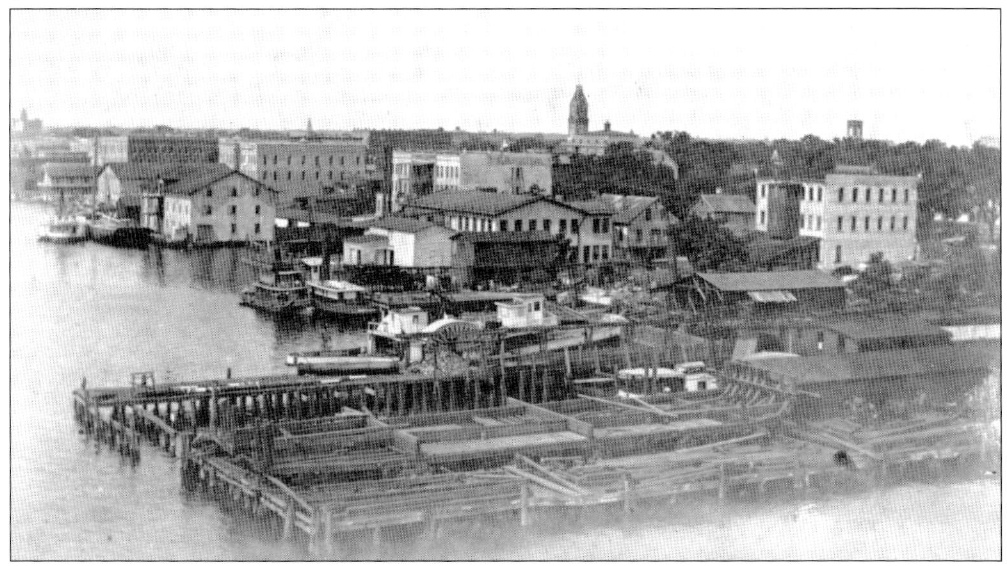

Capt. James Gilman Merrill moved to Jacksonville from Charleston, South Carolina, in 1866 following the Civil War. In Jacksonville, he started a blacksmith and ironwork shop for marine repairs. Merrill's sons Gene and Alex took over the business in 1879. In 1895, the Merrill-Stevens Engineering Company was incorporated. Merrill's friend Arthur Stevens, an engineer and naval architect, was also involved with the business. The first Merrill-Stevens location was on Bay Street on the St. Johns River. This photograph of downtown Jacksonville and the St. Johns shows Merrill-Stevens in the 1890s. (Jacksonville Historical Society.)

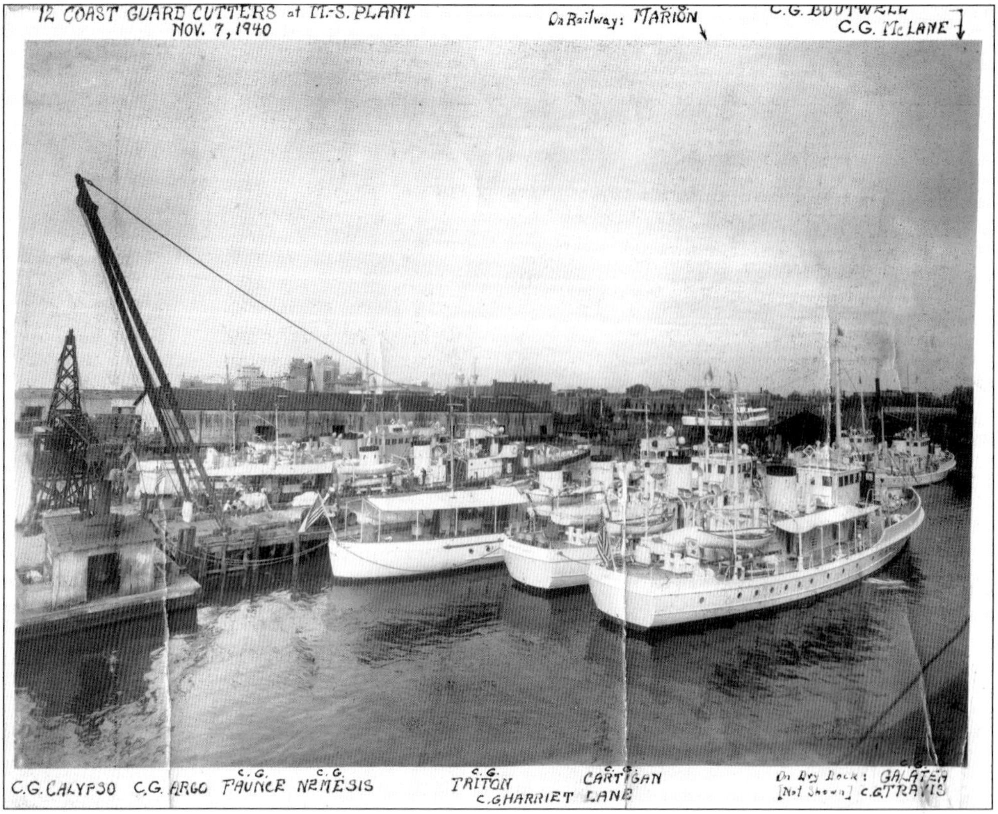

The Great Fire of 1901 destroyed the Merrill-Stevens wharves on Bay Street. The firm decided to expand operations after the fire by focusing more on shipbuilding than repair. Merrill-Stevens built a new plant and facility at the present-day location of the Jacksonville Shipyards. During World War I, the company was bought by the Emergency Fleet Corporation to produce ships for the US Merchant Marine. After the war, the Emergency Fleet Corporation sold the business back to Gene Merrill. It was reorganized as Merrill-Stevens Dry Dock and Repair Company. This photograph shows US Coast Guard cutters at Merrill-Stevens in 1940. (Jacksonville Historical Society.)

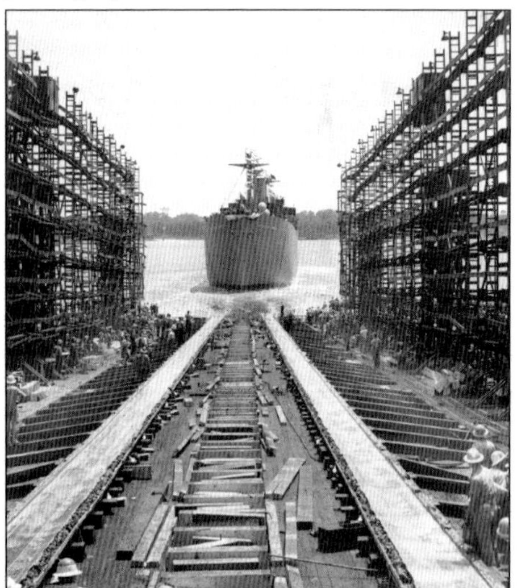

In 1942, the St. Johns River Shipbuilding Company was created by Merrill-Stevens with an investment from the US Military Commission to build Liberty ships, cargo ships built under the Emergency Shipbuilding Program for the American war effort. During the war, the company produced 82 ships with an employee force topping out at around 20,000 in 1944. This photograph shows the Liberty ship SS *William Byrd* launching into the St. Johns River in 1943. (Jacksonville Historical Society.)

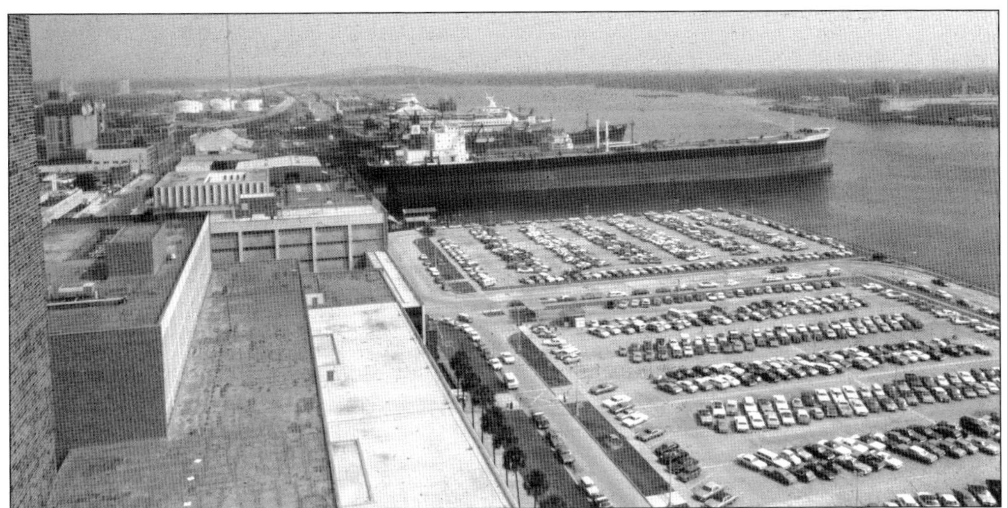

In 1953, Merrill-Stevens leased its shipyard to Rawls Brothers Contractors and relocated to Miami. Rawls Brothers renamed the shipyard to Rawls Brothers Shipyard. In 1963, Rawls Brothers sold the shipyard to Bill Lovett, who renamed it Jacksonville Shipyards. Lovett sold the shipyard to Fruehauf Corporation in 1969. Jacksonville Shipyards became the city's largest employer by 1977, but business steadily declined in the 1980s. Terex Corporation acquired Freuhauf, including the Jacksonville Shipyards, in 1989, and closed the shipyards in 1992. This photograph of the Jacksonville Shipyards was taken in 1976. (State Archives of Florida.)

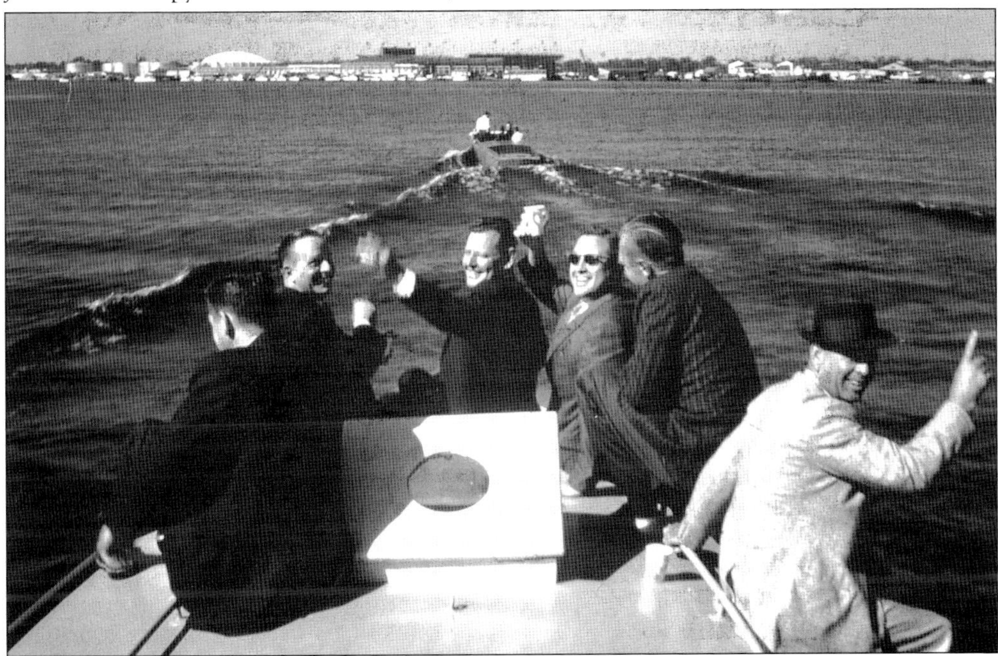

The Gator Bowl stadium first opened in 1928 and has hosted the annual Gator Bowl college football game since 1946. The stadium is also host to the Florida-Georgia game, which is nicknamed "the World's Largest Outdoor Cocktail Party." The location of the stadium by the river makes it a prime destination for boaters to either attend a game or simply tailgate in the area. This photograph shows Jacksonville boaters traveling across the St. Johns to the Gator Bowl game in 1959. The stadium can be seen at top, with the Jacksonville Coliseum to the left. (Andrew R. Nicholas.)

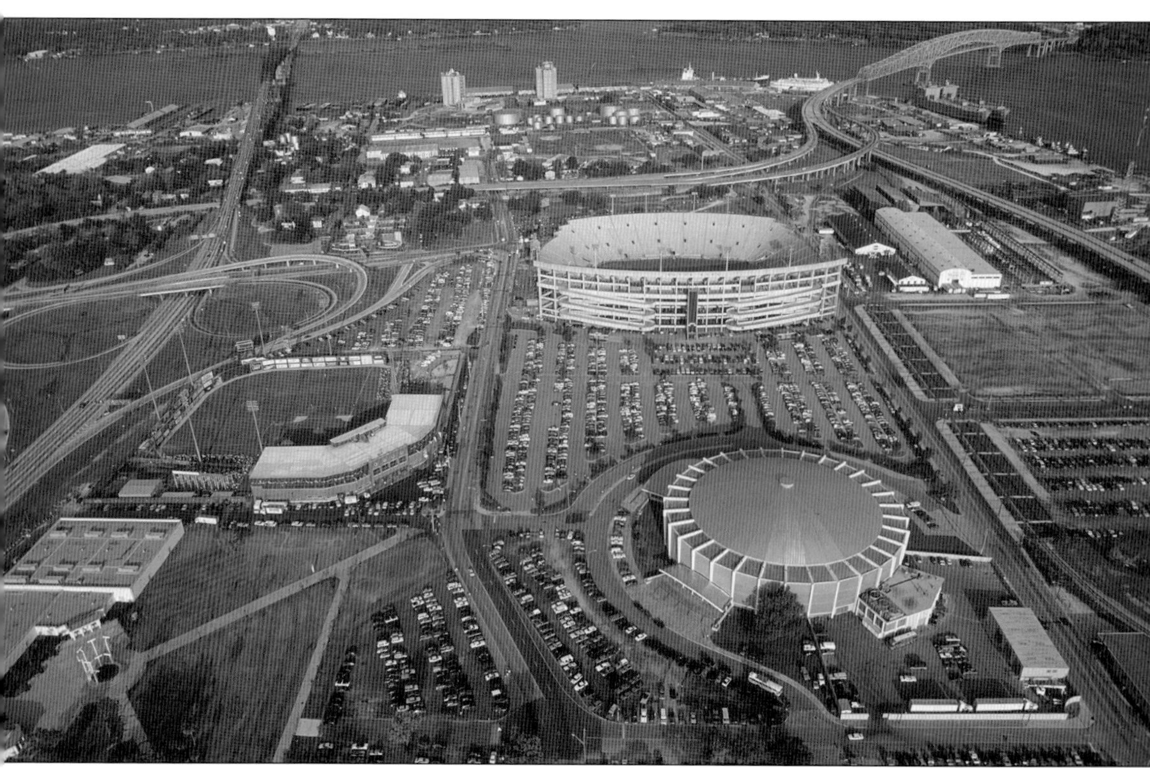

This photograph shows the Jacksonville Coliseum, Wolfson Park, and Gator Bowl stadium in 1991. The coliseum opened in 1960 and was Jacksonville's main arena for events and concerts until 2003, when it was demolished for the present-day Veterans Memorial Arena, built on the same site. Wolfson Park was a baseball park that first opened in 1954 for the short-lived Jacksonville Braves and then the Jacksonville Suns. It was demolished in 2002 for the new 121 Financial Ballpark that opened in 2003. The Jacksonville Suns were later renamed the Jacksonville Jumbo Shrimp due to the popularity of shrimping on the St. Johns River. The Gator Bowl stadium first opened in 1927 as Fairfield Stadium. In 1948, it was renamed the Gator Bowl after it first began hosting the annual college football Gator Bowl game. In 1994, Jacksonville was awarded an NFL franchise, the Jaguars. The Gator Bowl stadium was demolished, and in its place, a bigger stadium was built to accommodate the new NFL team. Jacksonville Municipal Stadium opened in 1995 and was renamed Alltel Stadium in 1997, EverBank Field in 2010, and TIAA Bank Field in 2018. Throughout the continual changes to the stadiums, coliseums, and arenas, the St. Johns River continues to flow around Commodore Point.

Gulf Life Insurance Company acquired property on the Southbank for a new headquarters. In 1966, construction for a 28-story building began. The Gulf Life Tower opened in 1967 as Jacksonville's tallest building. This photograph shows the tower under construction in 1966, as seen from the St. Johns River. In 1993, Gate Petroleum acquired the building and rebranded it as Riverplace Tower. (Andrew R. Nicholas.)

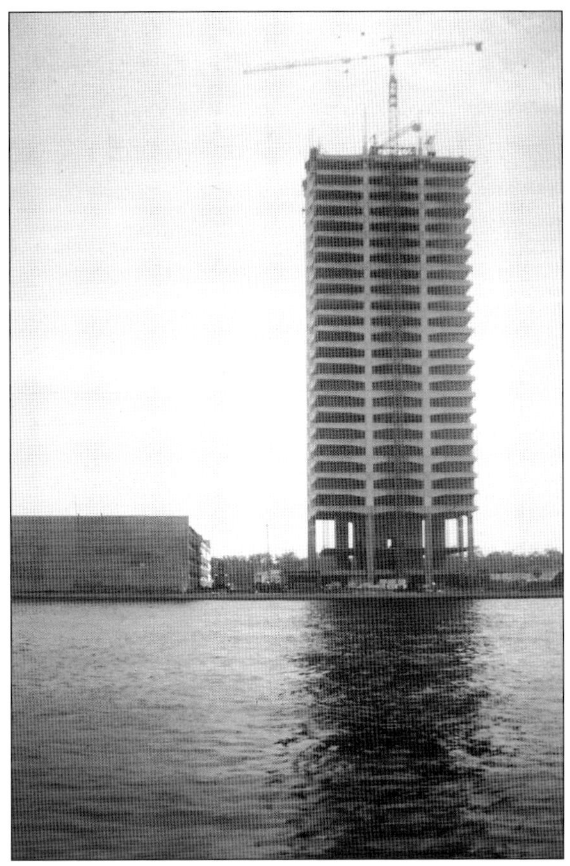

George Williams Gibbs founded Gibbs Gas Engine Company in 1908. The company manufactured a fuel-efficient marine engine and built ships. The Gibbs shipyards were on the Southbank at the present-day Crowne Plaza Hotel. By the 1940s, the Gibbs shipyards expanded all the way to the present-day Duval County education building. This photograph shows the shipyards in 1960. (State Archives of Florida.)

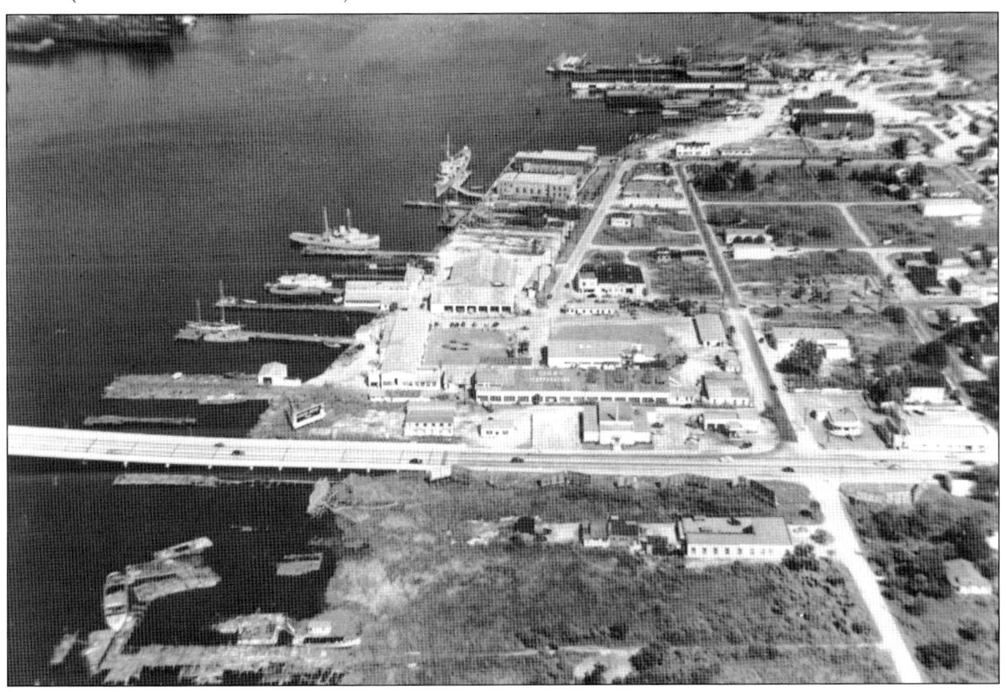

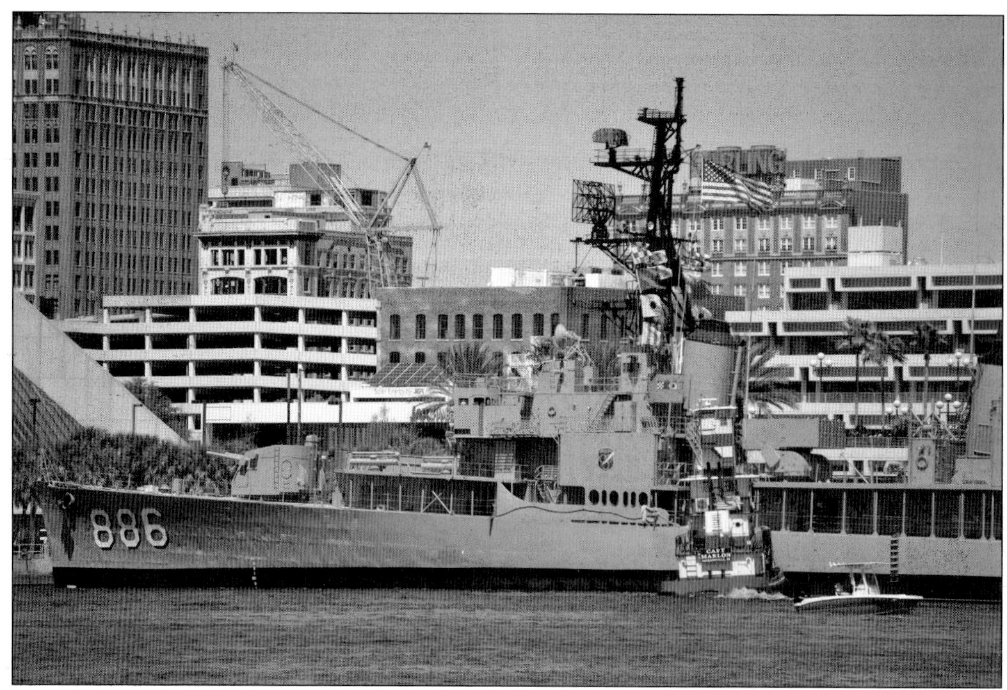

The USS *Orleck* (DD-886) is a Gearing-class destroyer launched in 1945. It was named after Lt. Joseph Orleck, the captain of the USS *Nauset* (AT-89), a Navajo-class tugboat in service during World War II. The *Nauset* was sunk by the Luftwaffe on September 9, 1943. Orleck chose to go down with the *Nauset*. The *Orleck* participated in the Korean War and Vietnam War. In 1982, the ship was transferred to Turkey for use in the Turkish navy, where it was renamed the TCG *Yücetepe*. In 2000, the destroyer was sent to Texas, where it was returned to its former name and became a museum ship. In 2010, the *Orleck* was moved to Lake Charles, Louisiana. In 2021, it was moved to Port Arthur, Texas, for restorations. In March 2022, the *Orleck* arrived in Jacksonville, where it will be part of the Jacksonville Naval Museum on the St. Johns River. This photograph of the *Orleck* was taken on March 26, 2022, when it first arrived in Jacksonville. (Andrew R. Nicholas.)

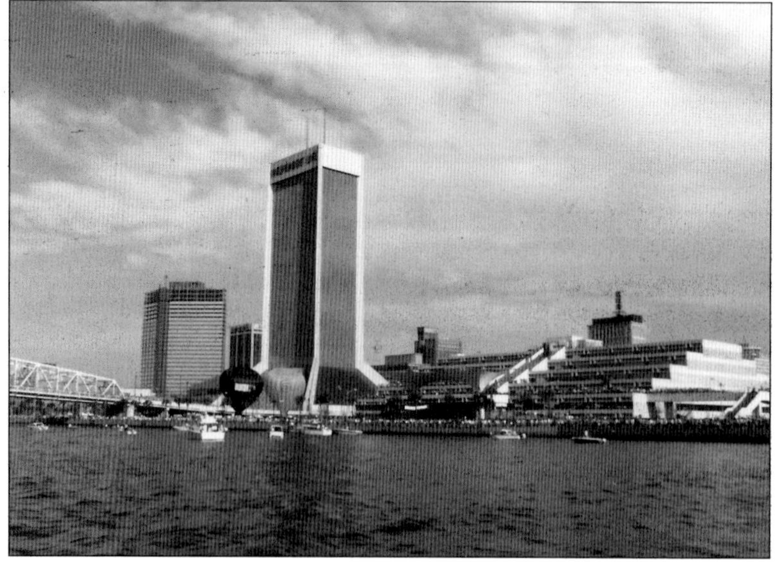

River Day was a short-lived event in Jacksonville to celebrate a cleaner and safer St. Johns River. It began in 1977 after cleanup of the river was completed. This photograph shows River Day celebrations in 1982. (Andrew R. Nicholas.)

This is a map of Jacksonville and the St. Johns River in 1887. No bridges over the St. Johns yet existed in the area, making ferry travel the only option. Jacksonville consisted of only the north bank of the river. The south bank consisted of South Jacksonville and Saint Nicholas. (State Archives of Florida.)

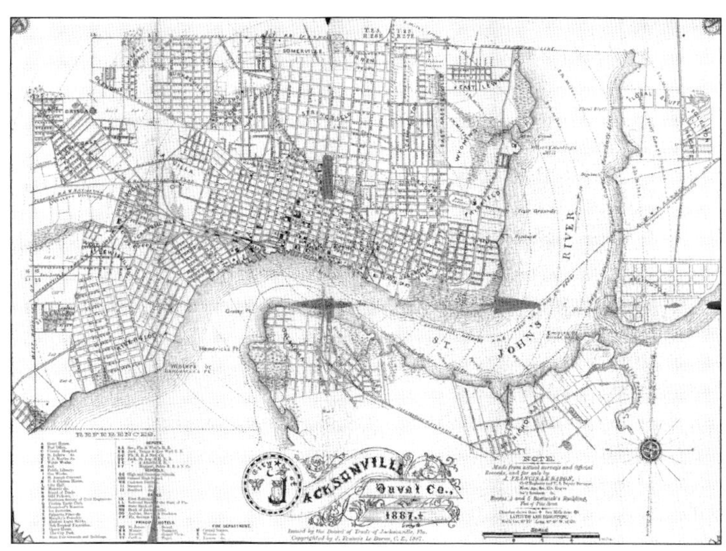

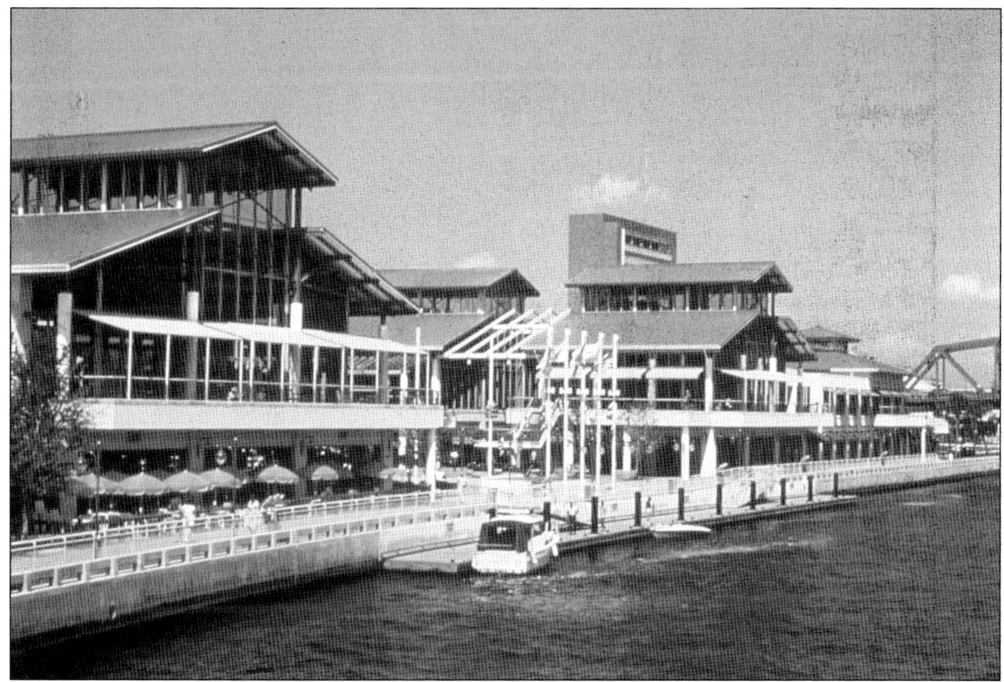

Jacksonville Landing was a two-story building on the north bank of the St. Johns River with shops, restaurants, and a floating dock for boaters. It opened in 1987 and became a popular destination for tourists. This photograph shows Jacksonville Landing in 1987. In the 2010s, business declined, leading it to close in 2019. The Jacksonville Landing was demolished in October 2019, leaving an empty field of grass in its place. As of 2022, plans are underway to convert the property into a riverfront park. (State Archives of Florida.)

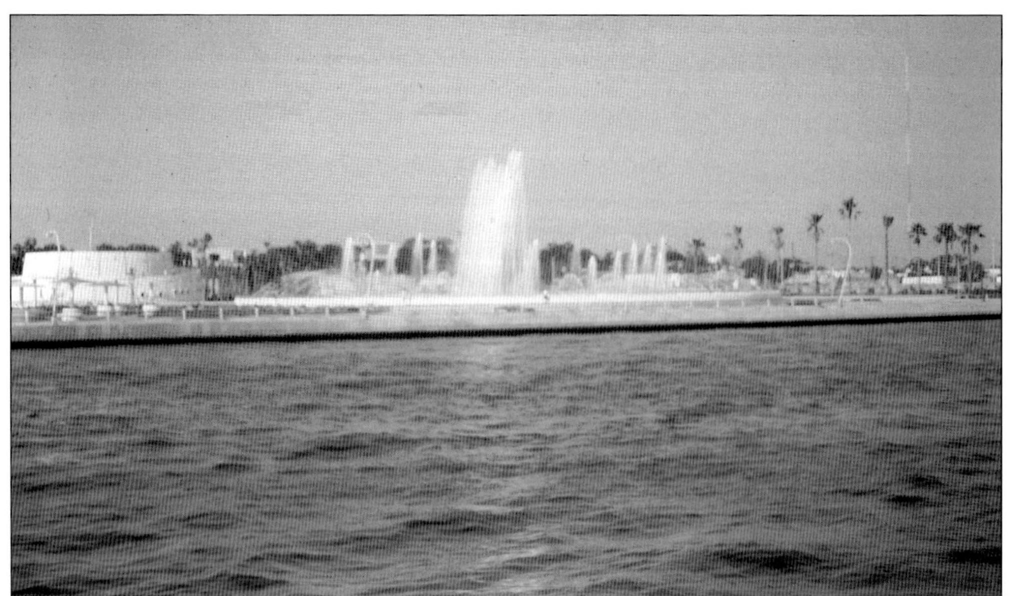

Friendship Fountain is on the Southbank near Main Street Bridge. The fountain was designed by Taylor Hardwick and opened in 1965. This photograph was taken from the St. Johns River in 1967. Note that there were no buildings behind Friendship Fountain at the time. (Andrew R. Nicholas.)

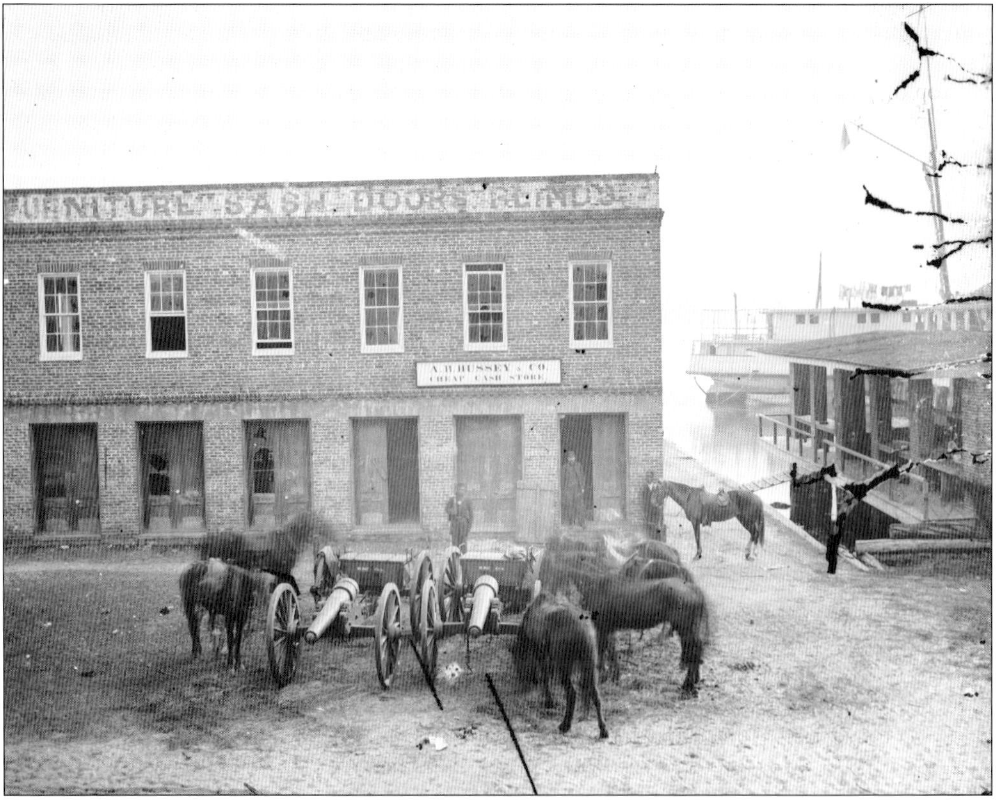

This photograph shows Jacksonville under Union occupation in 1864. A Union ship can be seen on the St. Johns River in the background. (Library of Congress.)

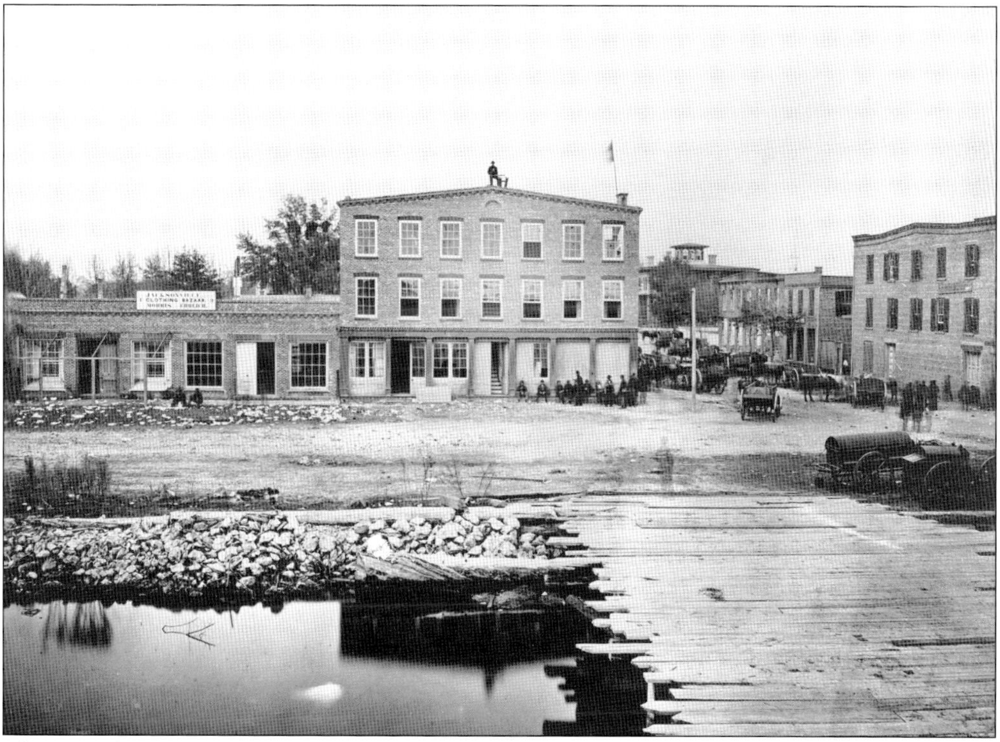

This is a photograph of Jacksonville from a Union steamship on the St. Johns River in 1864. On top of the building at center is a Union soldier on guard duty. To the left is a store called Jacksonville Clothing Bazaar. (Library of Congress.)

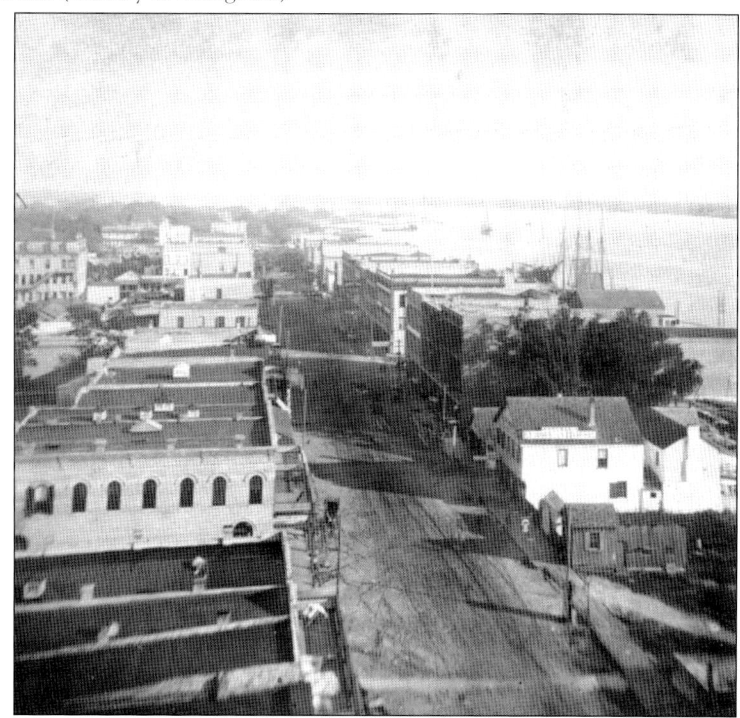

This photograph shows Jacksonville in 1876. The St. Johns River is on the right. Commodore Point can be seen in the far distance where the river flows around and continues flowing north. Twenty-five years later, the majority of the buildings in this photograph would burn down in the Great Fire of 1901. (New York Public Library.)

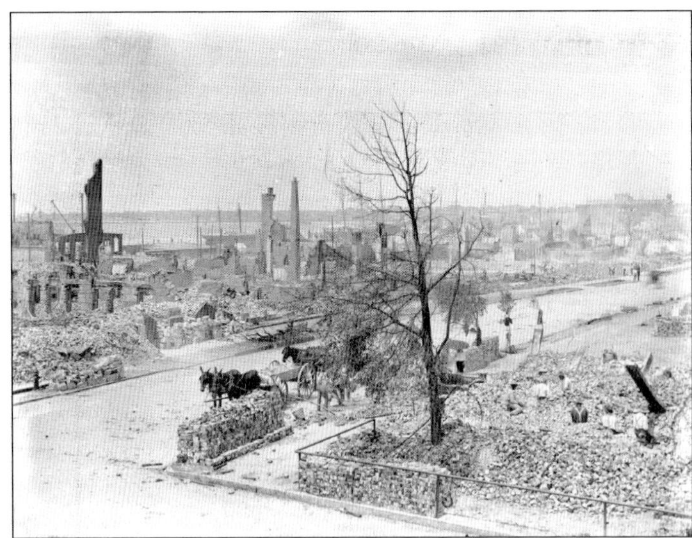

The Great Fire of 1901 destroyed the majority of the present-day area of downtown Jacksonville. Over 2,000 structures burned down, but only seven people were killed. This photograph shows the cleanup after the fire. In the far distance are the St. Johns River and the Florida East Coast Railway bridge. (Jacksonville Historical Society.)

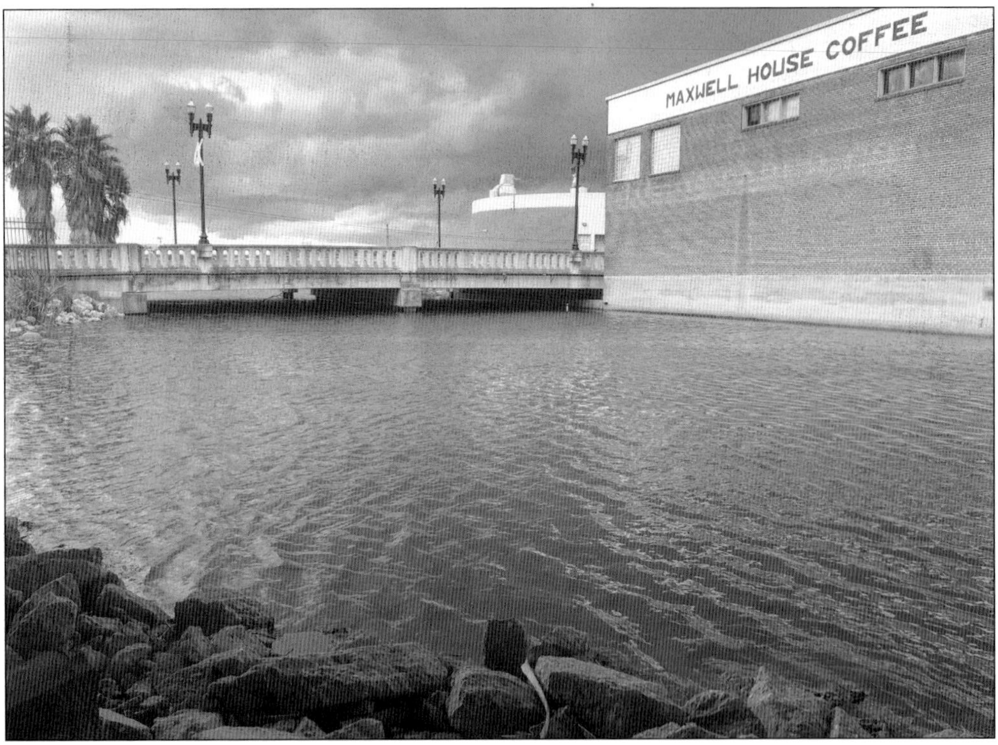

Hogans Creek is a 2.6-mile waterway in downtown Jacksonville. It flows through Warren M. Schell Jr. Memorial Park, Henry J. Klutho Park, and Springfield Park, then into the St. Johns River between the Maxwell Coffee House and Intuition Ale Works. During the Great Fire of 1901, Hogans Creek became a natural firebreak, stopping the flames from spreading farther east. Architect Henry J. Klutho and engineer Charles Imeson created the Hogans Creek Improvement Project in 1929–1930 to better control flooding and make the creek more appealing. Although Klutho's plans did make it look more appealing to an extent, the park was neglected over the years. The creek continues to be neglected into the 21st century, with debris and pollutants flowing out into the river. This photograph shows the creek in 2022. (Andrew R. Nicholas.)

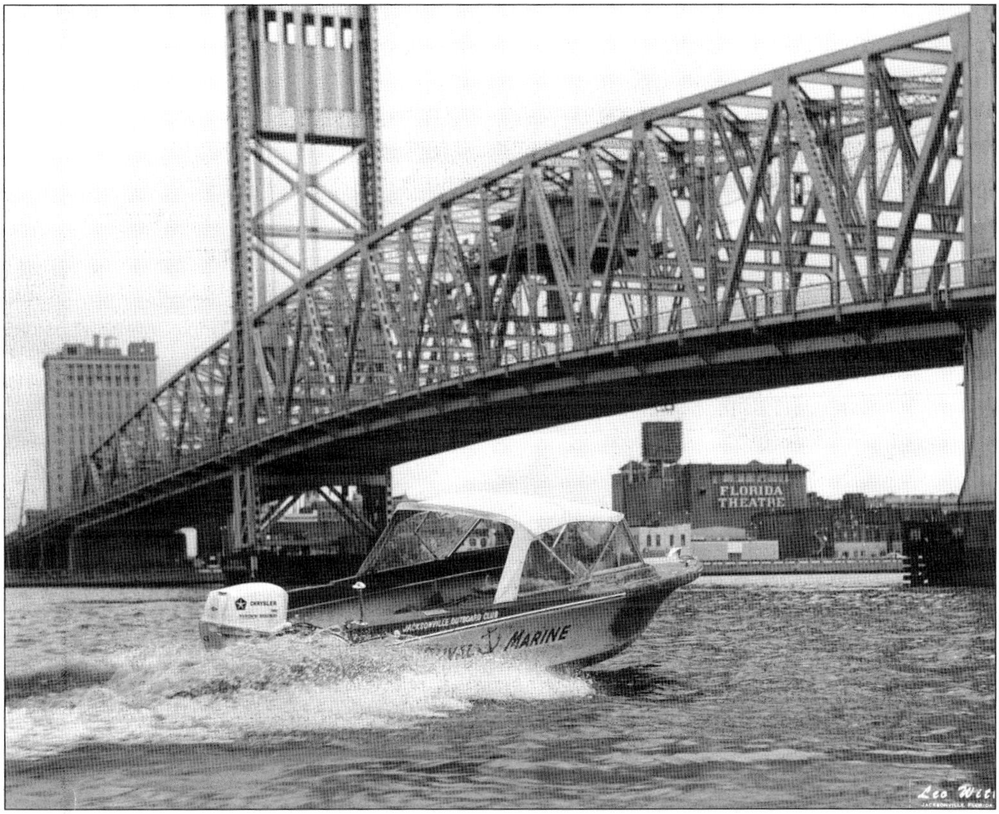

The Main Street Bridge began construction in 1938 and opened in 1941. It was built like the neighboring St. Johns River Bridge as a vertical lift bridge to allow larger marine vessels through. The bridge connects the Southside to downtown Jacksonville over a narrow part of the St. Johns River that was once called the Cow Ford. This photograph shows a boat going east under the bridge in the 1960s. The outboard motor is a Chrysler. (Jacksonville Historical Society.)

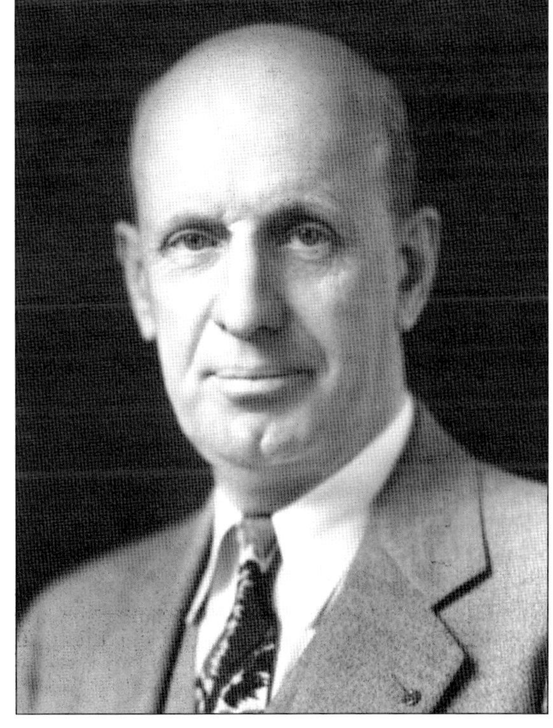

John Thomas Alsop Jr. was born on August 10, 1874, in Enfield, South Carolina. He was mayor of Jacksonville from 1923 to 1937 and again from 1941 to 1945. The Main Street Bridge in downtown Jacksonville was officially named the John T. Alsop Jr. Bridge in 1957. (Jacksonville Historical Society.)

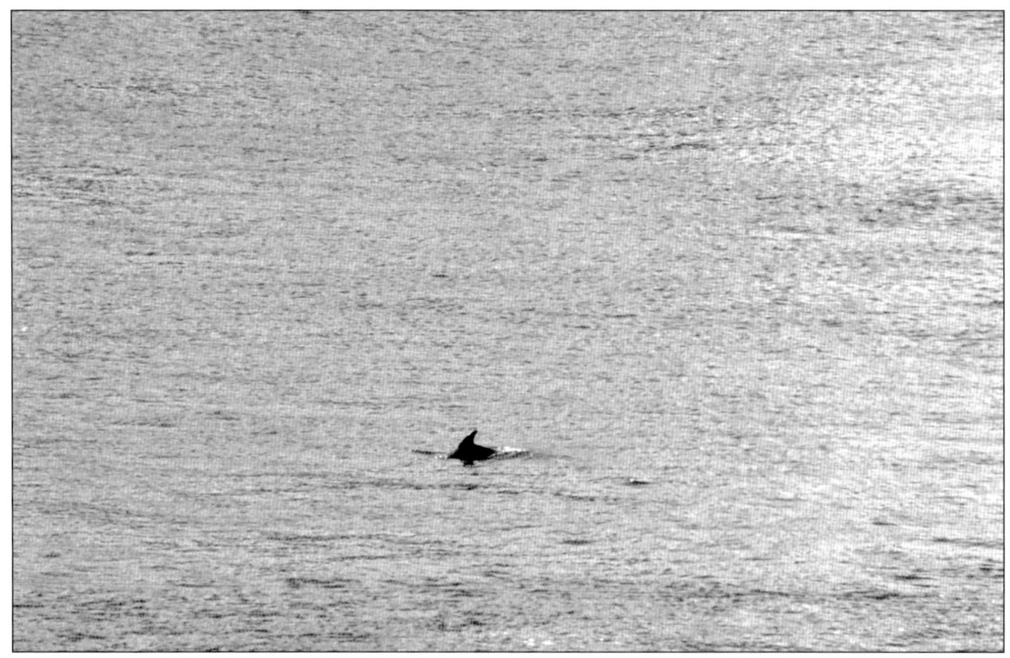

Dolphins are a common sight on the St. Johns River in Jacksonville, making the St. Johns River a theater of dolphin activity. This photograph of a dolphin was taken on the left side of the Acosta Bridge in 2022. (Andrew R. Nicholas.)

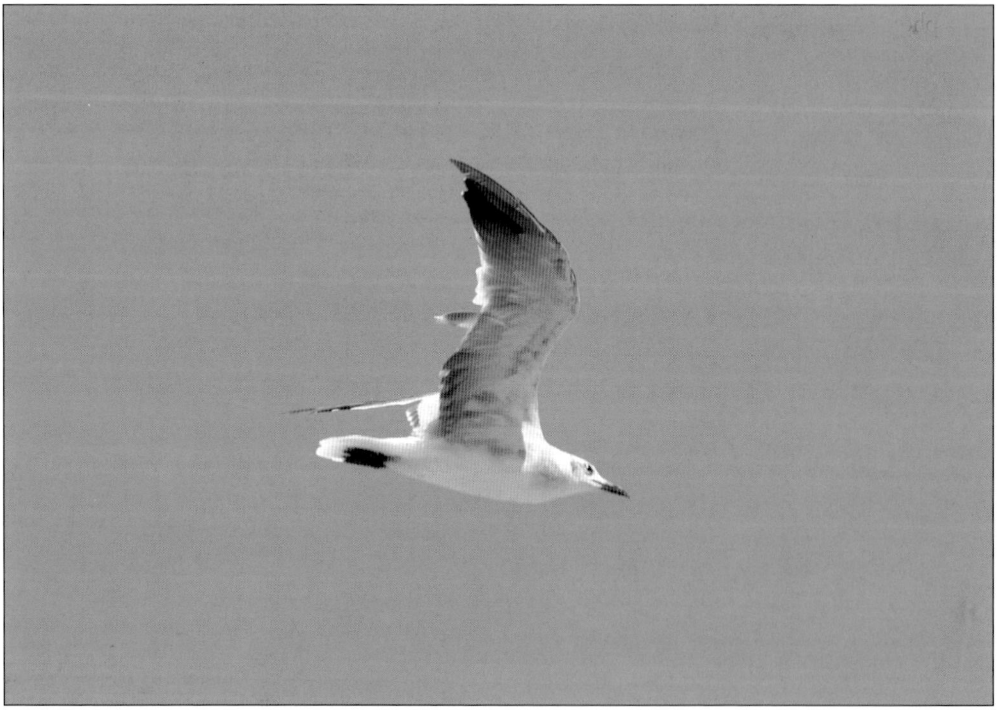

Seagulls are commonly found in cities near the ocean. The seagull in this photograph was flying over the St. Johns River. (Andrew R. Nicholas.)

Before bridges dotted the landscape of Jacksonville, there were ferries to transport people and vehicles across the St. Johns River. Before the 1920s, there were no bridges in the downtown area for cars to travel over the river. This photograph shows the ferry *South Jacksonville* with a load of people and cars in the 1910s. (West Volusia Historical Society.)

Today, there are five bridges for vehicles and two for pedestrians. Despite these bridges, there is still a St. Johns River Taxi that transports passengers across the river. The river taxi operates at several locations in the vicinity of downtown. This photograph shows the *Miss Hadley* river taxi approaching Friendship Fountain in 2022. (Andrew R. Nicholas.)

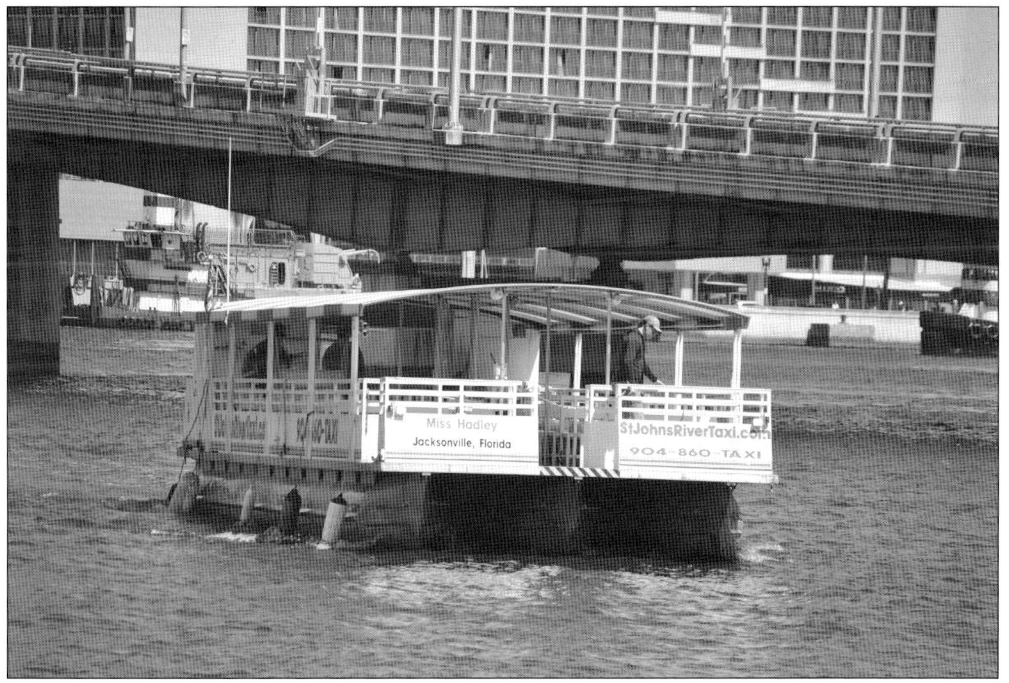

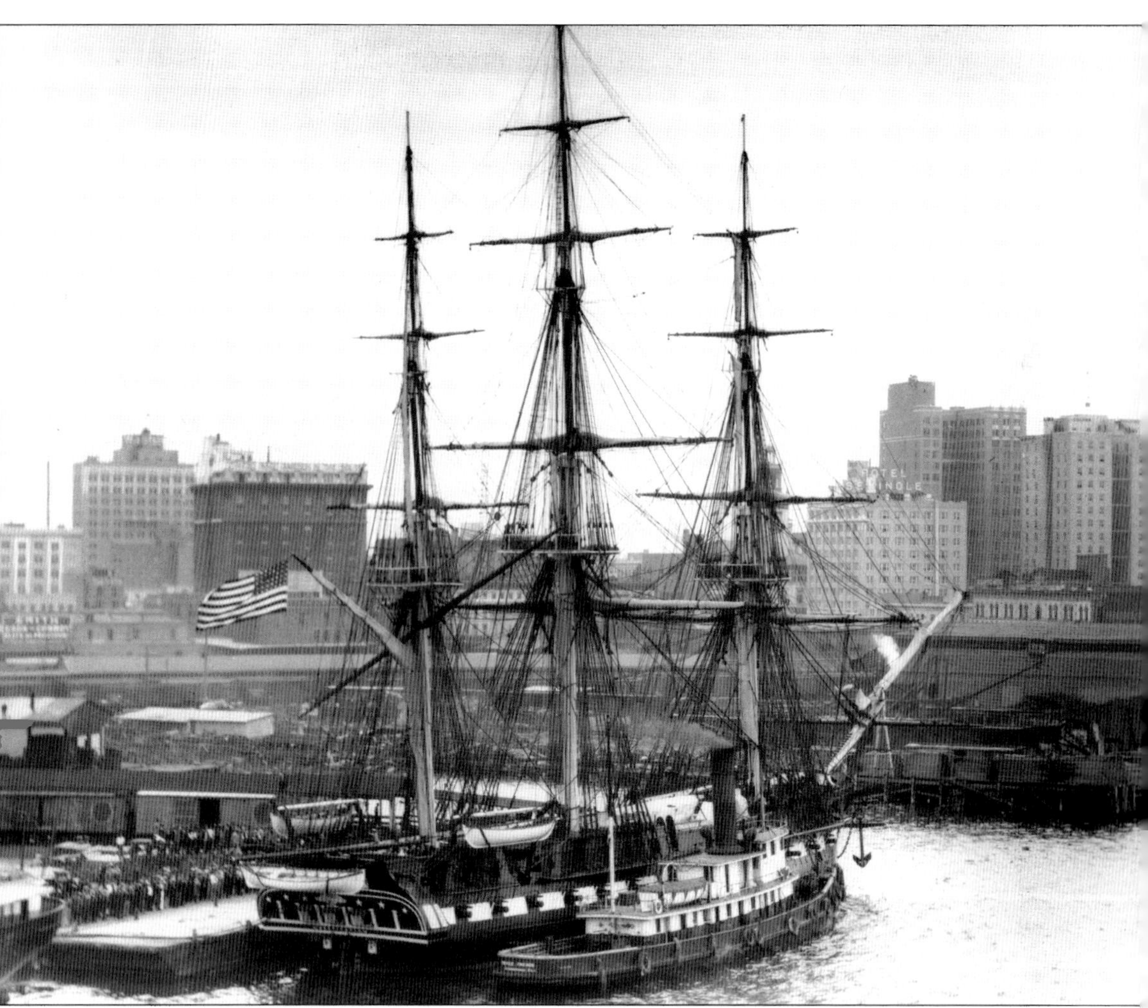

The USS *Constitution* was launched in 1797 as one of the first ships for what would become the US Navy. It became famous in the War of 1812 when it defeated five British warships. What makes the *Constitution* unique is that it is still around today. This photograph shows the *Constitution* docked on the St. Johns River at the Williamson Tire Company in Jacksonville on December 16, 1931. An estimated 6,000 Jacksonville residents visited the ship in Jacksonville. The Hotel Seminole at right center is on the location of the present-day Bank of America Tower. (Jacksonville Historical Society.)

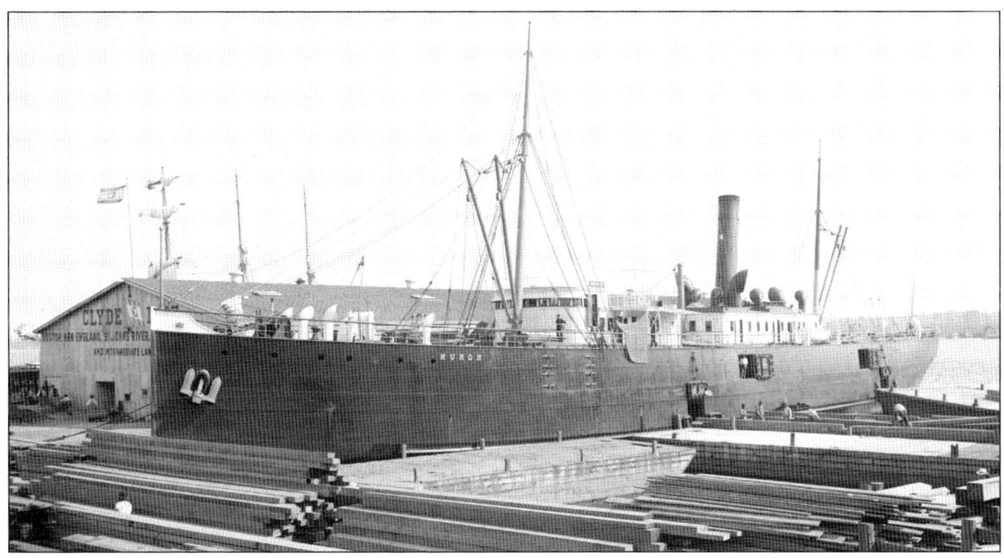

The Clyde Steamship Company operated steamship routes to various places on the east and west coasts of the United States. Clyde steamships also offered service out of Jacksonville to places like New York City and Boston. This photograph from around 1903 shows the SS *Huron* docked at a Clyde Line terminal in Jacksonville, near the present-day location of the CSX building. (Library of Congress.)

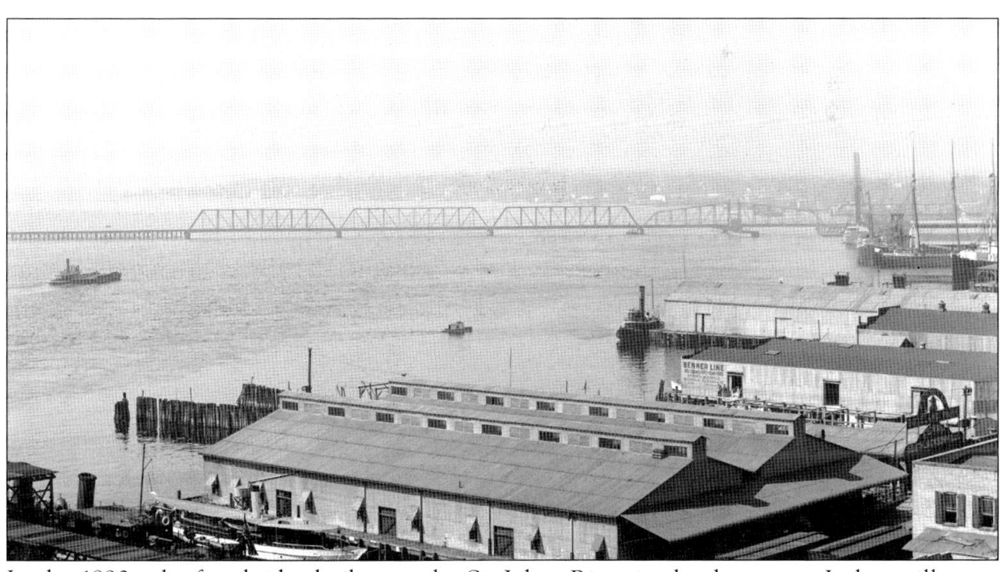

In the 1890s, the first bridge built over the St. Johns River in the downtown Jacksonville area opened. It was commissioned by Henry Flagler to allow his Florida East Coast Railway to travel over the river into South Jacksonville. It was a single-track swing bridge that could turn to allow marine traffic to pass through. This photograph from 1910 shows the bridge in the distance. (Library of Congress.)

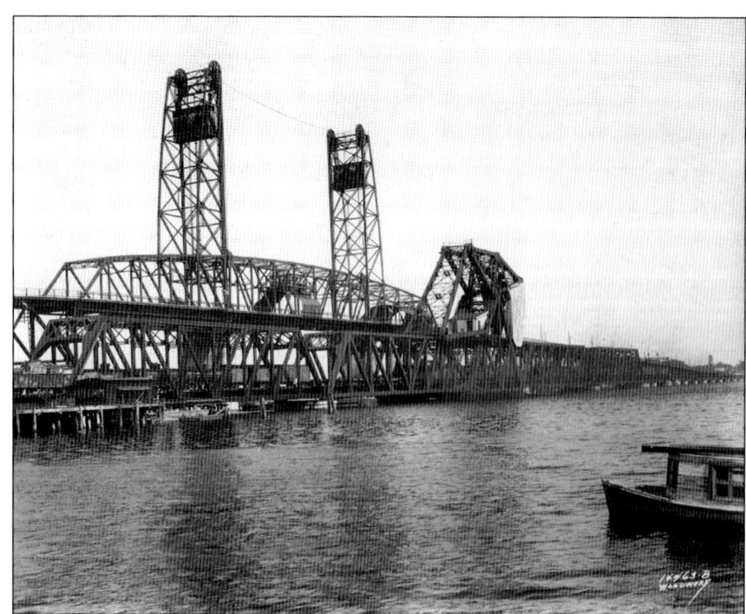

The St. Johns River Bridge was a three-lane steel vertical-lift bridge connecting South Jacksonville to Jacksonville. It was the first bridge for automobiles and pedestrians to cross the St. Johns River. This photograph of the bridge and the FEC Strauss Bridge was taken in 1927. (Jacksonville Historical Society.)

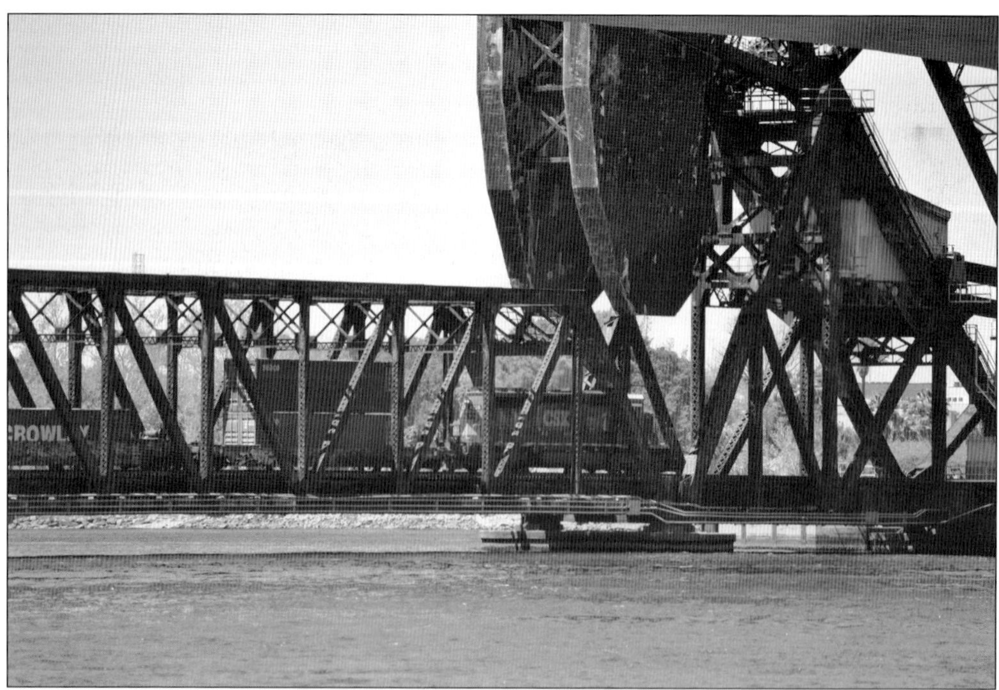

The FEC Strauss trunnion bascule bridge opened in 1925 as a double-track railroad bridge. It was built to replace Flagler's single-track railroad bridge. The bridge is always in the upright position until a train approaches, causing it to go down. The designer of the bridge was Joseph Strauss, notable as the chief engineer of the Golden Gate Bridge. This photograph shows the FEC Strauss Bridge in the down position to allow a CSX train with a full load to cross over the St. Johns River in 2022. (Andrew R. Nicholas.)

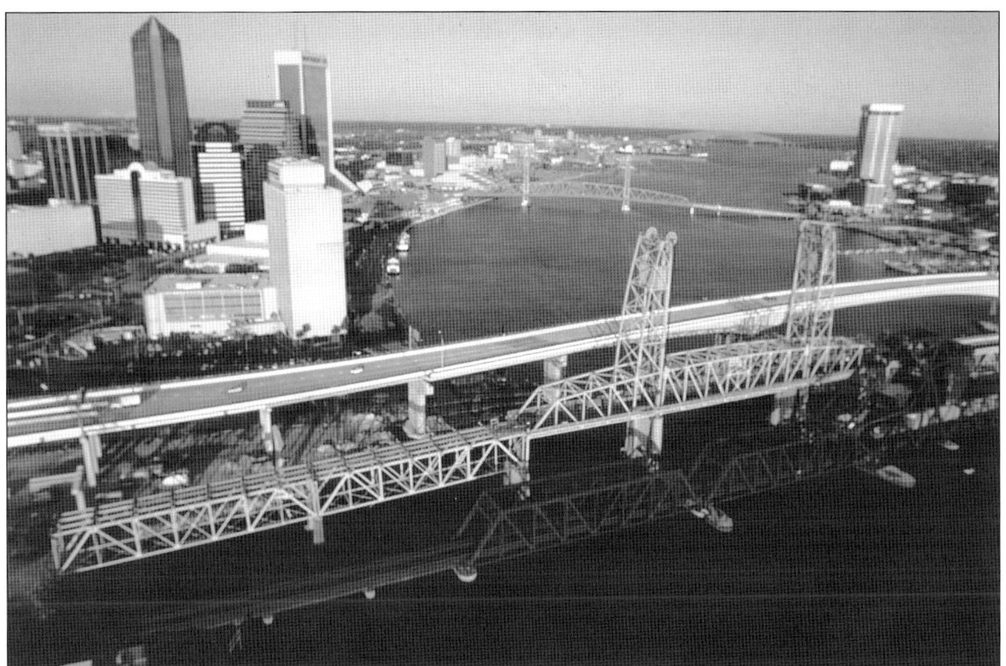

The St. Elmo W. Acosta Bridge began construction in 1990 to replace the 70-year-old St. Johns River Bridge. The Acosta Bridge was built higher to allow vessels through and was not a lift bridge like the older bridge. This photograph from 1994 shows the Acosta Bridge in use while the St. Johns River Bridge is being prepped for demolition. (University of North Florida.)

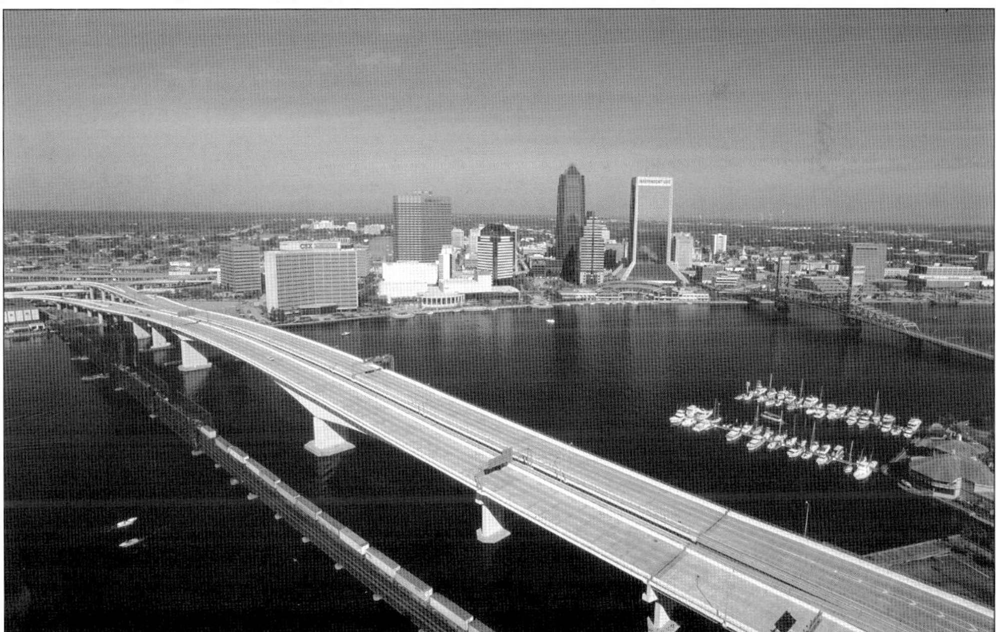

This is a photograph of downtown Jacksonville in 1997. The Acosta Bridge is seen going over the St. Johns River next to the FEC Strauss Bridge. River City Brewing Company is on the right, where the boats are docked. River City Brewing closed in 2021 and was demolished in 2022. (University of North Florida.)

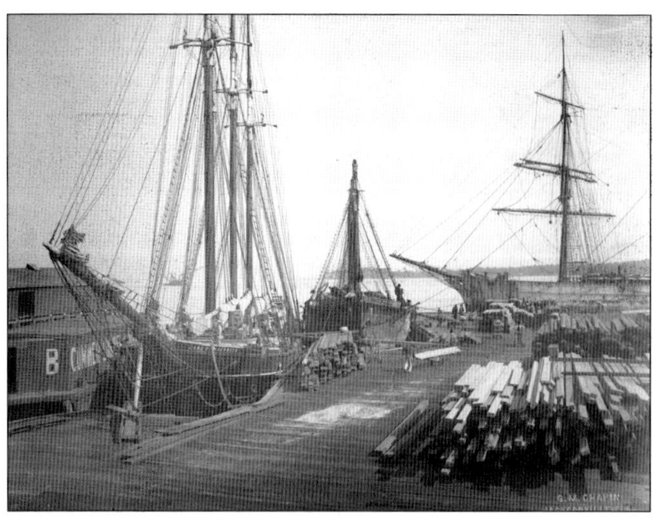

Wellington Willson Cummer was born on October 21, 1848, in Toronto, Ontario. In 1896, he relocated his family from Michigan to Jacksonville, where he started a lumber business called the Cummer Lumber Yard near McCoys Creek. Cummer had a railroad built to transport lumber from Florida to his lumber yard. This photograph of the Cummer Lumber Yard was taken in the 1910s. (Jacksonville Historical Society.)

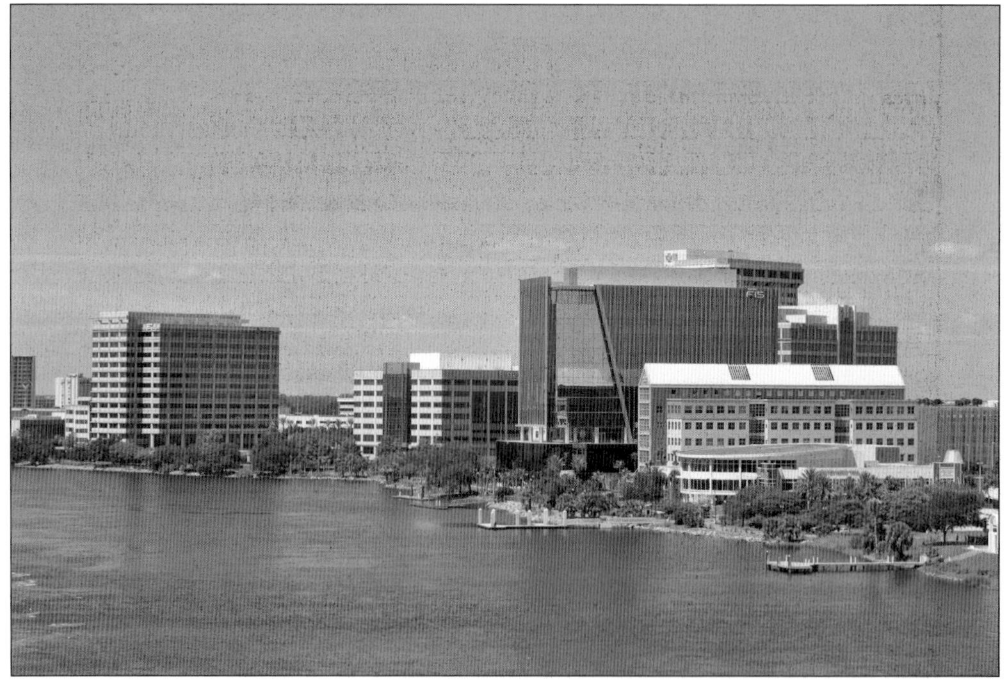

Brooklyn is a neighborhood on the St. Johns River in the vicinity of downtown Jacksonville. It was part of Phillips Dell's Spanish land grant called Dell's Bluff. Miles Price acquired Dell's Bluff in 1866. In 1868, he sold the southern part of the land to John Murray Forbes and retained the northern half. Price created the residential neighborhood called Brooklyn out of his half, while Forbes laid the foundation for present-day Riverside. Toward the end of the 20th century, the Brooklyn area was transforming into a commercial hub rather than a residential neighborhood. It continues to grow with further commercial buildings and new modern apartments near the St. Johns River. This photograph shows Brooklyn with commercial buildings on the river in 2022. (Andrew R. Nicholas.)

On the Southbank between the Acosta Bridge and Fuller Warren Bridge is Baptist Health, comprising six hospitals including Wolfson Children's Hospital. This photograph shows Baptist Health on the St. Johns River in 2022. (Andrew R. Nicholas.)

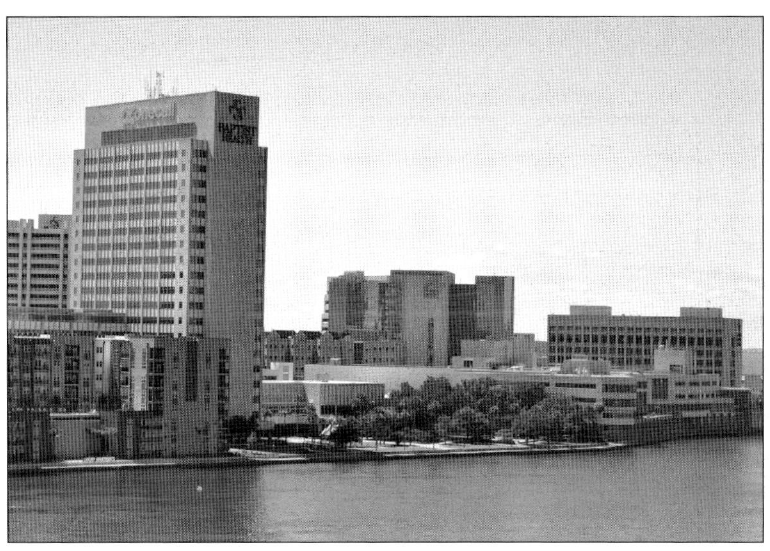

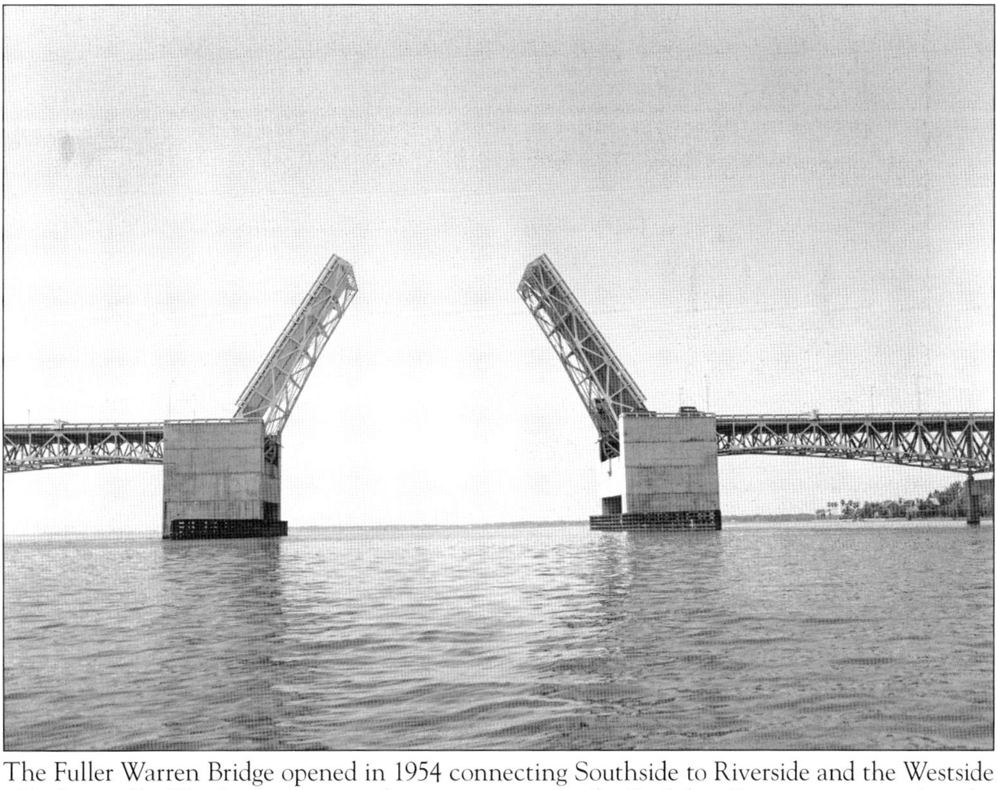

The Fuller Warren Bridge opened in 1954 connecting Southside to Riverside and the Westside of Jacksonville. The bridge was an alternate route over the St. Johns River as compared to the nearby St. Johns River Bridge, which almost takes the same route over the river. The bridge was four lanes wide with a center drawbridge. Tolls were collected from 1954 to 1988. The bridge is named after Fuller Warren, governor of Florida from 1949 to 1953. (State Archives of Florida.)

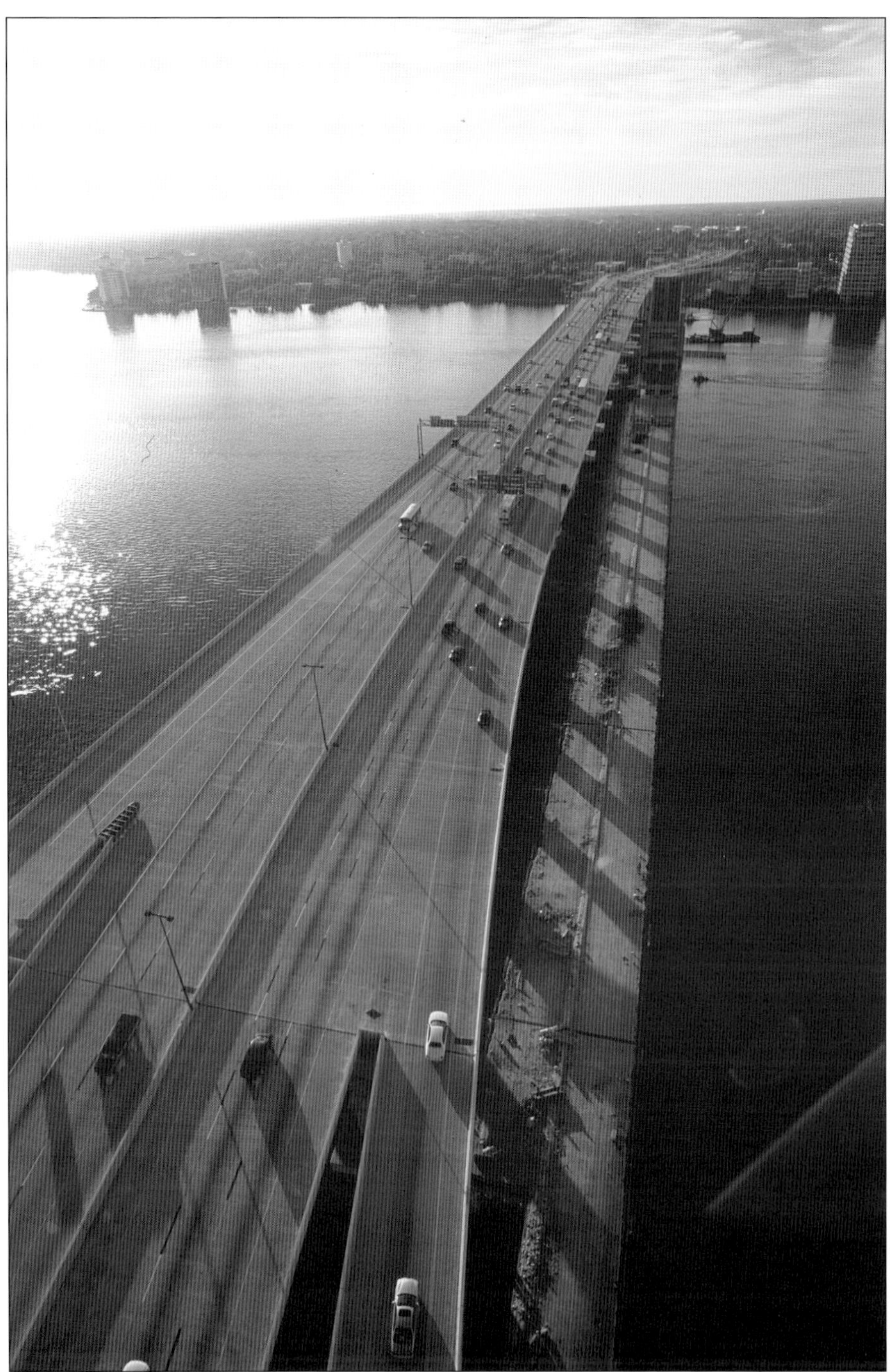

In 2000, construction started for a new eight-lane bridge began next to the Fuller Warren Bridge. In April, a portion of the new bridge was opened for Interstate 10 eastbound to Interstate 95 southbound. The bridge was fully opened in 2002, making it easier for traffic compared to the previous four-lane bridge. The new bridge was simply called the Fuller Warren Bridge, while the older bridge was left to be gradually demolished. The older Fuller Warren Bridge was completely demolished in 2007. (University of North Florida.)

Four

The Journey South

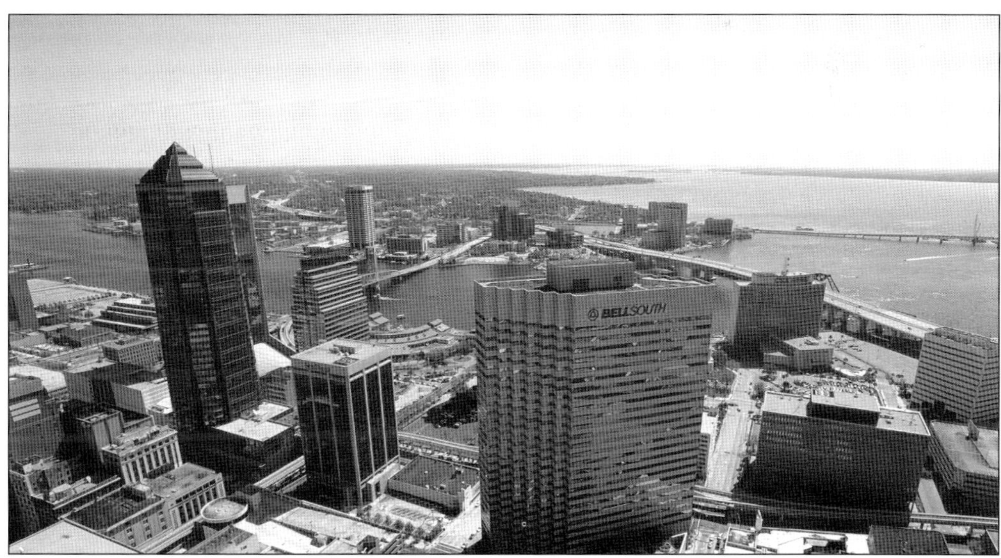

The St. Johns River south of Jacksonville grows to around two miles wide all the way down to Palatka. This aerial photograph of Jacksonville in 1998 shows a narrow St. Johns River in the city. The Fuller Warren Bridge, at left center, is where the river begins to grow wider. (University of North Florida.)

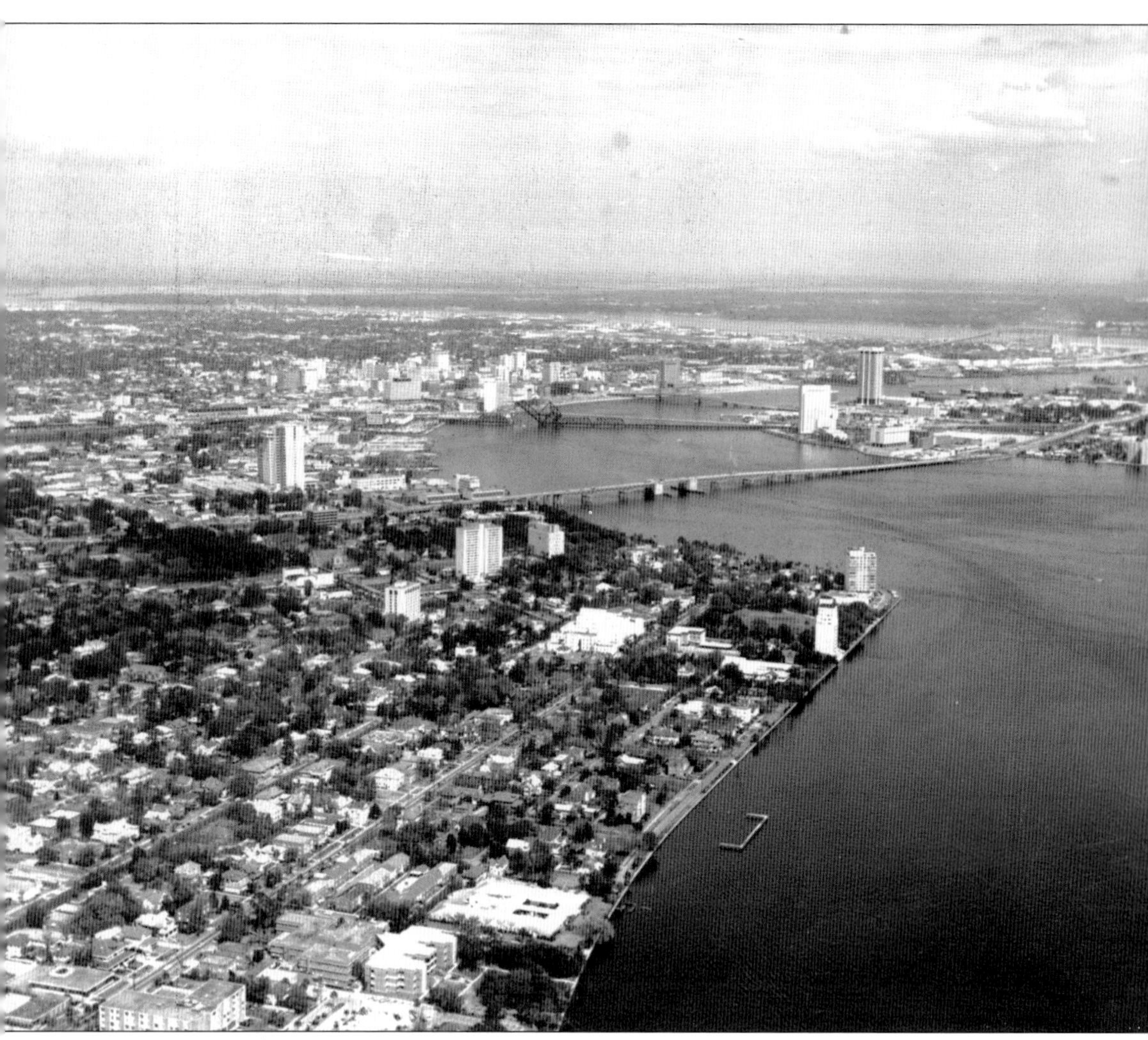

Riverside first began as a Spanish land grant in 1801 owned by Phillip Dell called Dell's Bluff. Ownership of Dell's Bluff later went to Miles Price, who sold part of it in 1868 to Edward M. Cheney and Boston developer John Murray Forbes, who began the development of Riverside. In 1887, Jacksonville annexed Riverside and nearby Brooklyn. Riverside grew, with mansions, bungalows, and a wide variety of dwellings. The name was fitting, since the St. Johns River flows on the eastern side of it. This aerial photograph shows Riverside with downtown Jacksonville in the distance in the 1970s. The river is seen flowing around the bend of Riverside, continuing north and then turning east. (Jacksonville Historical Society.)

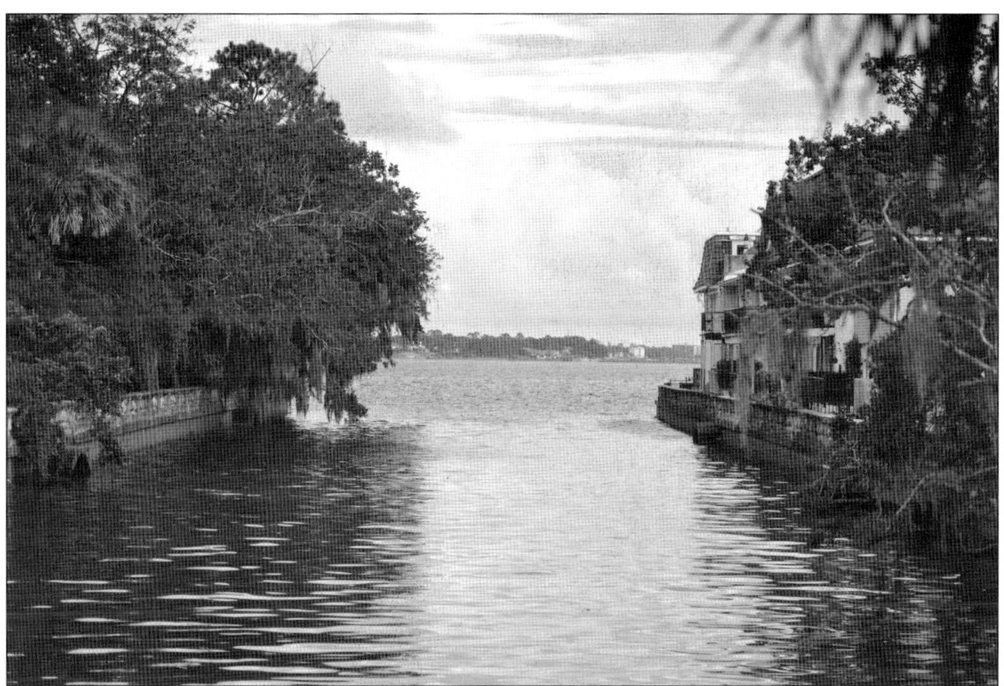

Avondale also developed out of the former Dell's Bluff. In 1884, developers attempted to create a community called Edgewood but were unsuccessful. In 1920, Telfair Stockton and an investment group purchased Edgewood and the surrounding land to develop an upscale neighborhood. The name of Stockton's development was Avondale, after a Cincinnati neighborhood of the same name. Avondale, like Riverside, also has the St. Johns River on its eastern side. Avondale also has Willow Branch Creek, which flows through a canal and then out into the St. Johns. The creek also flows through Willowbranch Park, where Willow Branch Library is. This photograph shows Willow Branch Creek flowing into the St. Johns at Yacht Basin Park in 2022. (Andrew R. Nicholas.)

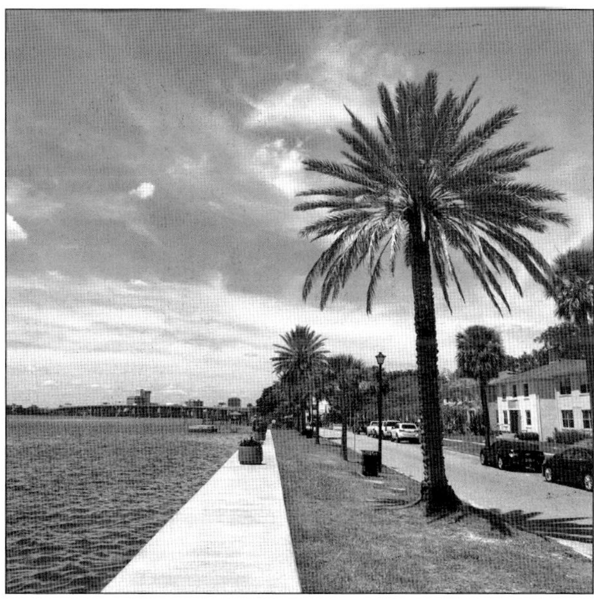

In 1793, a Spanish land grant was issued in the present-day area of San Marco. Albert Gallatin Philips developed a 450-acre plantation called Red Bank in 1854. Isaac Hendricks took over ownership of nearby land, and by 1850 had married Elizabeth Hudnall, another landowner in the area. Margaret, the daughter of Isaac and Elizabeth, married Albert Philips. In 1873, Elizabeth sold the eastern portion of her land to Harrison Reed, who began the first development of South Jacksonville. In 1882, Elizabeth developed the western portion, calling it Oklahoma. This photograph shows Riverfront Park in San Marco overlooking the St. Johns River. (Andrew R. Nicholas.)

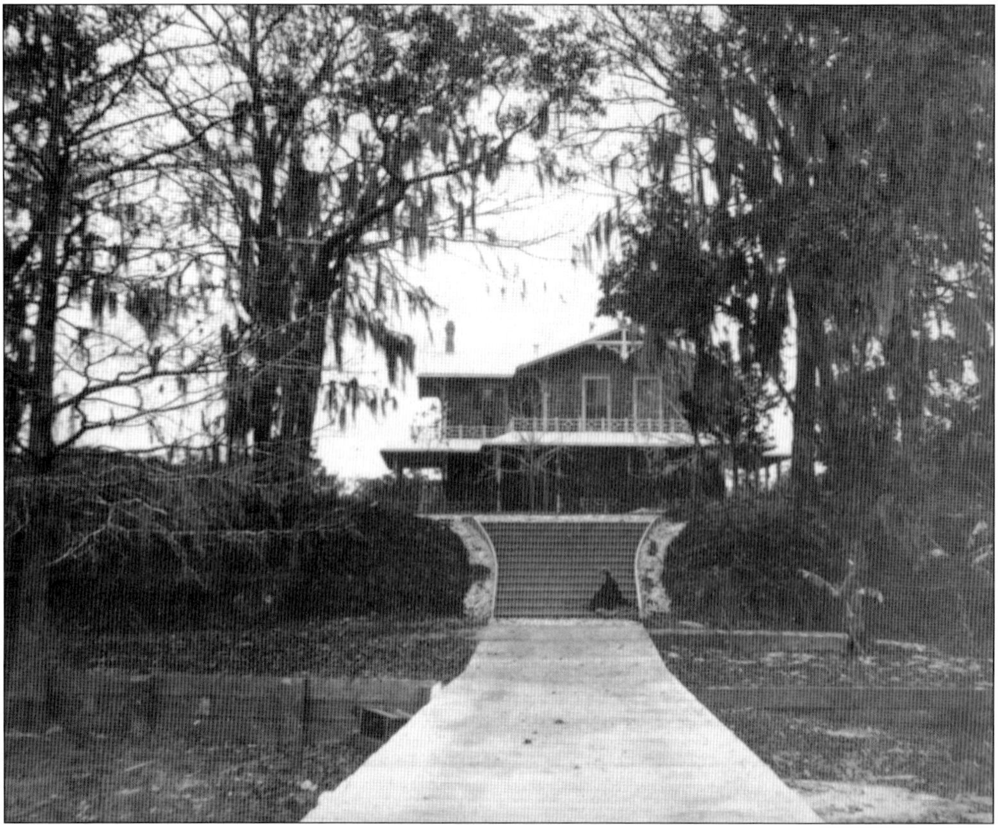

Harrison Reed's sister Martha Reed Mitchell and her husband, Alexander, built an estate called Villa Alexandria south of Oklahoma. This photograph from 1875 shows the Alexandria estate on the St. Johns River. It was demolished in 1926 for the present-day Swisher House, built in 1929. (New York Public Library.)

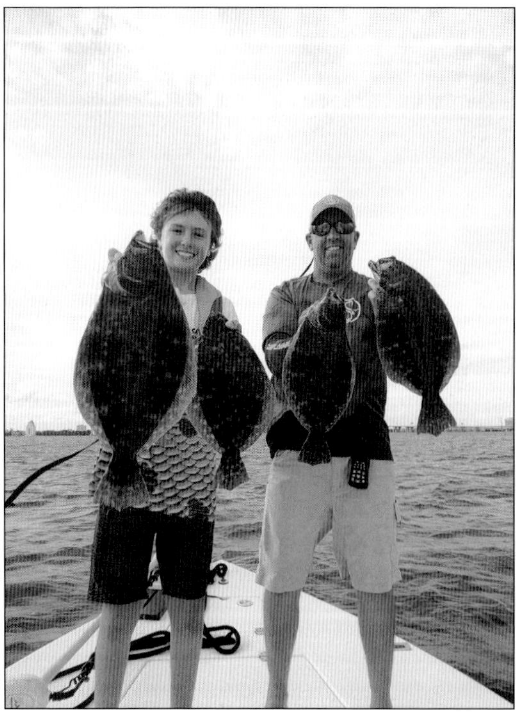

Flounders are found on the bottom of bodies of water. The St. Johns River has an abundance of flounders. This photograph shows two Jacksonville fishermen holding four flounders caught in the St. Johns near San Marco in 2020. (Jimmy Moore.)

Fishweir Creek is a tributary of the St. Johns River. Fishweir itself has two tributaries: Big Fishweir Creek, flowing west, and Little Fishweir Creek, flowing north. Fishweir Creek overall was once a deeper creek, but the buildup of sediment from urbanization has caused a decline in its natural habitat, and boating on it has become more difficult. This photograph shows several women on a canoe on Fishweir Creek around 1920, when the creek saw better days. (Jacksonville Historical Society.)

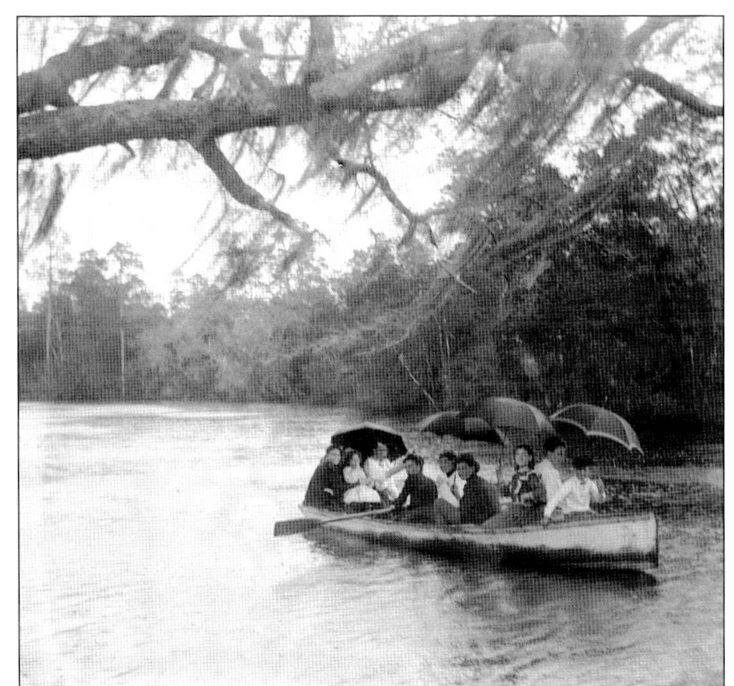

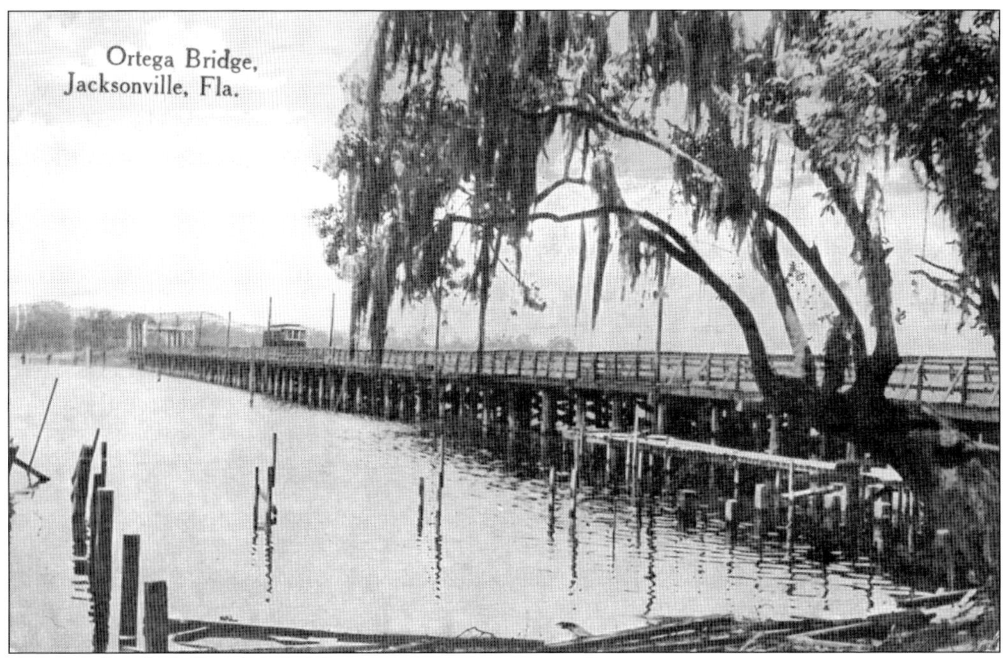

The wooden Ortega Bridge was built in 1908 for streetcar service between Ortega and Jacksonville. In 1927, the present-day two-lane drawbridge was built to place the wooden bridge. This postcard shows the wooden Ortega bridge in the 1910s. (Florida Historical Society)

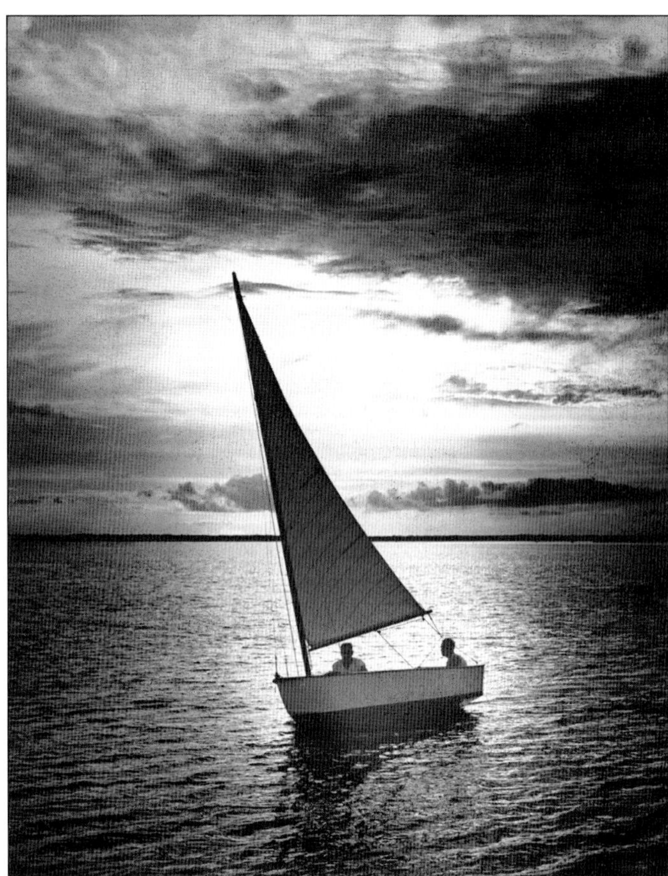

Ortega is bordered by the St. Johns River and the Ortega River. This photograph shows a sailboat near Ortega on the St. Johns in 1946. (State Archives of Florida.)

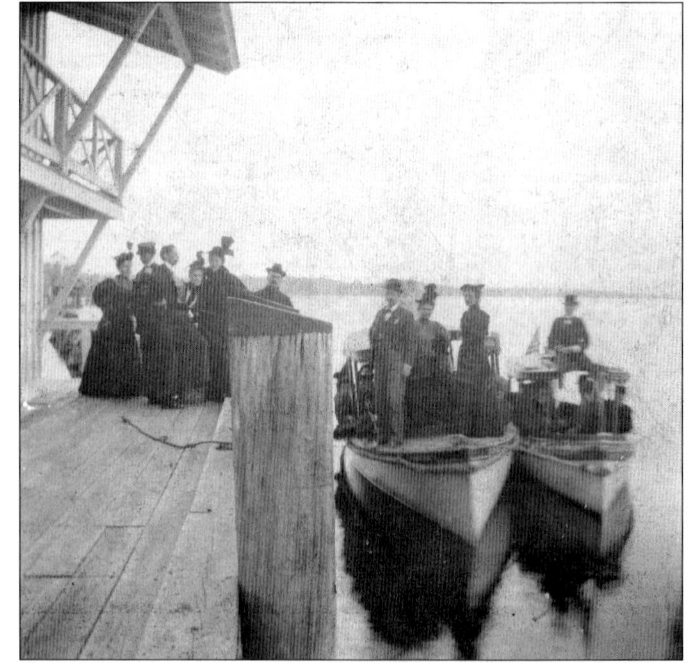

The Florida Yacht Club was established in 1876 to promote yachting and social enjoyment. The club was first located at the foot of Market Street in downtown Jacksonville until the Great Fire of 1901 burned it down. The club temporarily moved to Riverside Avenue, and in 1907 re-opened near the mouth of Willow Branch Creek. In 1928, the club moved to its present-day location in Ortega. This photograph from the 1890s shows members of the Florida Yacht Club at its first location on Market Street along the St. Johns River. (Jacksonville Historical Society.)

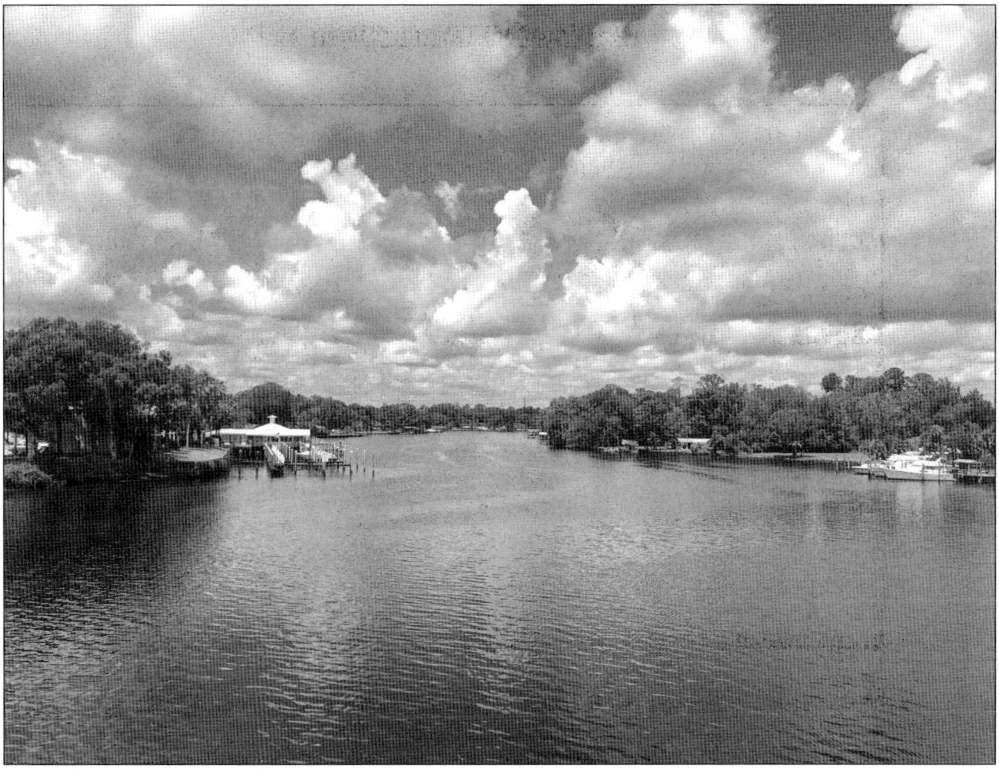

The Cedar River flows through the Westside past Lake Shore Boulevard, San Juan Avenue, Hyde Park, and Blanding Boulevard until connecting with the Ortega River and the St. Johns River. The seafood restaurant Cedar River Seafood was founded in 1977 on the Cedar River. This photograph shows the river looking north from the San Juan Avenue bridge in 2022. (Andrew R. Nicholas.)

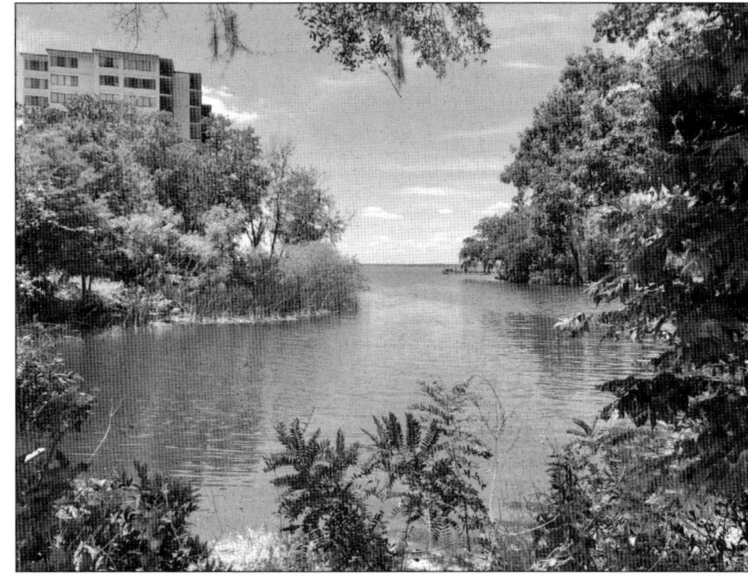

New Rose Creek flows under San Jose Boulevard and turns north through residential neighborhoods. This photograph shows the creek flowing into the St. Johns River in 2022. (Andrew R. Nicholas.)

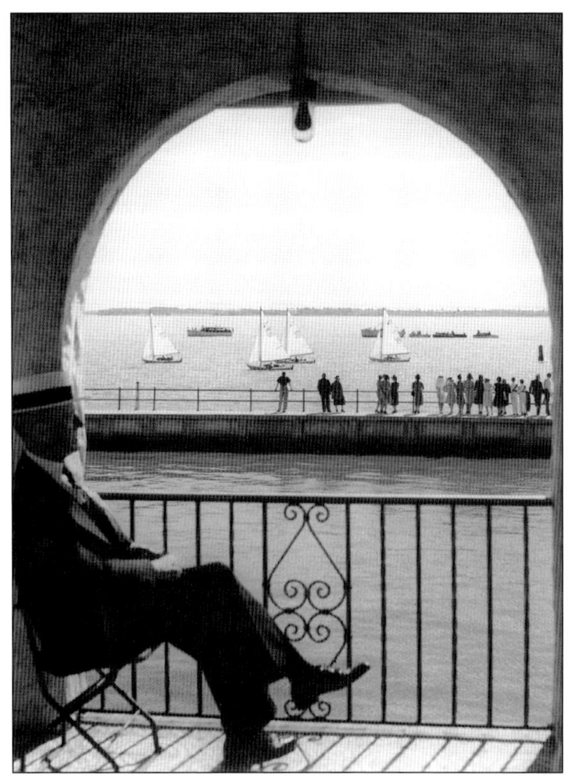

In 1926, Alfred I. duPont and his wife, Jessie Ball duPont, moved to Jacksonville from their large Nemours Estate in Wilmington, Delaware. The duPonts acquired six lots on the St. Johns River in San Jose, where a Mediterranean-style mansion was built. Alfred's brother-in-law Ed Ball supervised the construction of the mansion. It was completed in 1927 and called Epping Forest after the Balls' ancestral home in England. Nearby land was acquired, creating 60 acres for the Epping Forest property. This photograph shows a boat race on the St. Johns River viewed from Epping Forest in 1940. (State Archives of Florida.)

Goodbys Creek was developed in 1766 by Joseph Goodbee, who had a 250-acre farm on the north side of the creek. This photograph shows boats docked at Lakeside Marina on Goodbys Lake in 1960. (State Archives of Florida.)

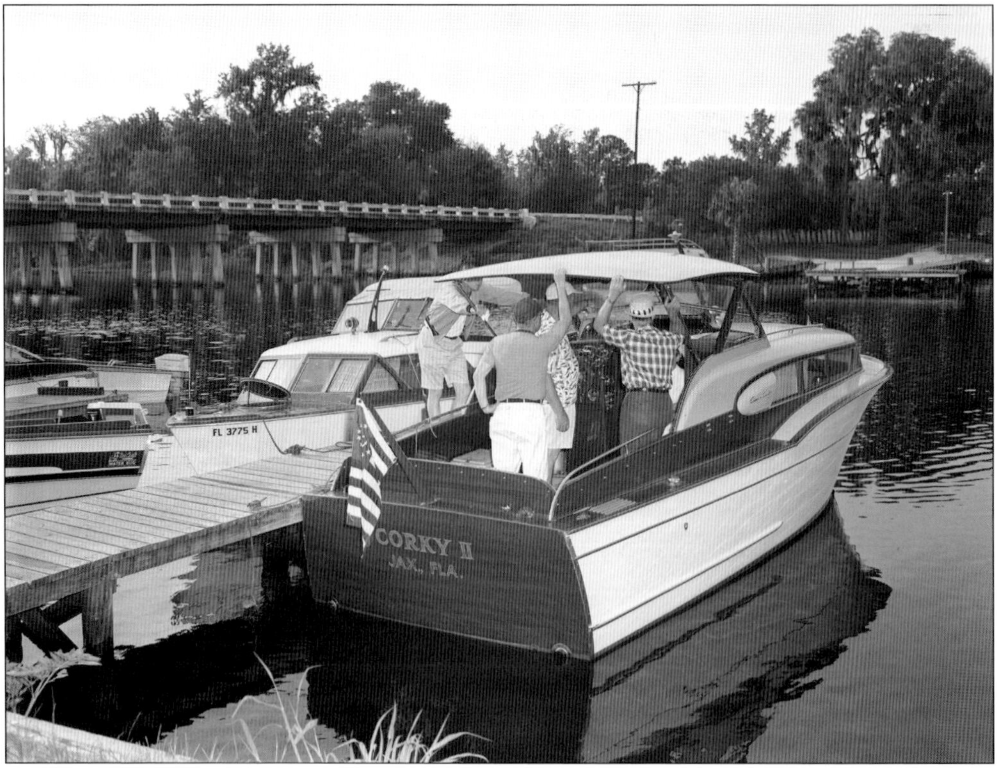

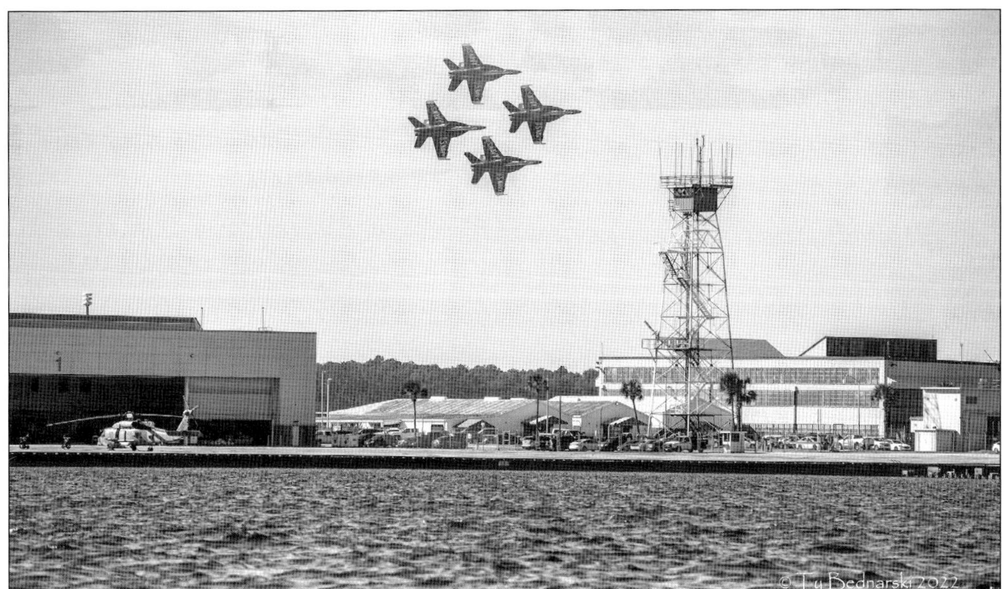

After World War II, Adm. Chester W. Nimitz decided to create a flight demonstration squadron to maintain public interest in naval aviation and the US Navy. The squadron is named the Blue Angels, and had its first demonstration at NAS Jacksonville in 1946. This photograph taken from a boat on the St. Johns River shows the Blue Angels performing at NAS Jacksonville in 2022. Boaters can anchor here to watch the Blue Angels perform during air shows. The home base of the Blue Angels is NAS Pensacola. (Ty Bednarski.)

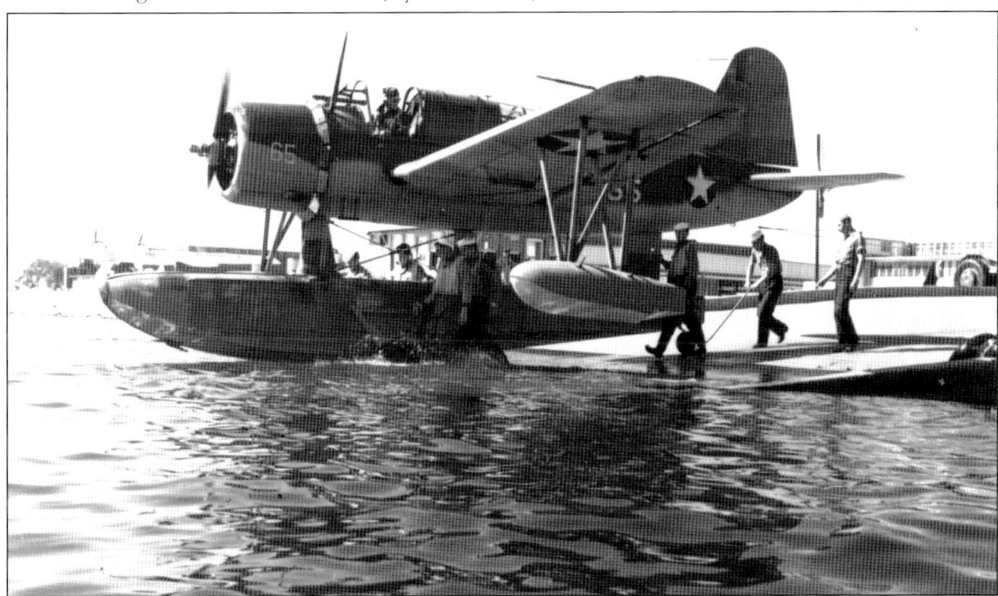

Across the St. Johns River from Goodbys Creek is Naval Air Station Jacksonville, commissioned in 1940. Before this, the area was a quartermaster training camp called Camp Joseph E. Johnston from 1917 to 1919. The camp was renamed Camp Clifford Foster after World War I and was used by the National Guard. During the Great Depression, it became a transient work camp. Today, NAS Jacksonville is the largest US Navy base in the southeast and is an integral part of Jacksonville. This photograph shows a seaplane at NAS Jacksonville in 1943. (Jacksonville Historical Society.)

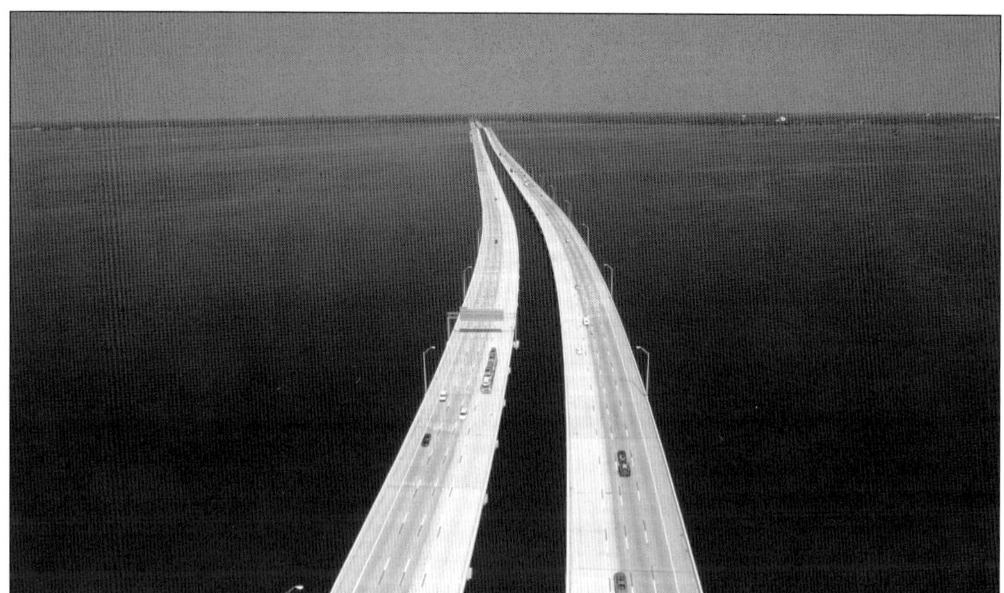

The Henry Holland Buckman Bridge opened in 1970 connecting Orange Park and the Westside of Jacksonville to the Mandarin area. The bridge is eight lanes wide and 3.07 miles long with its highest clearance at 65 feet. (University of North Florida.)

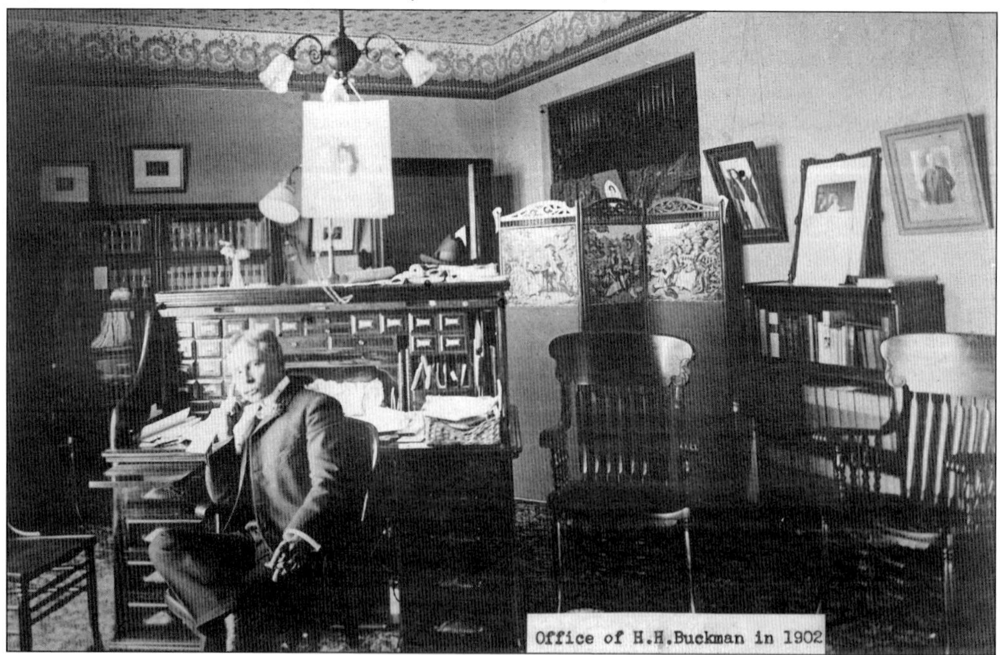

Henry Holland Buckman was born on June 20, 1858, in Jacksonville. He earned a law degree from Cumberland University in 1879 and became a successful attorney in Jacksonville. Buckman served in the Florida House of Representatives and authored the Buckman Act. In 1905, the act was passed by the Florida legislature, reorganizing Florida's higher educational system. The result of this was the creation of the present-day University of Florida, Florida State University, and Florida A&M University. This photograph shows Buckman in his office in 1902. (Florida Historical Society.)

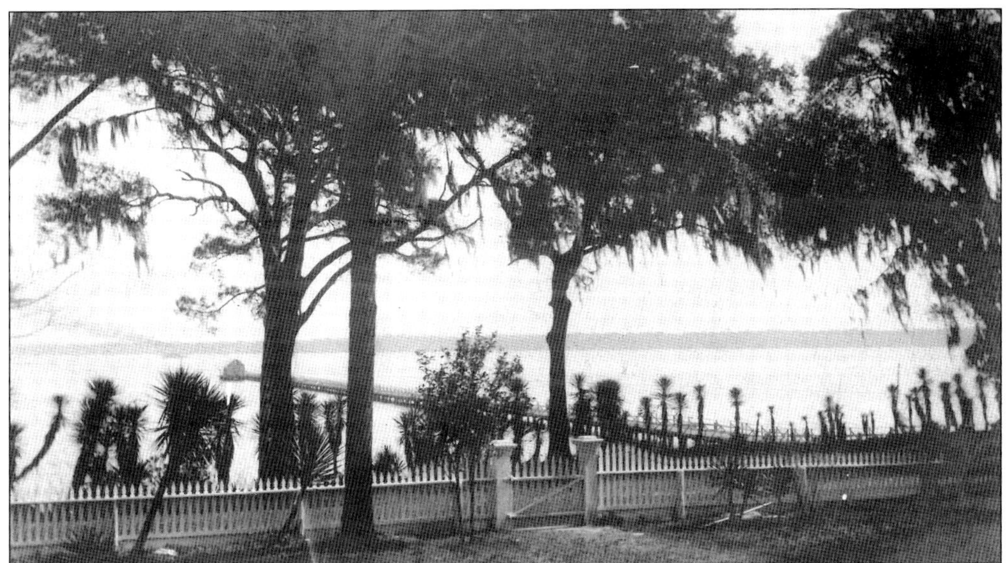

The present-day area of Orange Park was first known as Laurel Grove, where Zepheniah Kingsley owned a plantation. In 1877, the town of Orange Park was founded by the Florida Winter Home and Improvement Company. Orange Park was established on the St. Johns River and included the former Laurel Grove plantation. Orange trees were planted on new building lots and farm tracts to attract more people to the area. In 1879, the town was incorporated. (Florida Historical Society.)

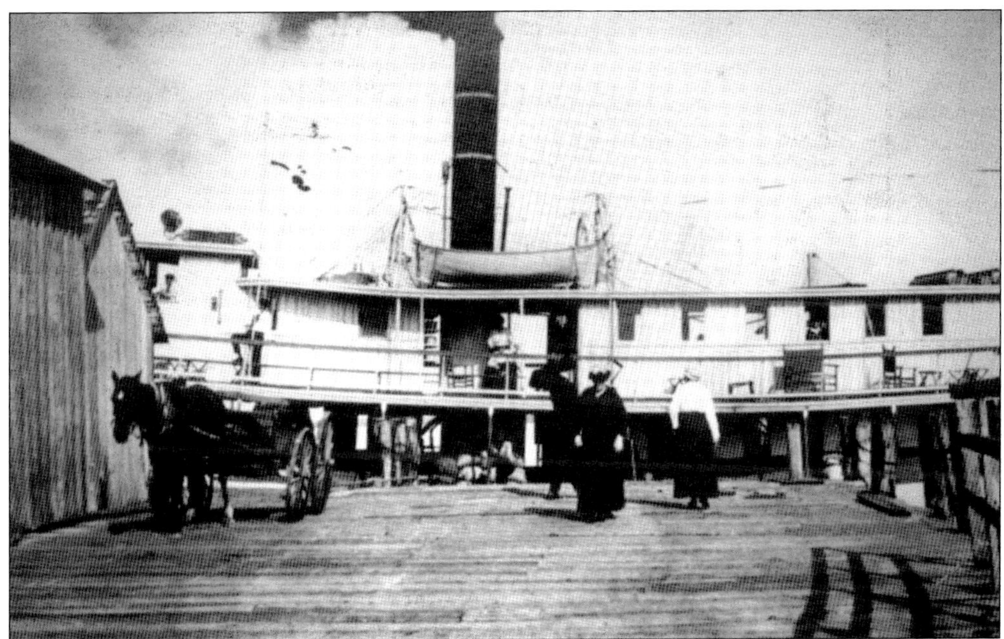

In 1893, the steamship *May Garner* was launched. Capt. Charles Edward Garner, owner of the Independent Day Line, named the ship after his daughter May. The *May Garner* operated on the St. Johns River from Green Cove Springs up to Orange Park. (Clay County Historical Archives.)

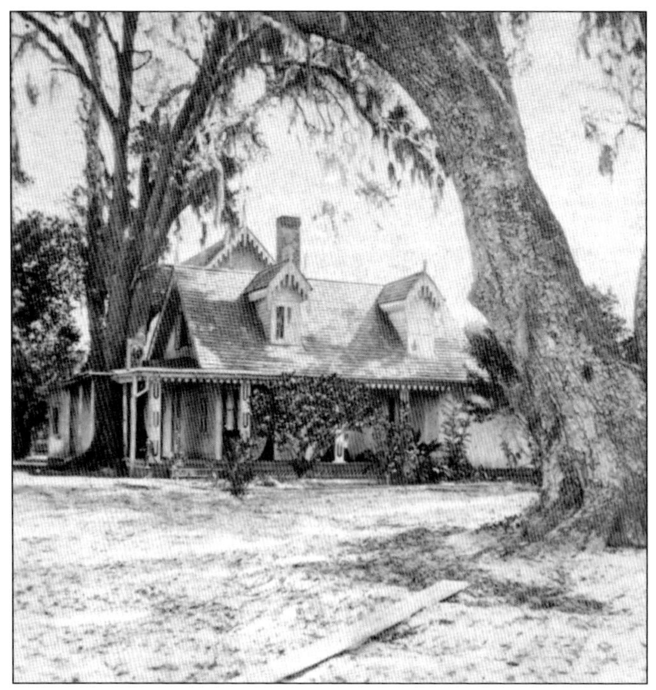

Harriet Beecher Stowe was born on June 14, 1811, in Litchfield, Connecticut. She grew up to be an abolitionist and a well-known author, publishing the novel *Uncle Tom's Cabin* in 1852. Her novel had a profound impact on public opinion of slavery in the United States and contributed to the growing divide that led to the Civil War in 1861. After the Civil War, Stowe bought property on the St. Johns River in Mandarin. The Harriet Beecher Stowe residence is seen in this photograph from the 1870s. While living in Mandarin, she wrote *Palmetto Leaves* about her time living in north Florida. (New York Public Library.)

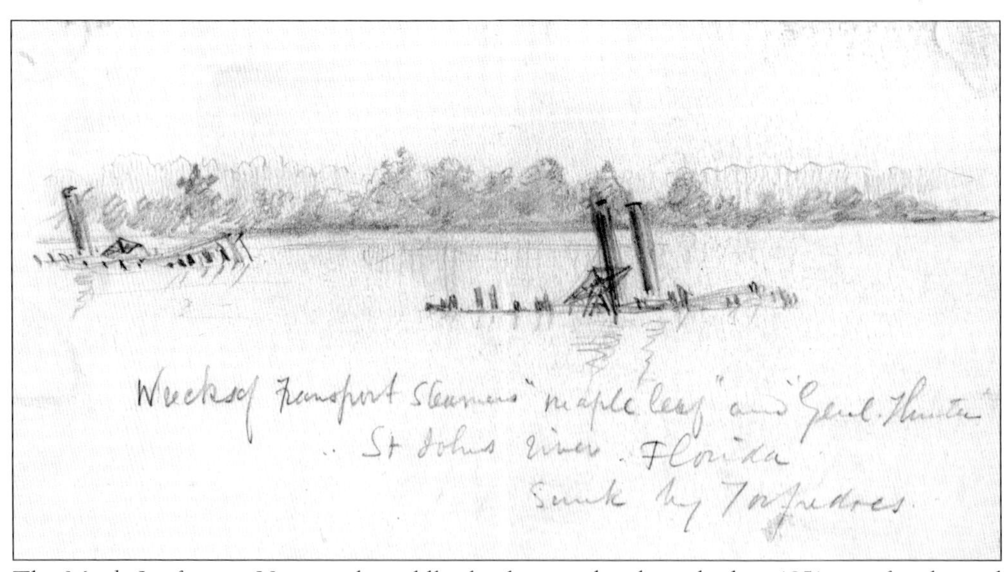

The *Maple Leaf* was a Union side-paddlewheel steamship launched in 1851 as a freight and passenger vessel. During the Civil War, it was a civilian merchant steamship chartered as a Union transport. On April 1, 1864, the *Maple Leaf* struck a Confederate mine off Mandarin, killing four and sinking into the St. Johns River. On April 16, the Union steamship *General Hunter* also hit a mine and sank. Alfred Waud, an artist well-known for making sketches during the Civil War, made this sketch of the sunken *Maple Leaf* and *General Hunter* in the river. (Library of Congress.)

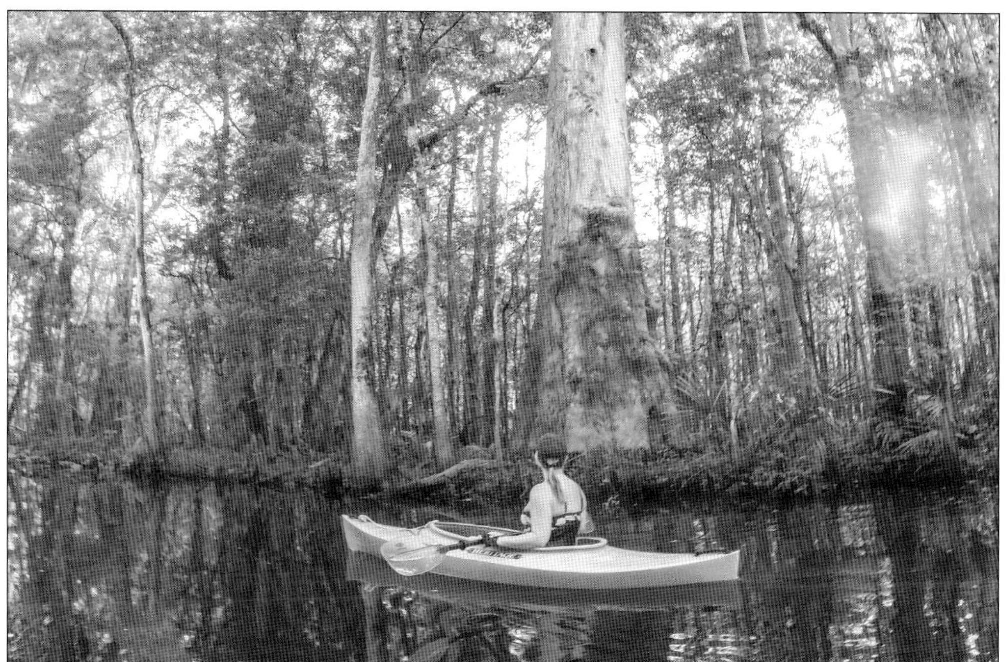

Francis Levett Sr. acquired 10,000 acres at present-day Julington Creek. Levett named his estate Julianton Plantation after his wife, Julia. The creek flows from the St. Johns River to the Julington Durbin Creek Nature Preserve, where it splits into two creeks. This photograph shows a woman in a kayak on the southern creek, Durbin Creek. (Rhonda Lovett.)

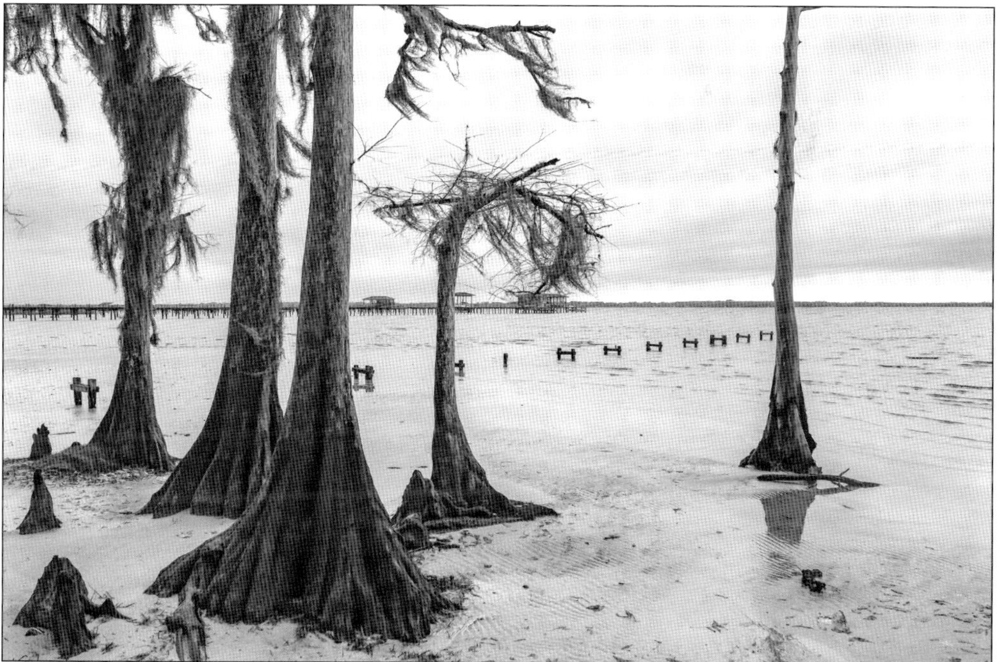

Alpine Groves Park was once an orange grove homestead in the 19th century. Today, there are still 19th-century structures on the property, including the Bennet House and the horse stables. This photograph shows the remains of a dock at Alpine Groves Park at low tide. (Rhonda Lovett.)

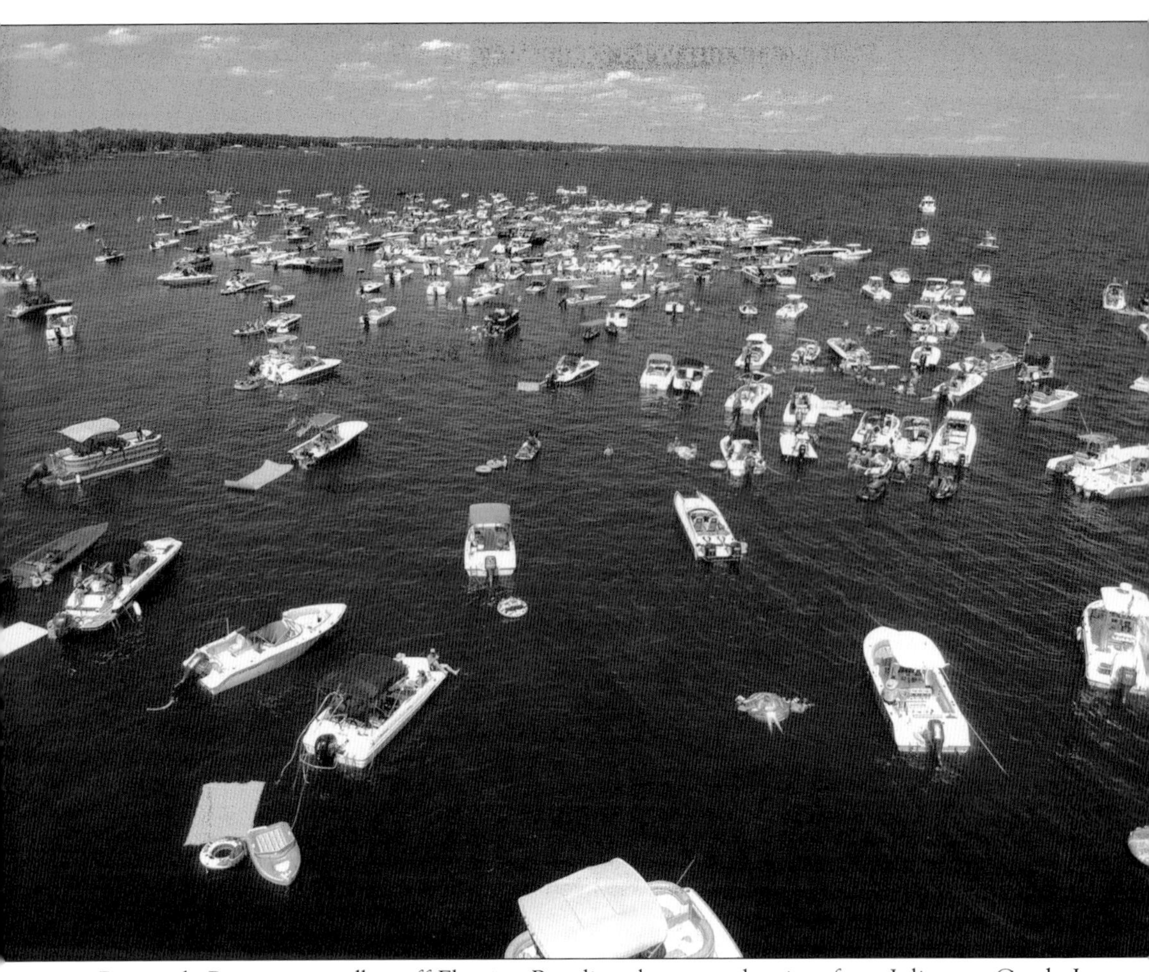

Pineapple Point is a sandbar off Fleming Bar directly across the river from Julington Creek. It has become a popular destination for boaters. This photograph of Pineapple Point was taken in 2021. (Brad Shubert.)

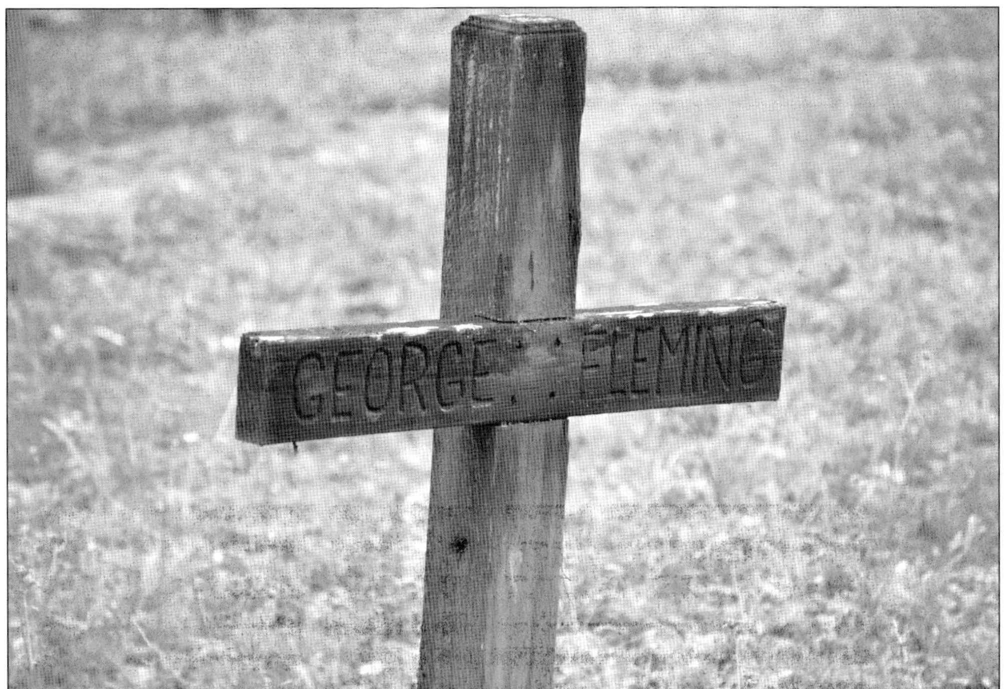

Irishman George Fleming settled at present-day Fleming Island in 1783 after receiving a Spanish land grant. Doctors Lake borders the northwest side of Fleming Island, with the St. Johns River flowing on its eastern side and then southwest as Black Creek. The western side of Fleming Island is marshland, which makes it technically not an island. This photograph shows Fleming's grave at Hibernia. (Andrew R. Nicholas.)

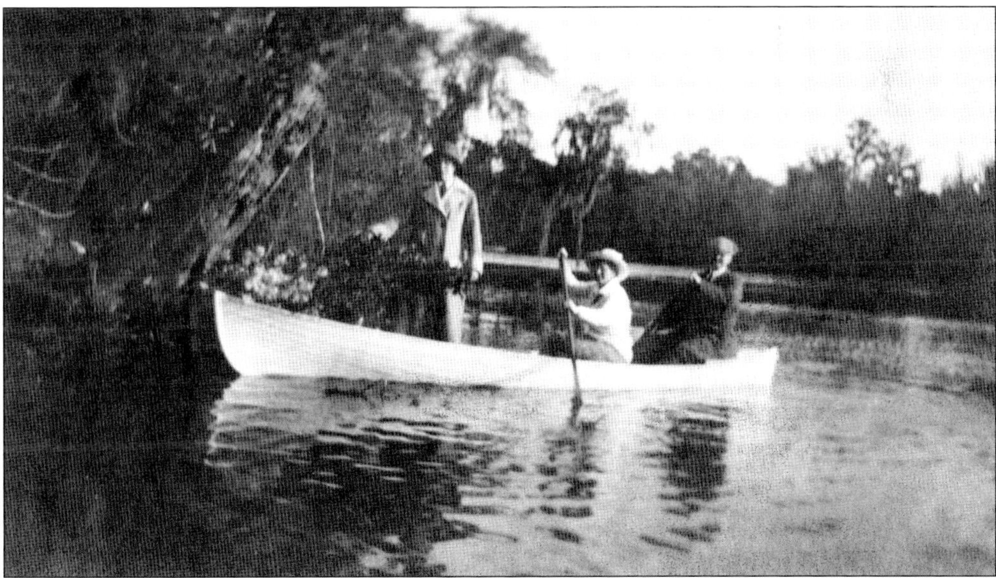

Fleming established Hibernia, which is the Latin name for Ireland, where he had his plantation. After his death in 1821, the plantation was transferred to his son Lewis Fleming. After the Civil War, the plantation was made a tourist resort. This photograph shows boaters on the St. Johns River near Hibernia in 1910. (State Archives of Florida.)

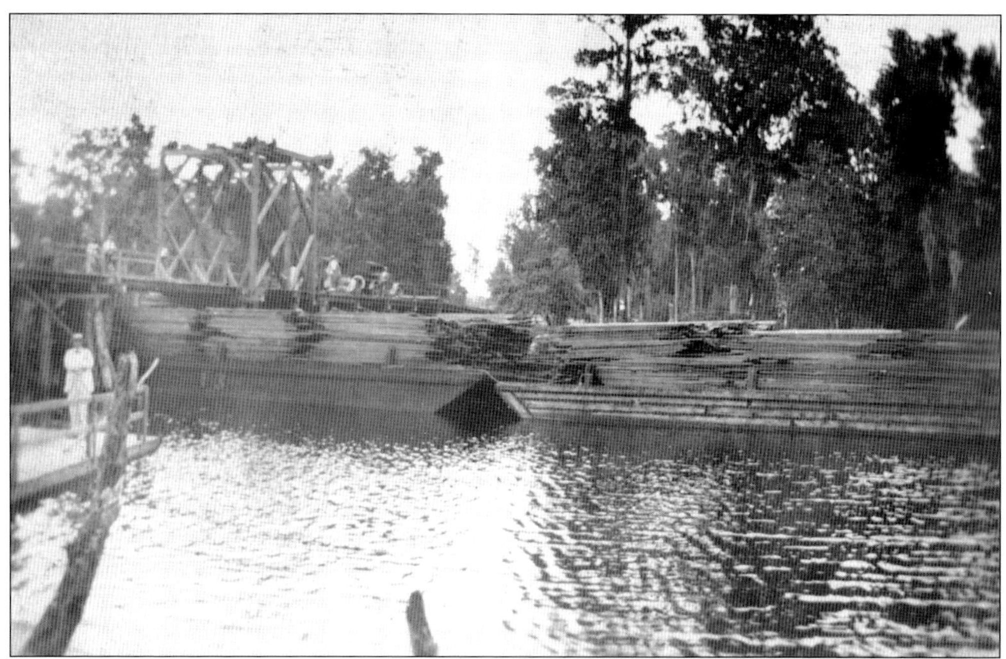

The area of Middleburg was first settled in the early 19th century as a ferry on Black Creek. In 1853, the town of Middleburg was founded near the middle of the Black Creek north and south tributaries. Middleburg traded in lumber and agriculture. This photograph shows barges full of lumber on Black Creek in the early 20th century. (State Archives of Florida.)

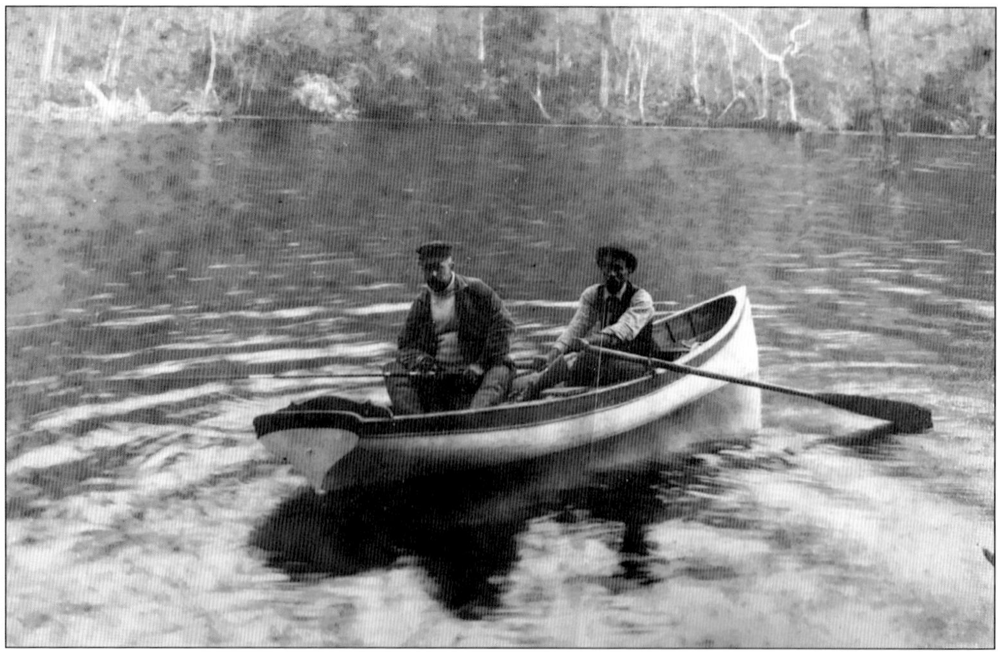

Black Creek is a 13-mile tributary of the St. Johns River that has two tributaries near Middleburg. The North Fork flows north toward Jennings State Forest. The South Fork flows south of Middleburg. It is near the confluence of the two forks where the town of Middleburg is located. This photograph shows two men rowing a canoe on Black Creek. (Clay County Archives.)

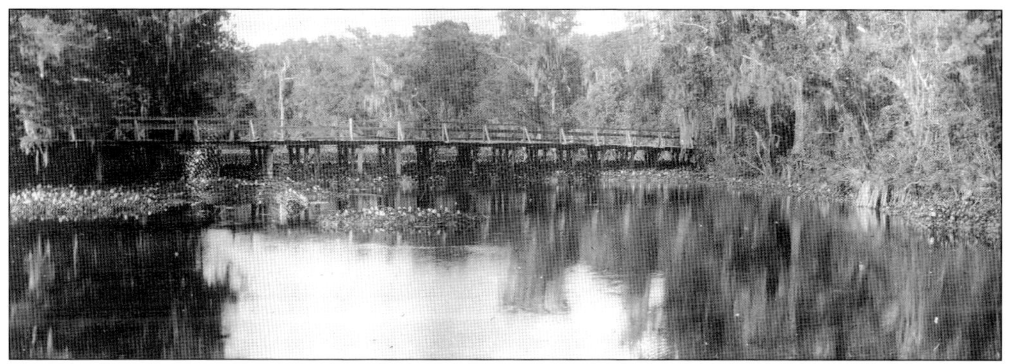

Governor's Creek is a small tributary of the St. Johns River. This photograph shows a bridge going over Governor's Creek in the early 20th century. (Clay County Archives.)

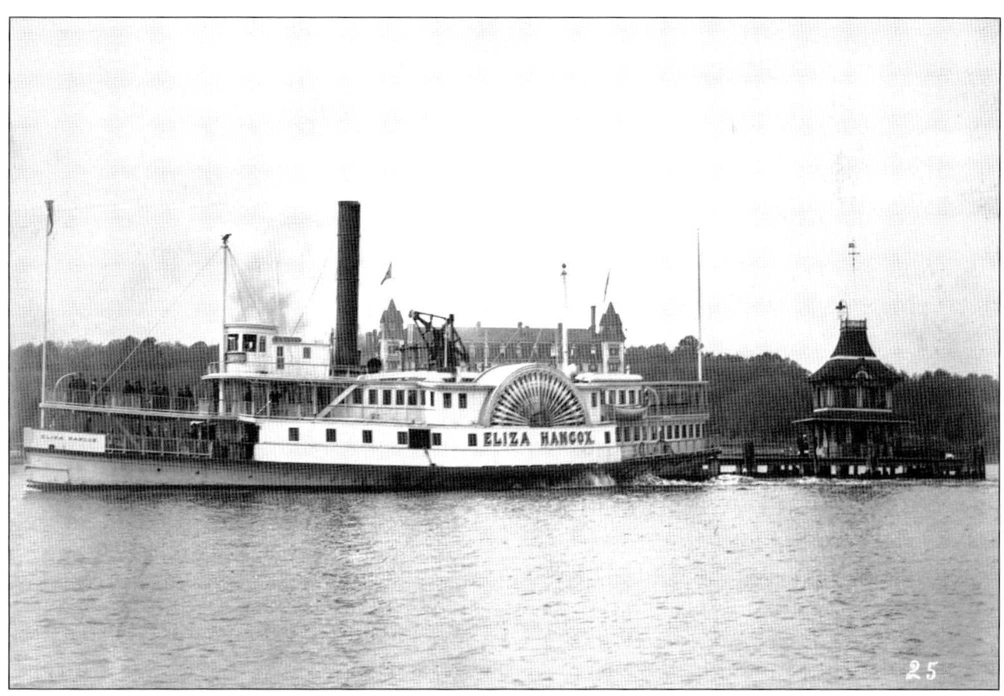

Magnolia Springs was a hotel on the St. Johns River near Green Cove Springs. This photograph shows the steamer *Eliza Hancox* docked on the river at Magnolia Springs around 1880. (State Archives of Florida.)

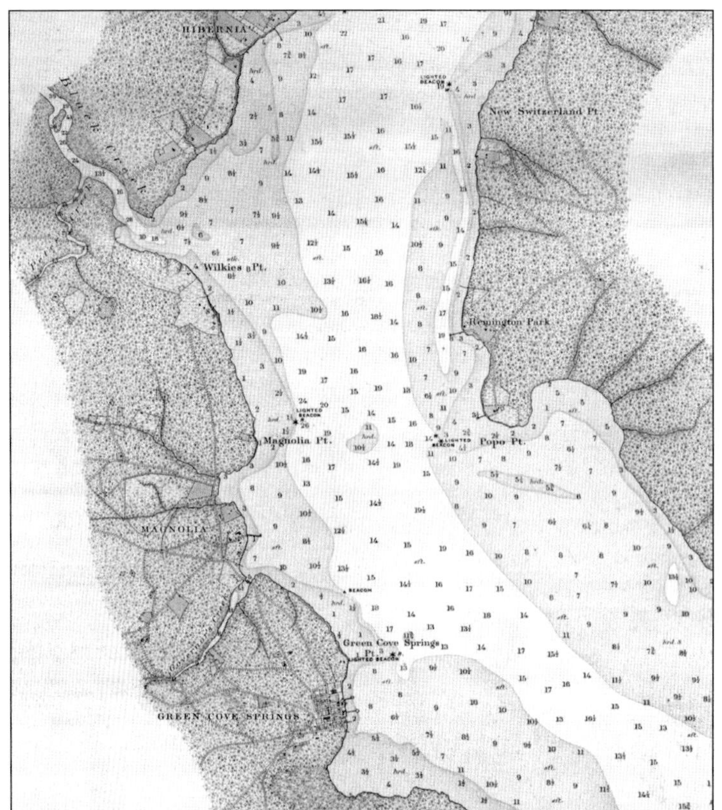

Green Cove Springs is a city on the St. Johns River and the county seat of Clay County. In the 1850s, landowners David Palmer and Sarah Ferris established the community of White Sulphur Springs. In 1866, the community was renamed Green Cove Springs and was incorporated in 1874. The community grew around a natural sulfur spring near the St. Johns called Green Cove Spring. (State Archives of Florida.)

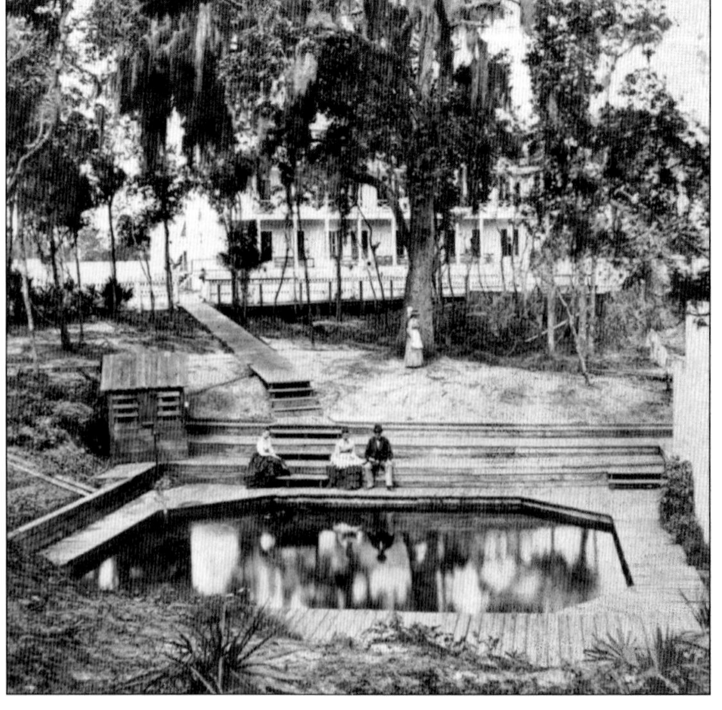

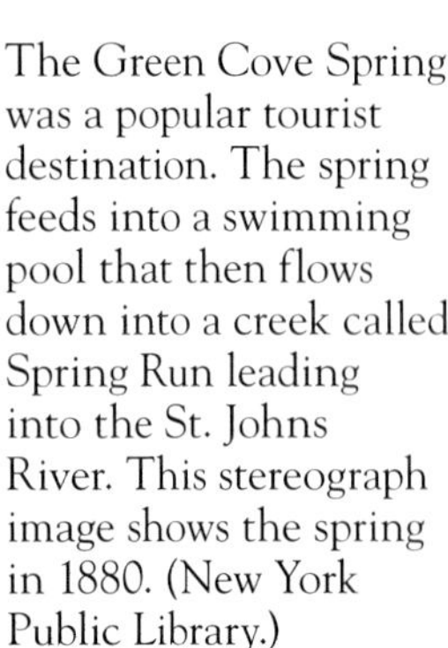

The Green Cove Spring was a popular tourist destination. The spring feeds into a swimming pool that then flows down into a creek called Spring Run leading into the St. Johns River. This stereograph image shows the spring in 1880. (New York Public Library.)

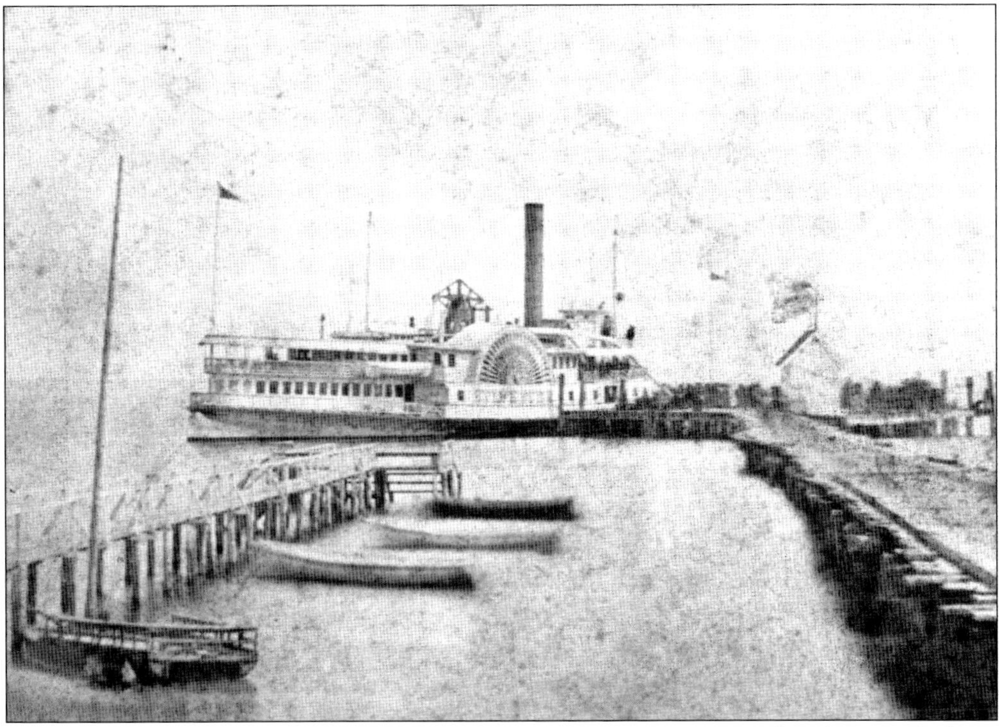

The *John Sylvester* was a steamer built in 1866 in Jersey City, New Jersey. This photograph shows the *Sylvester* docked at Green Cove Springs on the St. Johns River around 1870. In 1915, the steamer was renamed *Starlight* and then *Favorite* in 1925. (State Archives of Florida.)

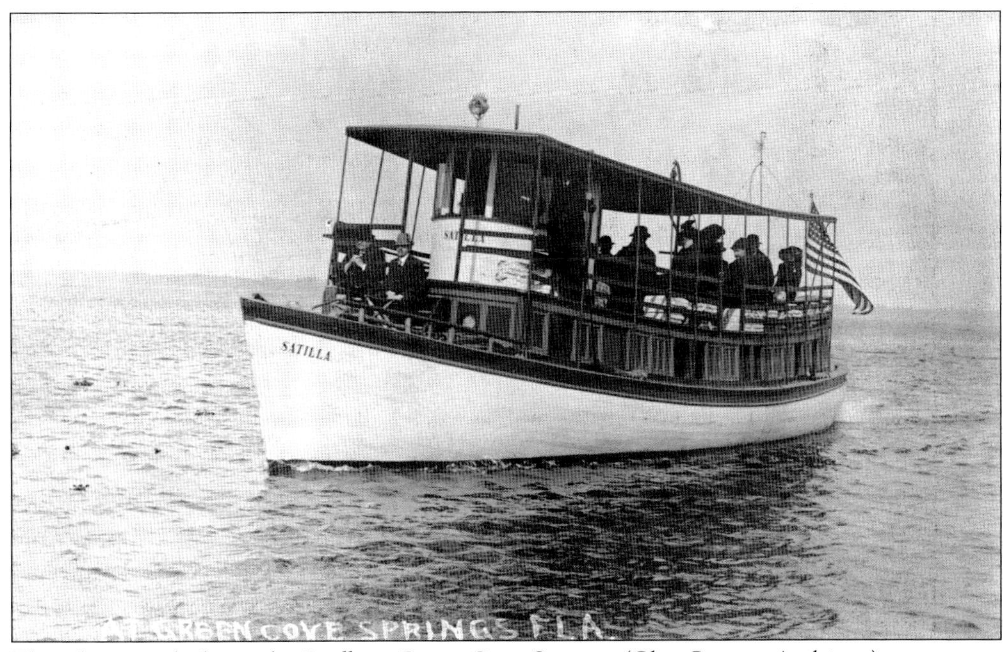

This photograph shows the *Satilla* at Green Cove Springs. (Clay County Archives.)

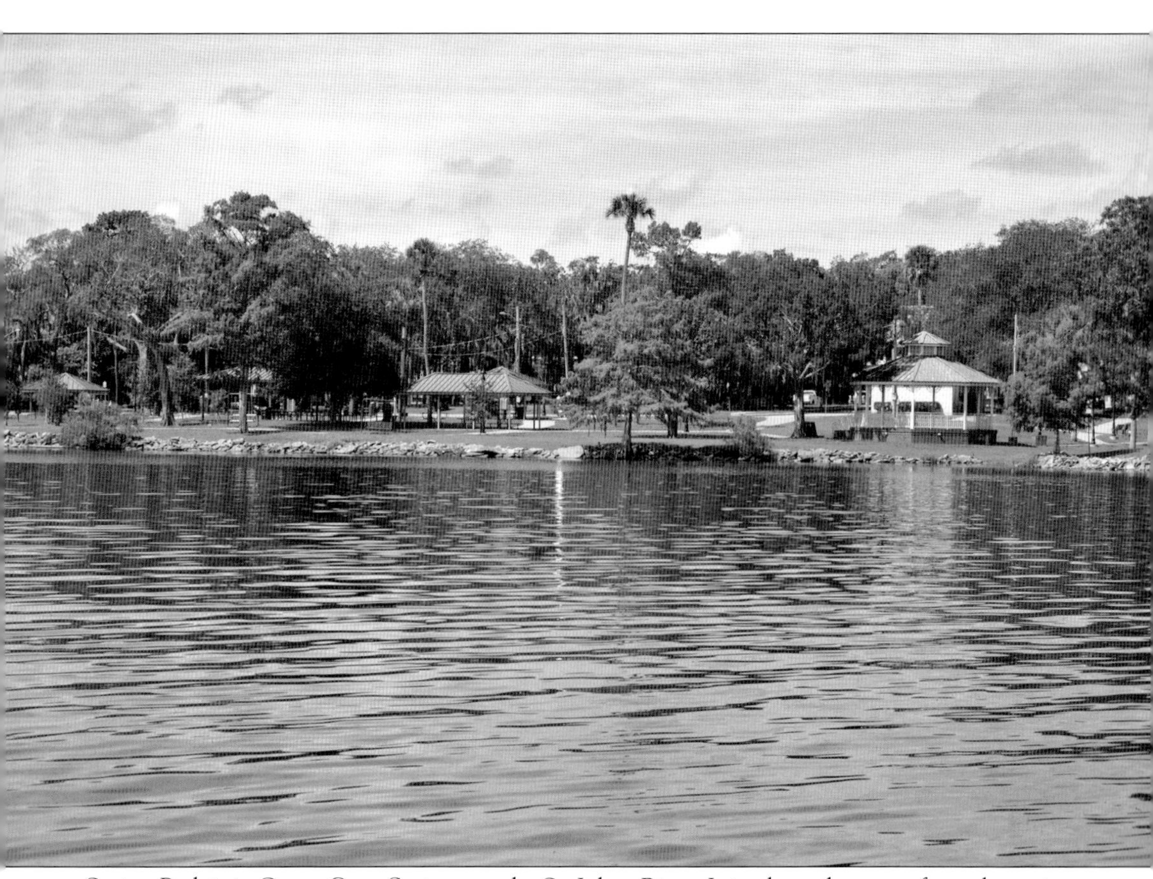

Spring Park is in Green Cove Springs on the St. Johns River. It is where the water from the spring flows out into the St. Johns. A pier is located at the park for fishing, walking, or docking. This photograph shows Spring Park from the pier in 2022. (Andrew R. Nicholas.)

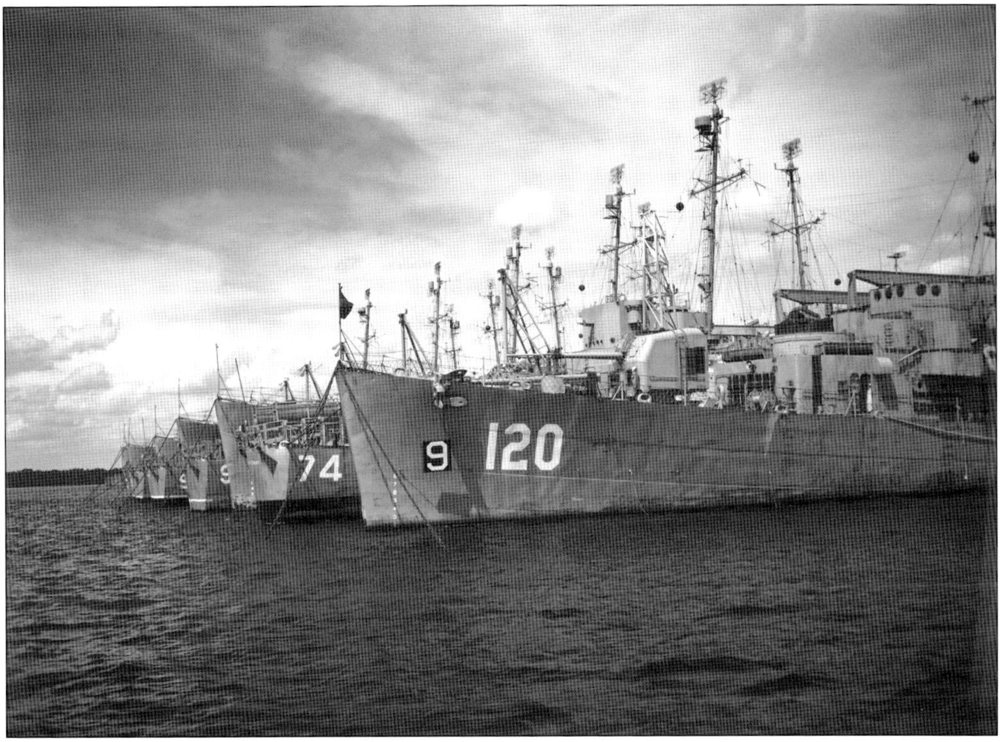

Naval Air Station Lee Field was established in 1940 to support the American war effort in World War II. In 1943, it was renamed Naval Air Station Green Cove Springs. NAS Green Cove Springs was near the St. Johns River south of downtown Green Cove Springs. After the war, it was reorganized into a naval auxiliary air station and then transferred to NAS Jacksonville. This photograph shows some of the Atlantic Reserve Fleet, Florida, at NAS Green Cove Springs around 1946. (State Archives of Florida.)

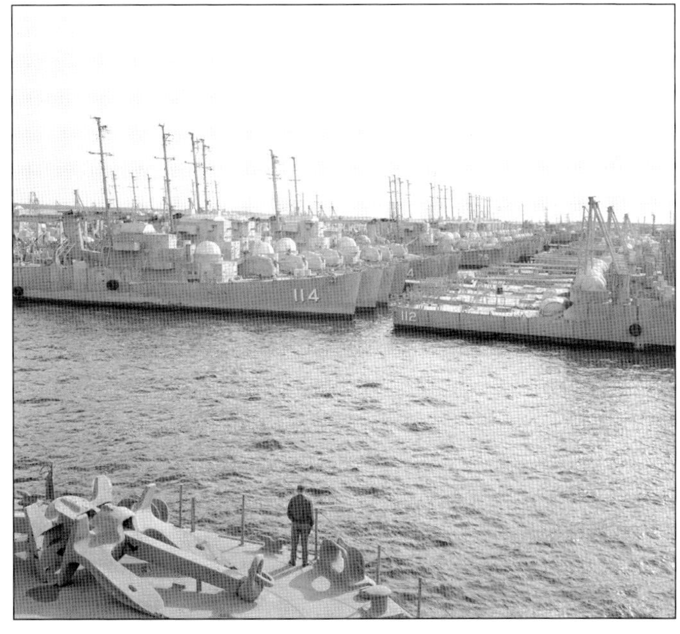

After World War II, the Atlantic Reserve Fleet, Florida, was established by Naval Air Station Green Cove Springs. The fleet was part of the US Navy reserve fleets, also called mothball fleet, which consisted of surplus ships kept ready in case of emergency. This photograph shows the mothball fleet of Green Cove Springs in 1958. (State Archives of Florida.)

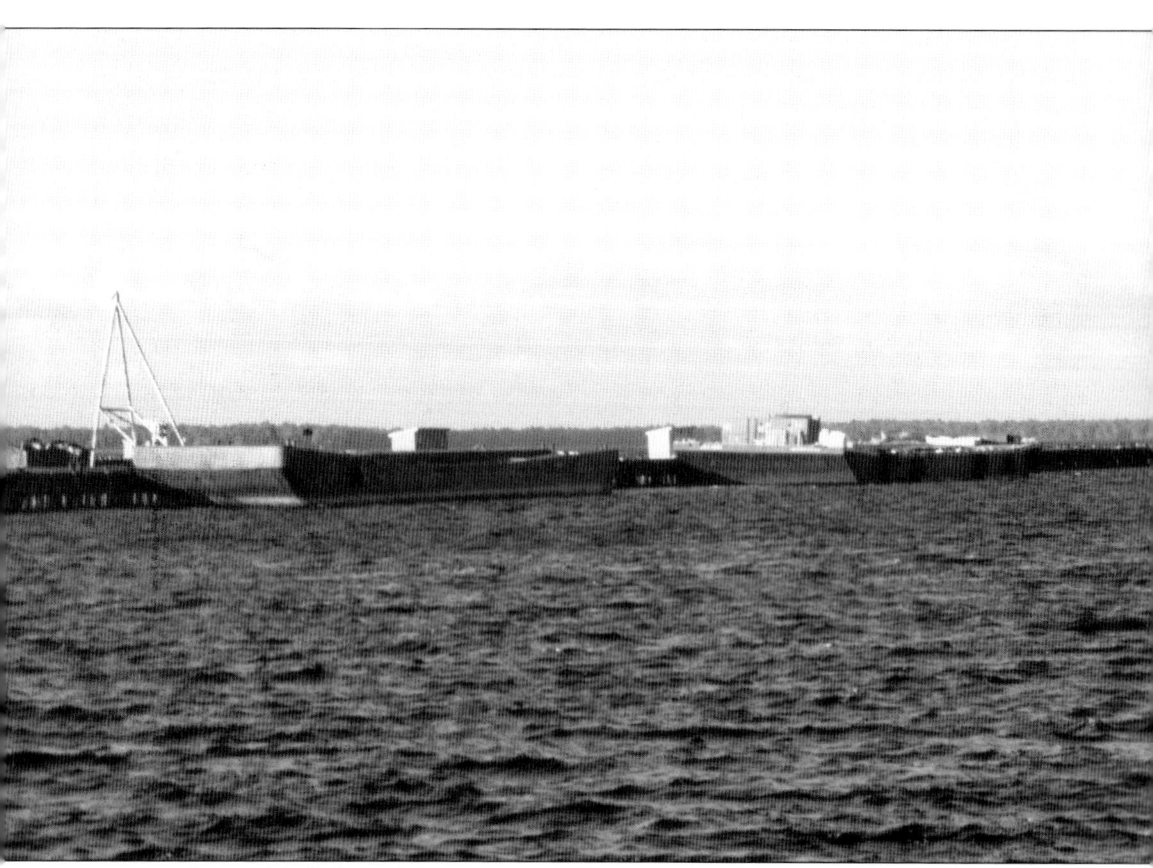

In 1962, the mothball fleet relocated to Texas and the naval station was transferred to Green Cove Springs. In 1965, the former naval station was sold to J. Louis Reynolds, and it later became Reynolds Industrial Park. This photograph shows barges on the St. Johns River docked at Reynolds Industrial Park in 1979. (State Archives of Florida.)

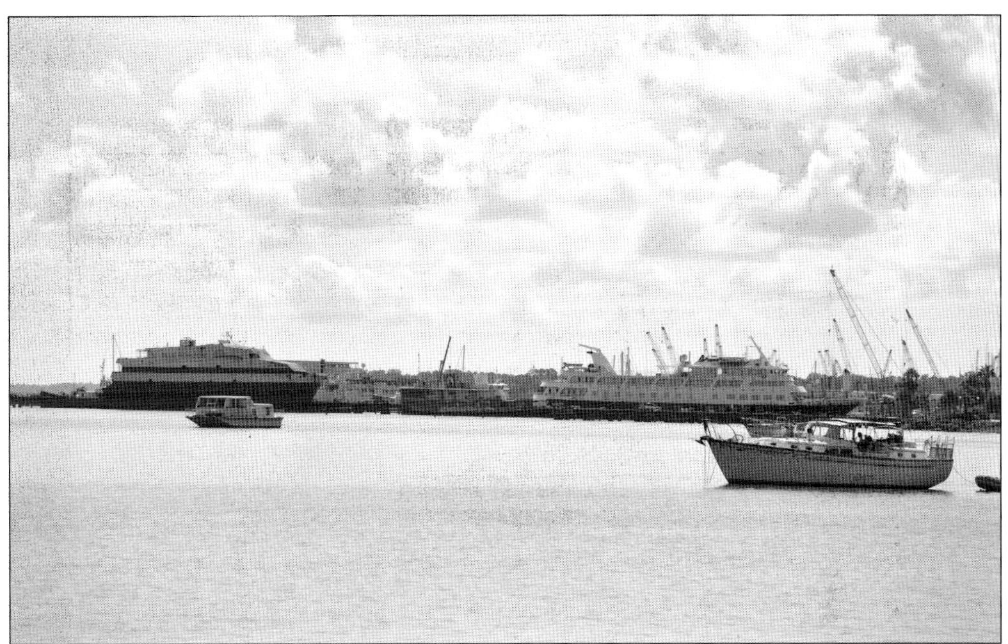

Reynolds Park continues to be an industrial park for ships and barges in the 21st century. This photograph from City Pier shows Reynolds Park busy with several large ships in 2022. (Andrew R. Nicholas.)

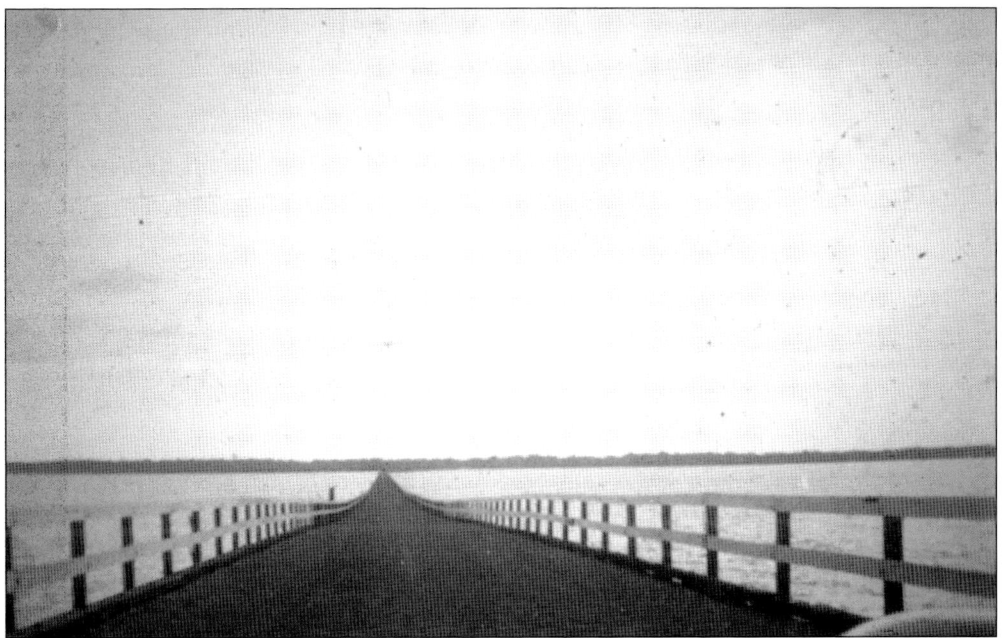

The first Shands Bridge was a wooden two-lane drawbridge built in 1928. In 1961, the present-day Shands Bridge was built. The old wooden bridge was demolished, leaving only a small portion at Green Cove Springs, with locals referring to it as "the Shands Pier." In October 2016, category five Hurricane Matthew destroyed the Shands Pier beyond repair. In 2022, the remnants of the pier were removed. (Clay County Archives)

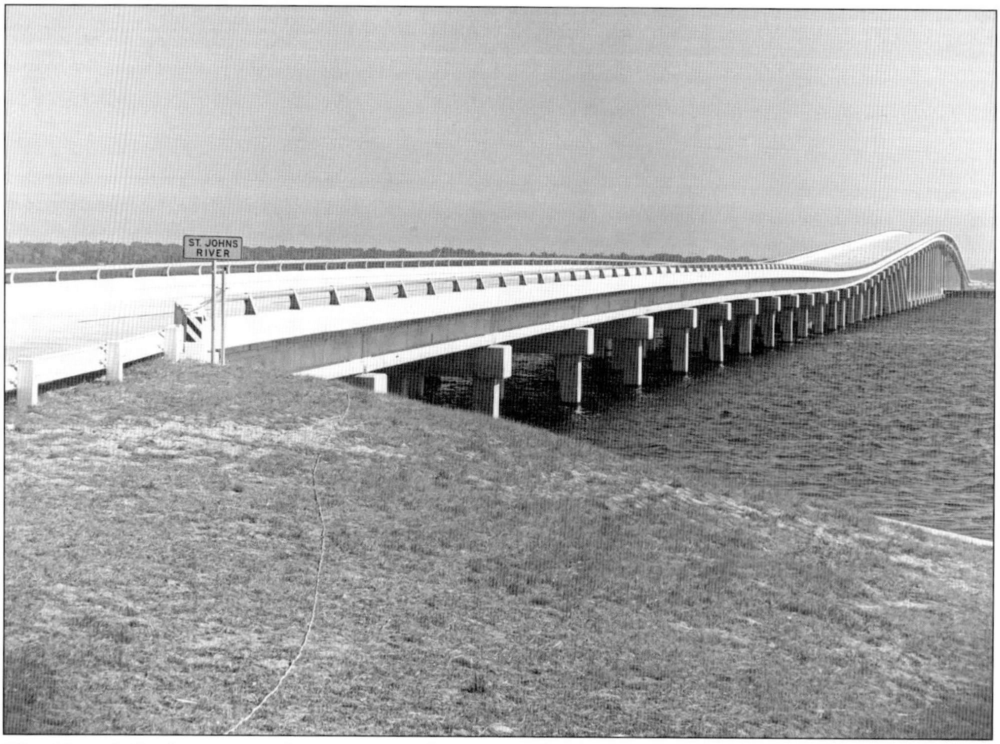

The Shands Bridge is a two-lane concrete beam-type bridge that opened in 1963. It is named after Alfred G. Shands, the brother of William Shands, an advocate for a teaching hospital in Florida, which later became UF Health Shands Hospital in 1958. A new four-lane bridge called First Coast Expressway will be built by 2030 to replace the Shands Bridge. (State Archives of Florida.)

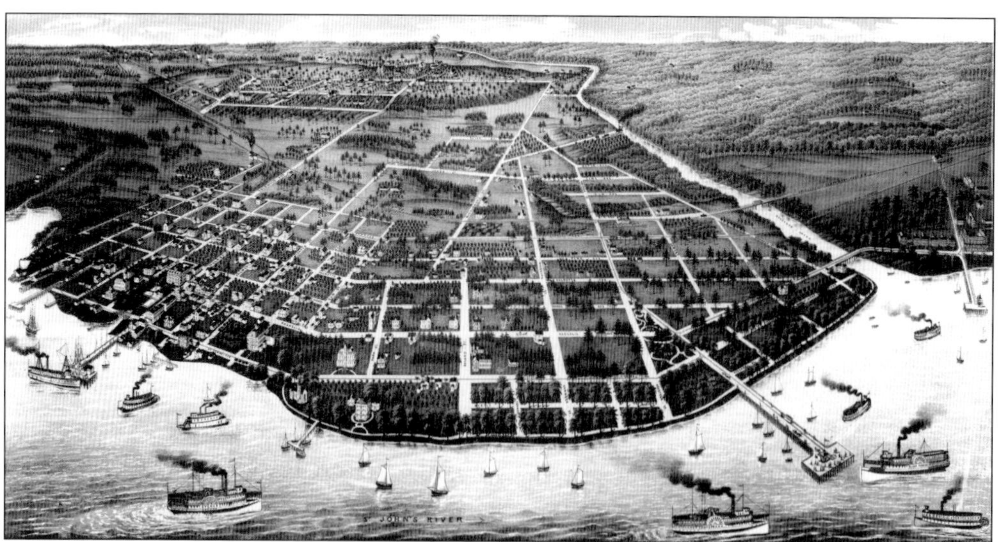

This is a bird's-eye view of Green Cove Springs in 1885. On the far left is where the present-day Green Cove Springs Public Pier and Spring Park is located. Governor's Creek can be seen on the far right going up to the top. On the right side of Governor's Creek is the Magnolia Hotel and dock. The long dock near Governor's Creek is at present-day Clay Street. (State Archives of Florida.)

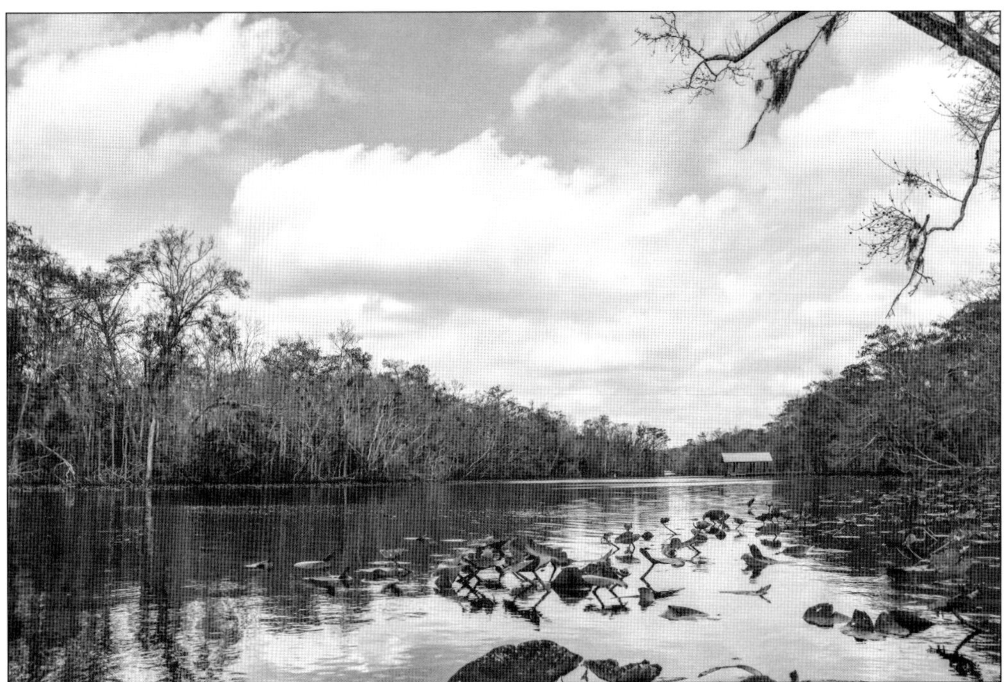

Trout Creek is a tributary of the St. Johns River that empties into Palmo Bay. This photograph was taken from a kayak on Trout Creek. (Rhonda Lovett.)

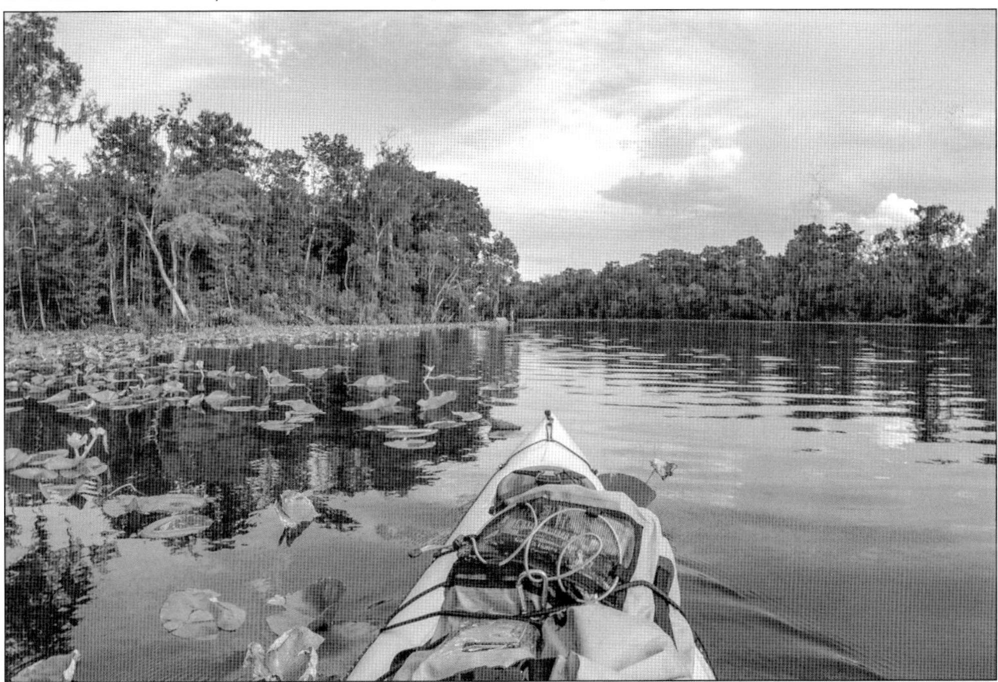

Six Mile Creek is a tributary of the St. Johns River that also empties out into Palmo Bay. The creek was first settled by Capt. William Rainsford when he received a grant of 1,000 acres in 1768 and established a water-powered sawmill. This photograph shows a kayaker on Six Mile Creek. (Rhonda Lovett.)

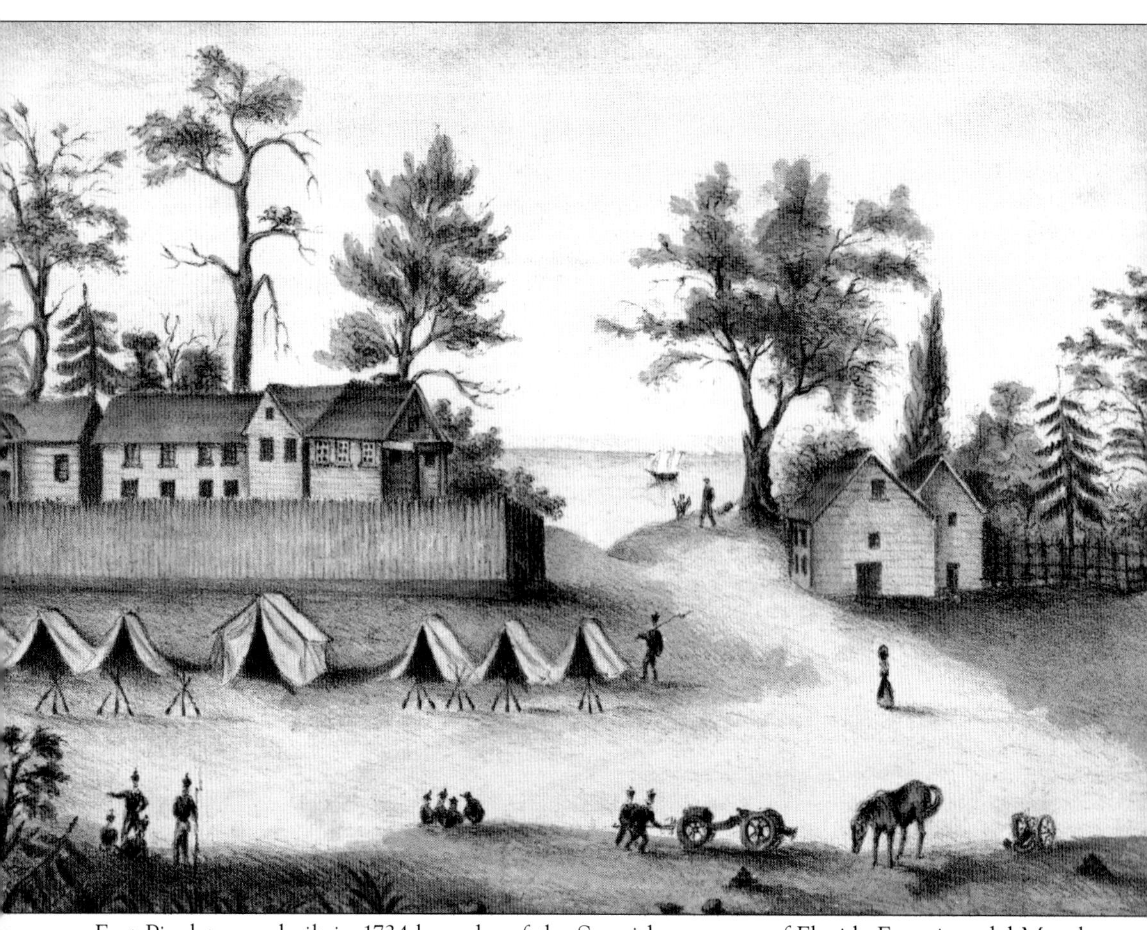

Fort Picolata was built in 1734 by order of the Spanish governor of Florida Francisco del Moral y Sánchez due to the continual tension between Spain and Great Britain. The fort was located on the eastern side of the St. Johns River about 20 miles west of St. Augustine, the capital of Spanish Florida. A similar Spanish fort called San Francisco de Pupo was built on the west side of the river near Fort Picolata. James Oglethorpe of Georgia invaded Florida in 1739 with a force of Scottish Highlanders and Native American allies. Oglethorpe's forces destroyed both forts and unsuccessfully laid siege to St. Augustine. Fort Picolata was later rebuilt by the Spanish. When the British acquired Florida in 1763, they continued to use Fort Picolata. The fort was then used by American forces when it was acquired by the United States in 1821. This sketch shows Fort Picolata in 1837, with the St. Johns River in the background. (Library of Congress.)

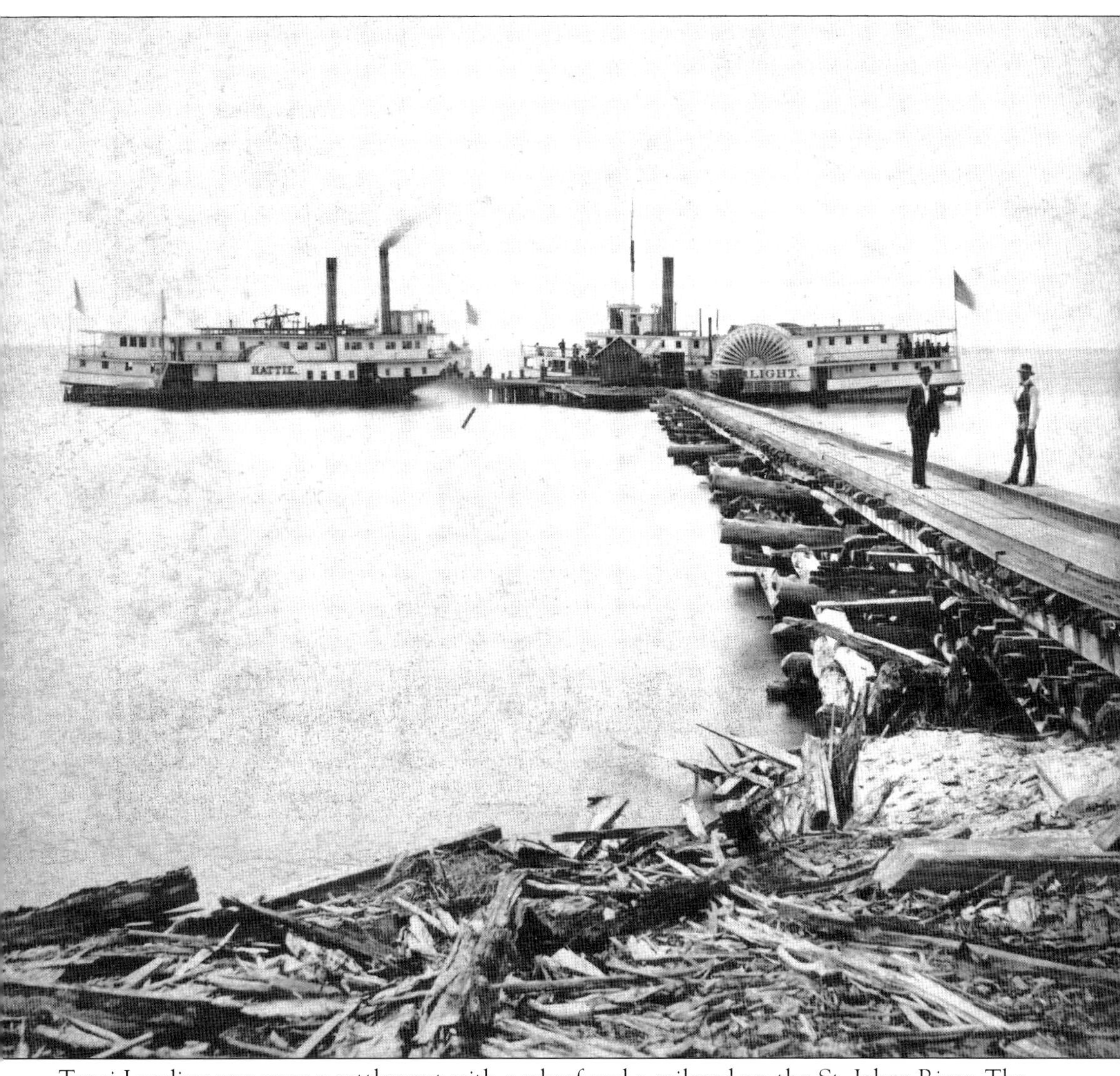

Tocoi Landing was once a settlement with a wharf and a railroad on the St. Johns River. The name is a Timucua word meaning water lily. It is also the name of a nearby creek, Tocoi Creek. This photograph shows the Tocoi wharf with the steamers *Hattie* and *Starlight* on the St. Johns in 1871. Tocoi gradually became a ghost town by the 20th century. The name has received renewed interest with the creation of Tocoi Creek High School, which opened in 2021 about three miles north of the creek. (State Archives of Florida.)

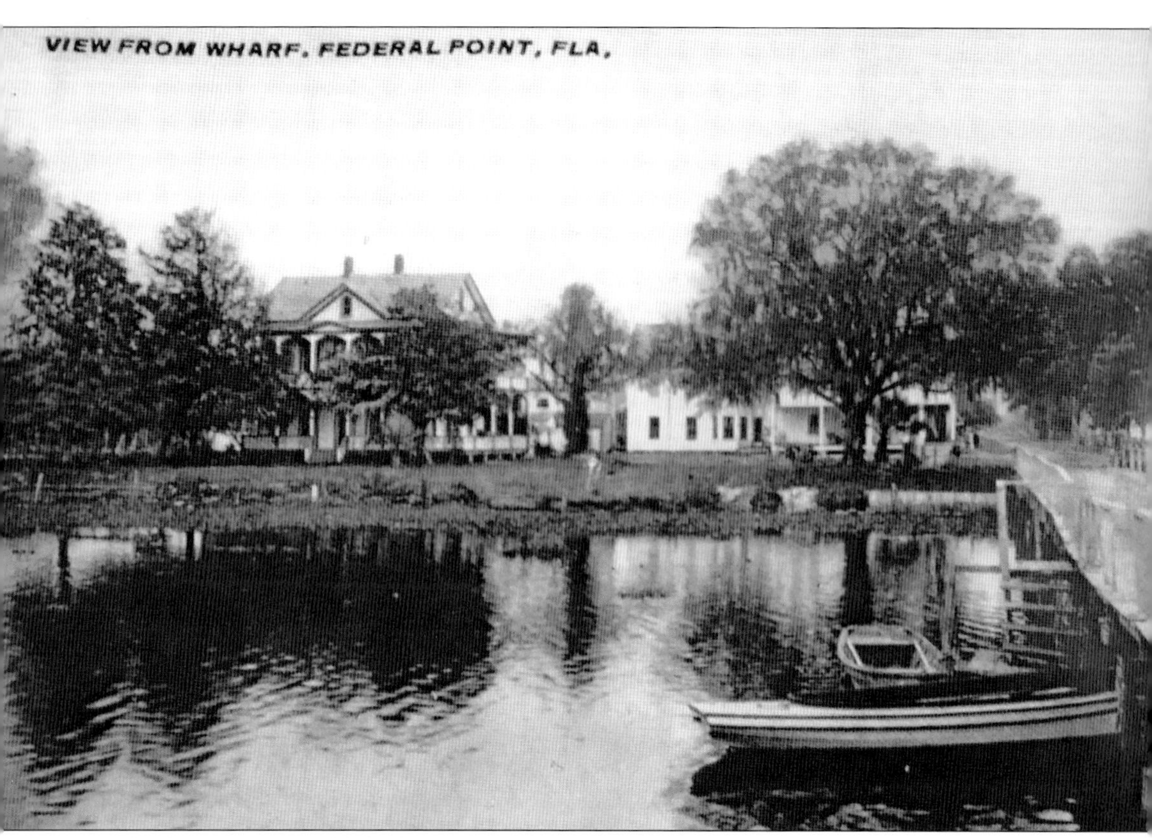

Federal Point was established in 1866 by J.F. Tenny and J.C. Folsom on the St. Johns River. It had a wharf for steamboats, a post office, two schools, and a church. The postcard shows Federal Point in the late 19th century. (West Volusia Historical Society.)

Five

To the Land of George

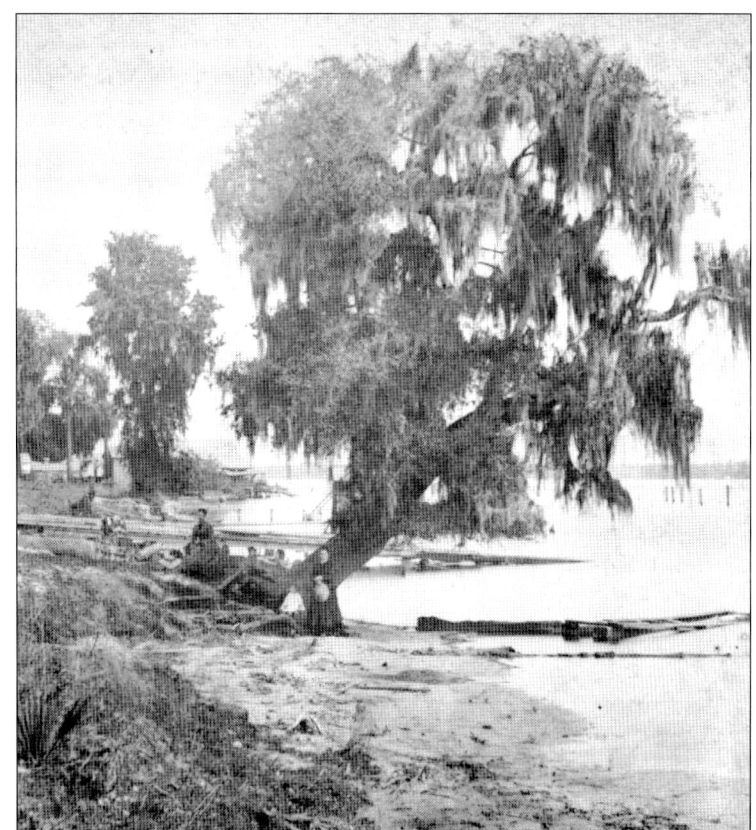

Palatka is on the St. Johns River and is the county seat of Putnam County. The Seminole settled in this area in the late 18th century. Its name comes from the Seminole word *pilo-taikita*, meaning "cow's crossing" or "crossing over." This photograph shows the river shoreline at Palatka in 1875. (New York Public Library.)

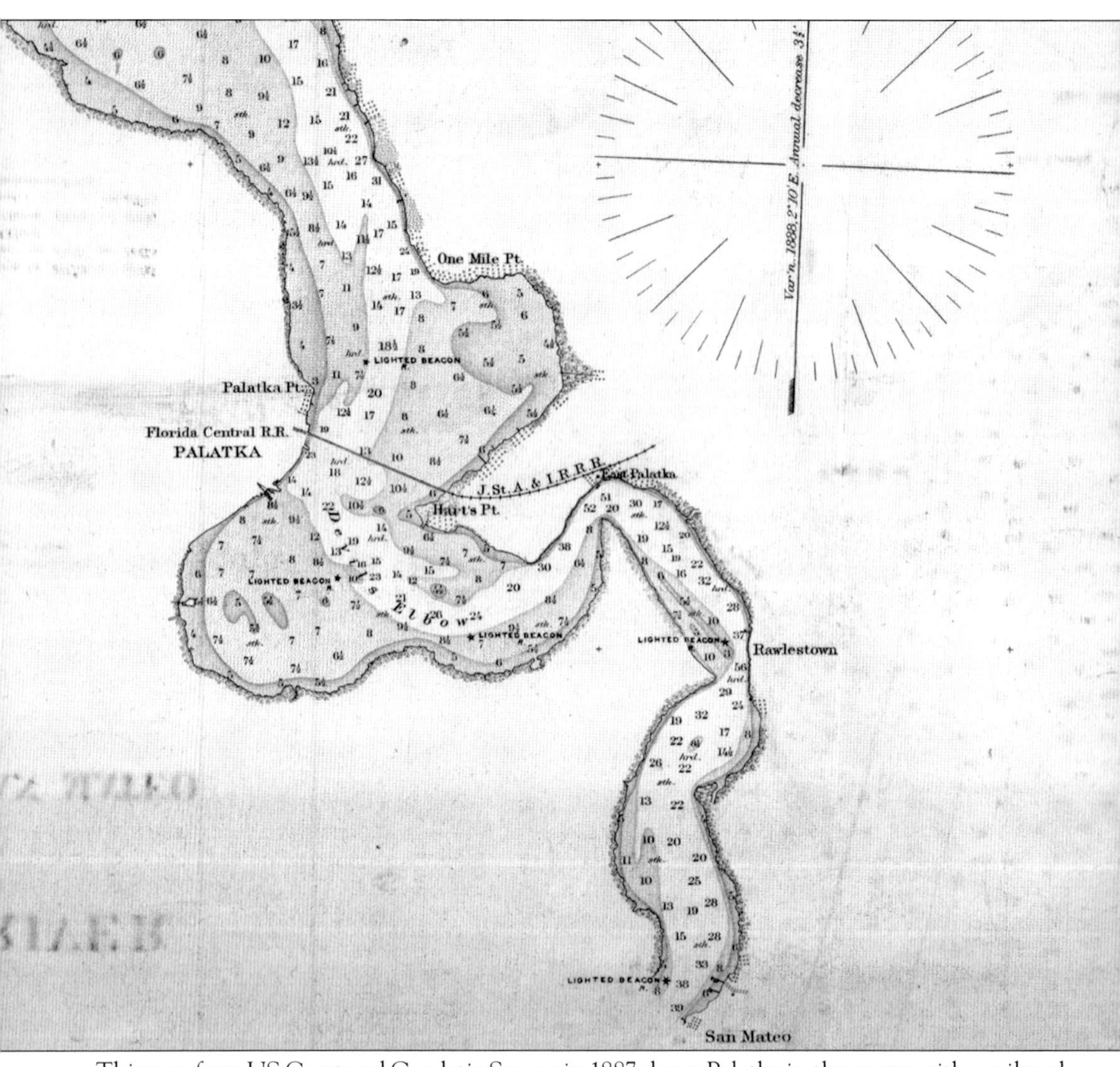

This map from US Coast and Geodetic Survey in 1887 shows Palatka in the center with a railroad bridge going over the St. Johns River. (State Archives of Florida.)

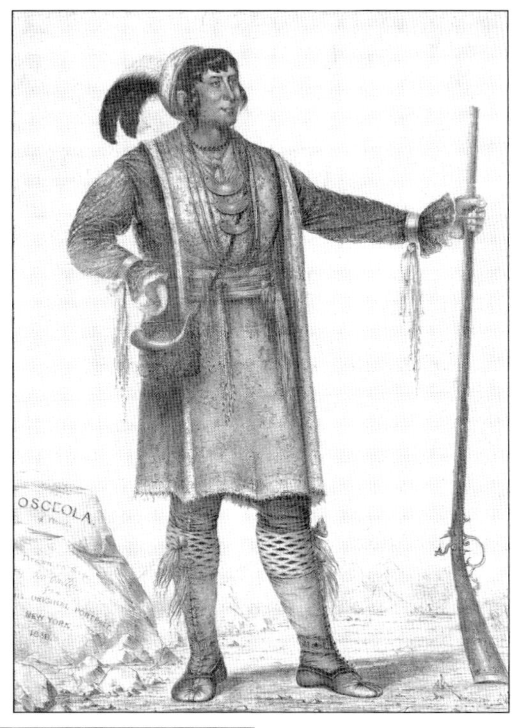

The Seminole originated with the Creek Native Americans of present-day Georgia and Alabama. Various bands of Creek, specifically Muscogee Creek, migrated south to Florida due to conflicts with Europeans and other Native American tribes. By the 1770s, this distinct Creek tribe in Florida was referred to as "Seminole," a name meaning "runaway" or "wild people." The Seminole became more distinct with the assimilation of the Native American Yuchi, Yamassee, some aboriginals, and especially runaway slaves. The United States came into conflict with the Seminole in 1817 with the First Seminole War, when Gen. Andrew Jackson invaded Spanish Florida and pushed them further south. The Second Seminole War erupted in 1835, after the passage of the Indian Removal Act of 1830 forced the Seminole to relocate to present-day Oklahoma. Osceola is considered the most influential leader of the Seminole. The sketch shows him posing with a rifle in 1838. (Library of Congress.)

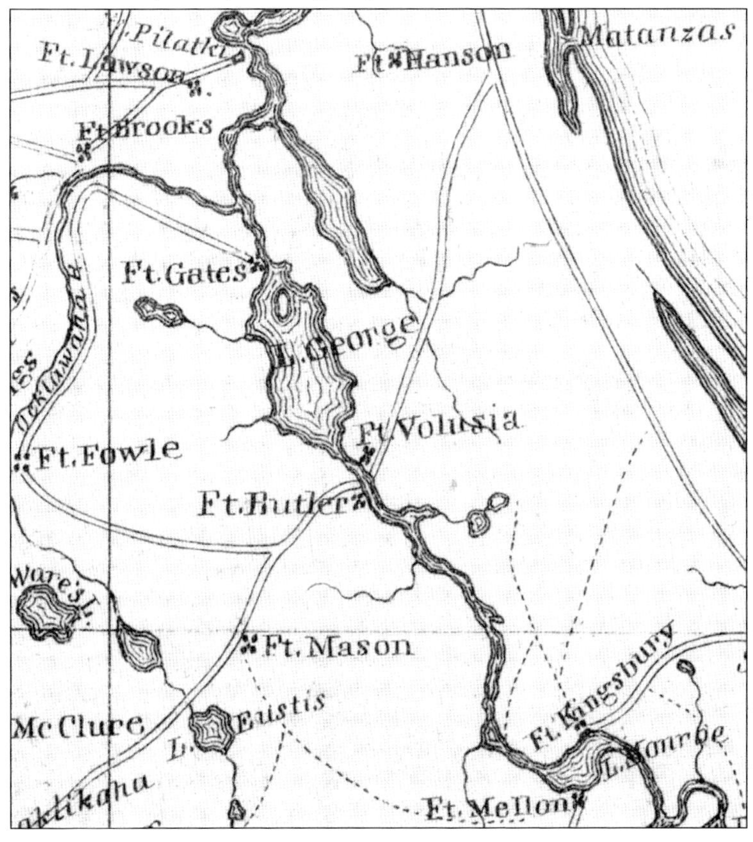

In the early 1820s, Palatka was founded as a trading post and ferry on the St. Johns River. During the Seminole Wars, Palatka was burned by the Seminoles in 1835. The US Army afterward built Fort Shannon in 1838 to defend Palatka and the nearby St. Johns. After the Seminole War in 1843, the fort was abandoned. This map from 1840 shows forts on the river during the war. (New York Public Library.)

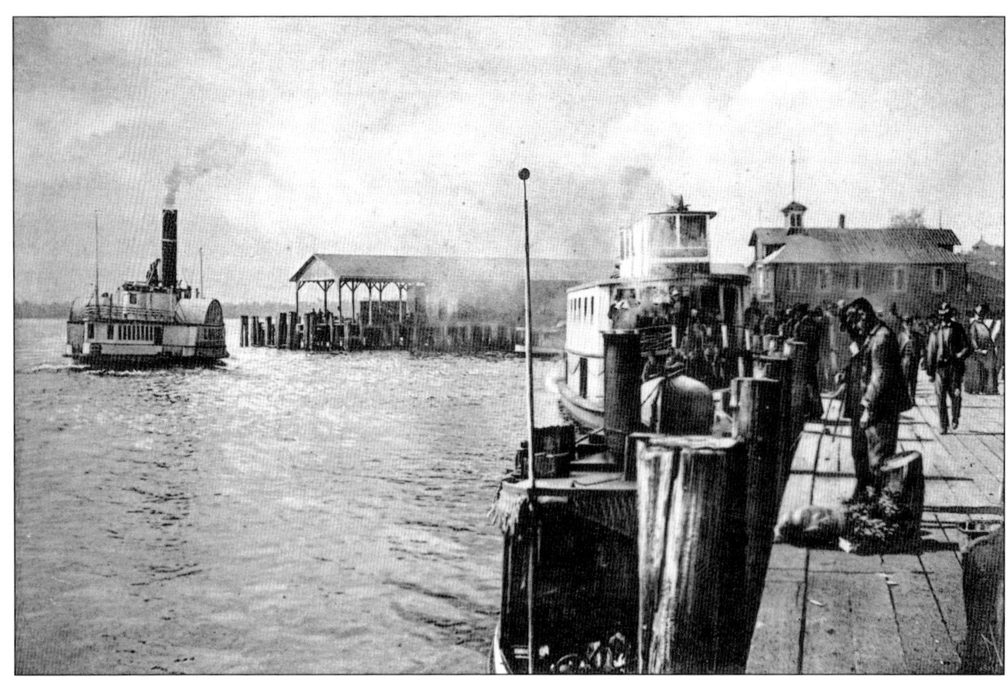

In 1849, Palatka became the county seat of Putnam County, and the town was incorporated in 1853. After the Civil War, Palatka grew to become a popular transportation hub for steamboats and the railroad. Tourism increased, making it a popular winter resort destination. This photograph shows the St. Johns River and docks at Palatka in 1890. (State Archives of Florida.)

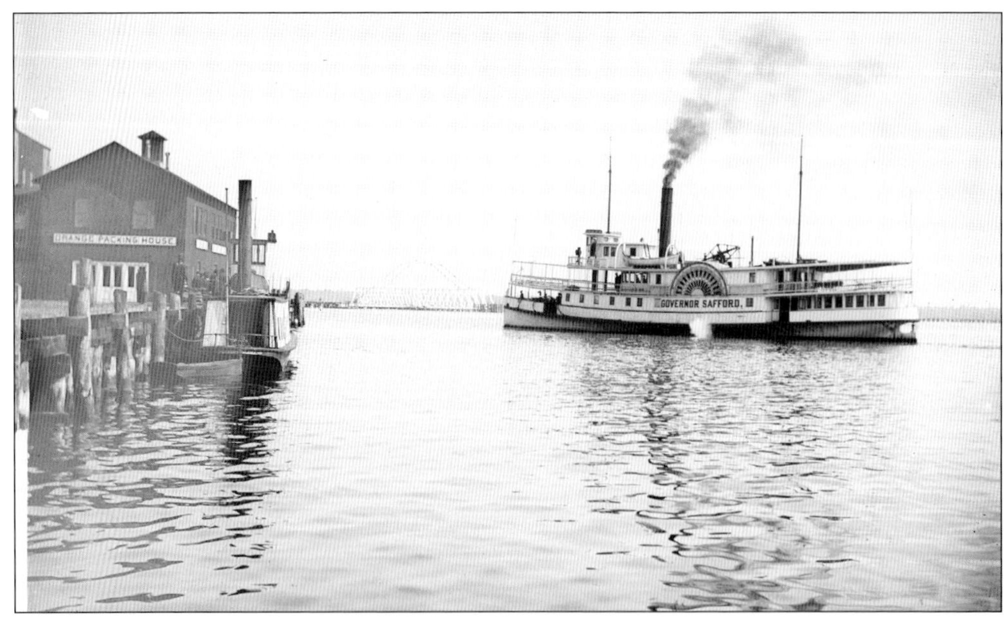

In 1884, Palatka was mostly burned down in a fire, but the town rebuilt with brick instead of wood. The 1894–1895 Great Freeze severely hurt the citrus industry, including transportation at Palatka. By the early 1900s, Palatka declined as a major tourist destination. This photograph shows the *Governor Safford* steamer on the St. Johns River at Palatka around 1910. (Library of Congress.)

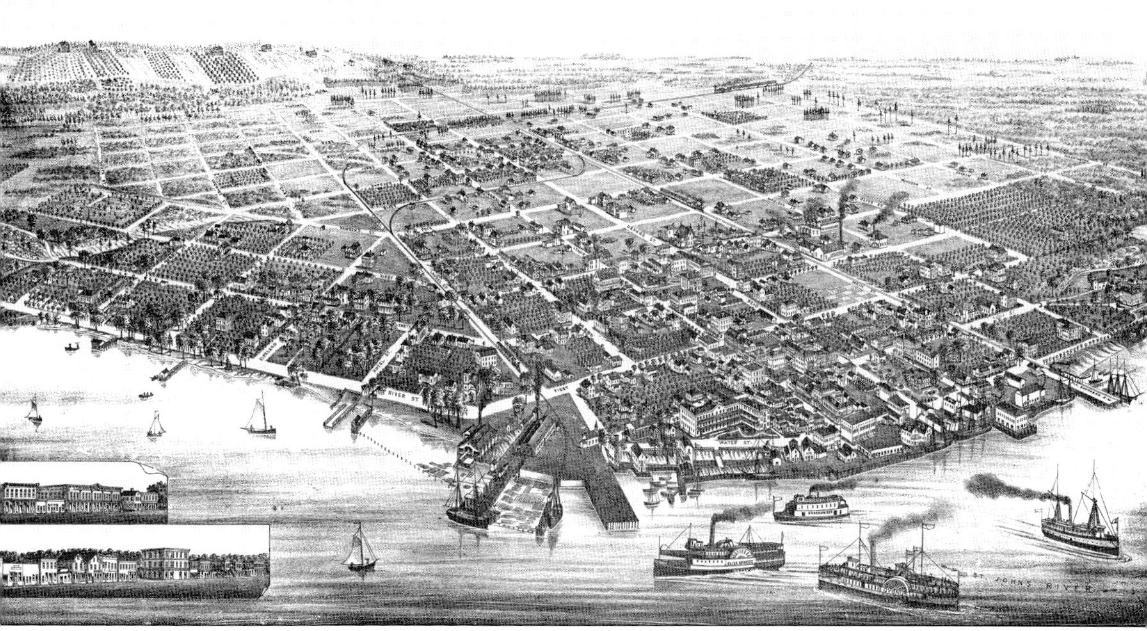

This is a bird's-eye view of Palatka in 1884. At the present-day area of Riverfront Park between Main Street and Laurel Street, steamships would load and unload goods. To the left of Laurel Street are residential docks that are still in use today. (State Archives of Florida.)

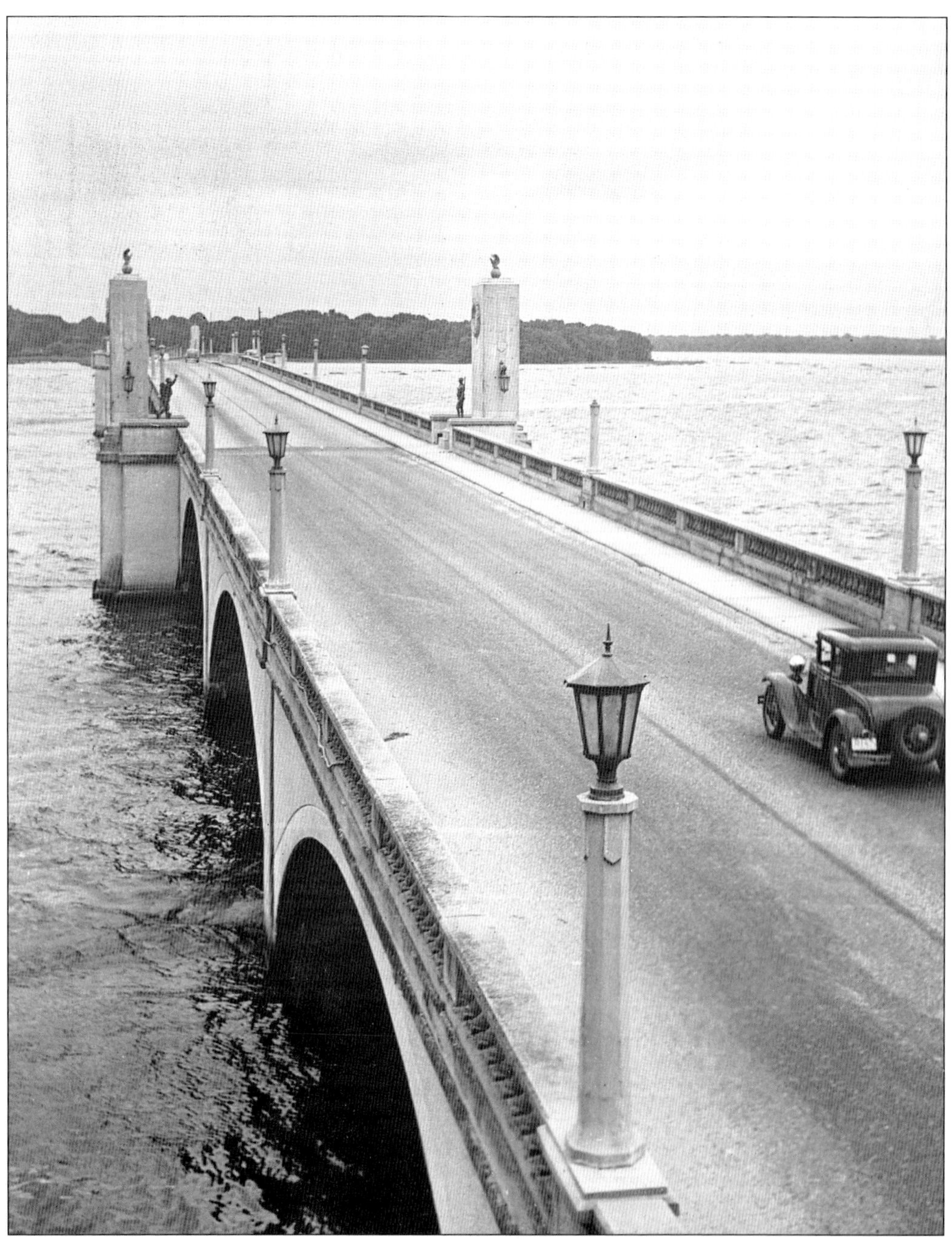

Memorial Bridge was built in 1927 over the St. Johns River, connecting Palatka with East Palatka. It was a two-lane drawbridge opening in the middle to allow large marine vessels through. This photograph of Memorial Bridge was taken in 1948. (State Archives of Florida.)

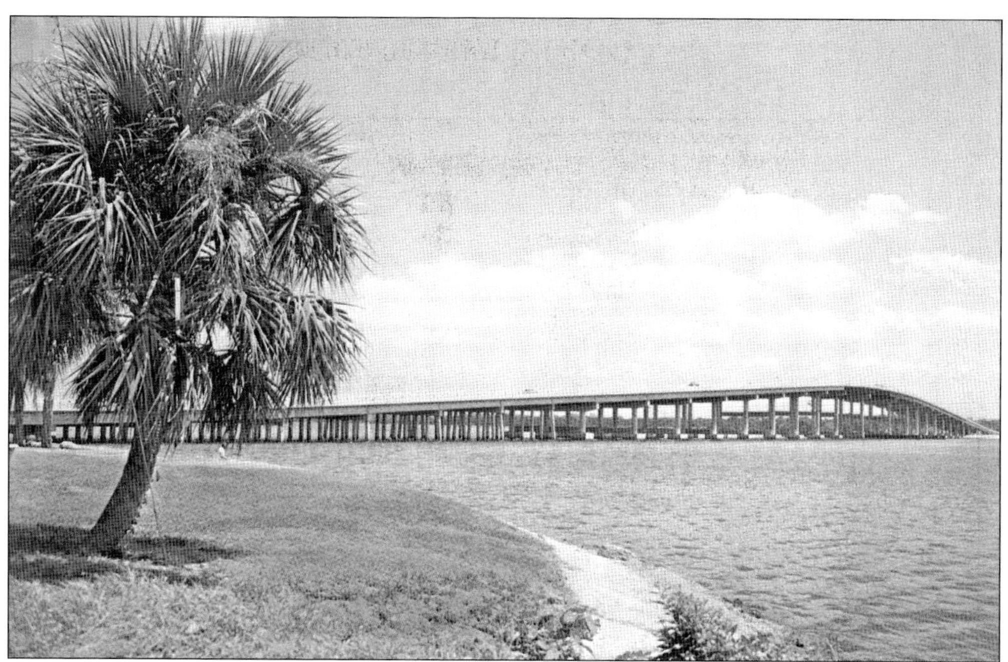

In 1976, Memorial Bridge was replaced with a newer four-lane bridge with a 65-foot clearance. This photograph of Memorial Bridge was taken at Palatka. (State Archives of Florida.)

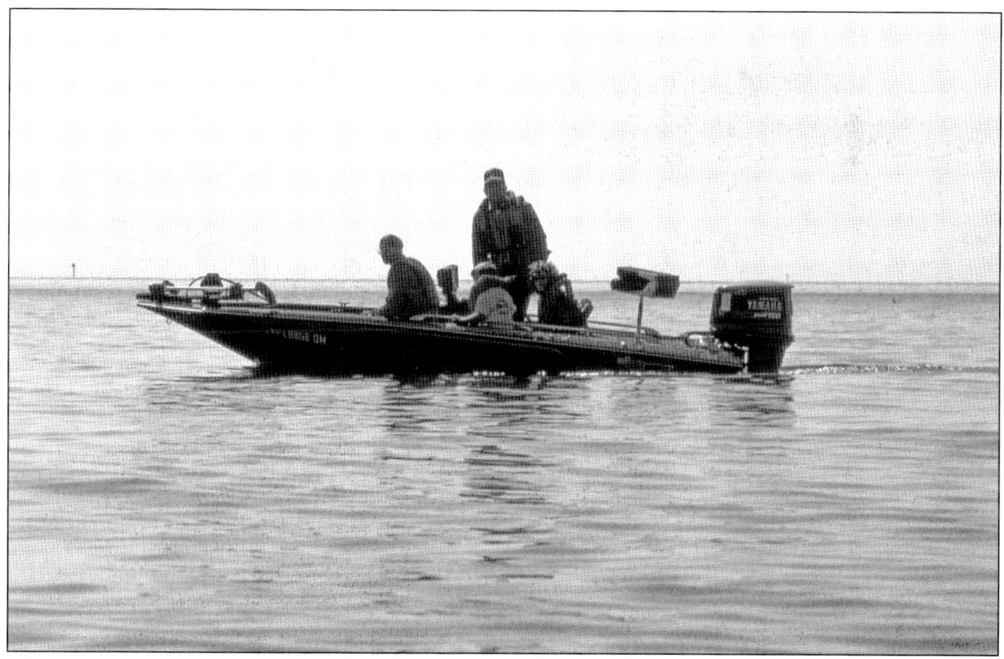

This photograph shows participants in the Bobby Brantley Legislative Bass Tournament at Palatka in the 1980s. The boat is a Skeeter Starfire with a Yamaha outboard motor. (State Archives of Florida.)

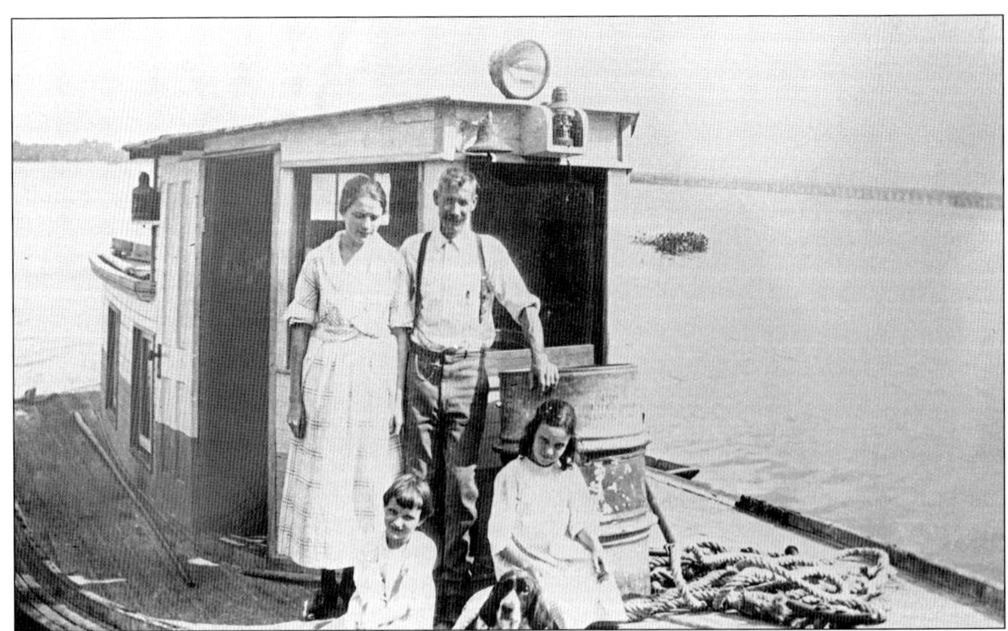

In 1765, Denys Rolle established the colony of Rollestown with around 200 indentured servants. Rollestown was abandoned in 1783 after Great Britain ceded Florida to Spain. The present-day town of East Palatka is located on the former site of Rollestown. This photograph shows a boat at East Palatka in 1920. (State Archives of Florida.)

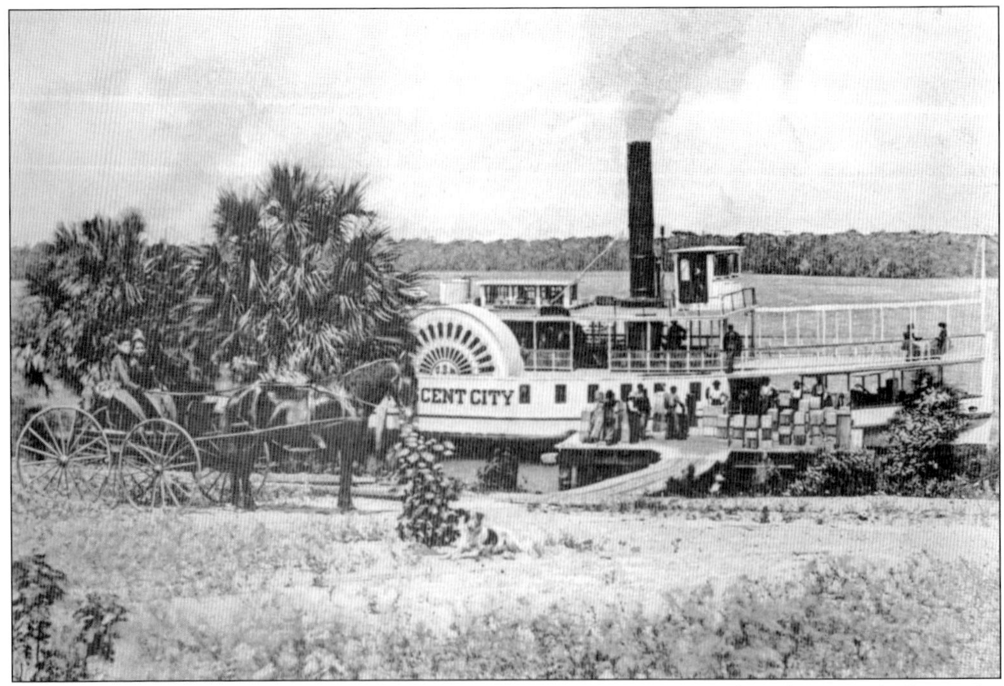

San Mateo was a small town settled in 1867 on the St. Johns River. This photograph shows the *Crescent City* steamer docked on the St. Johns at San Mateo in 1890. The steamer is being loaded with oranges. (State Archives of Florida.)

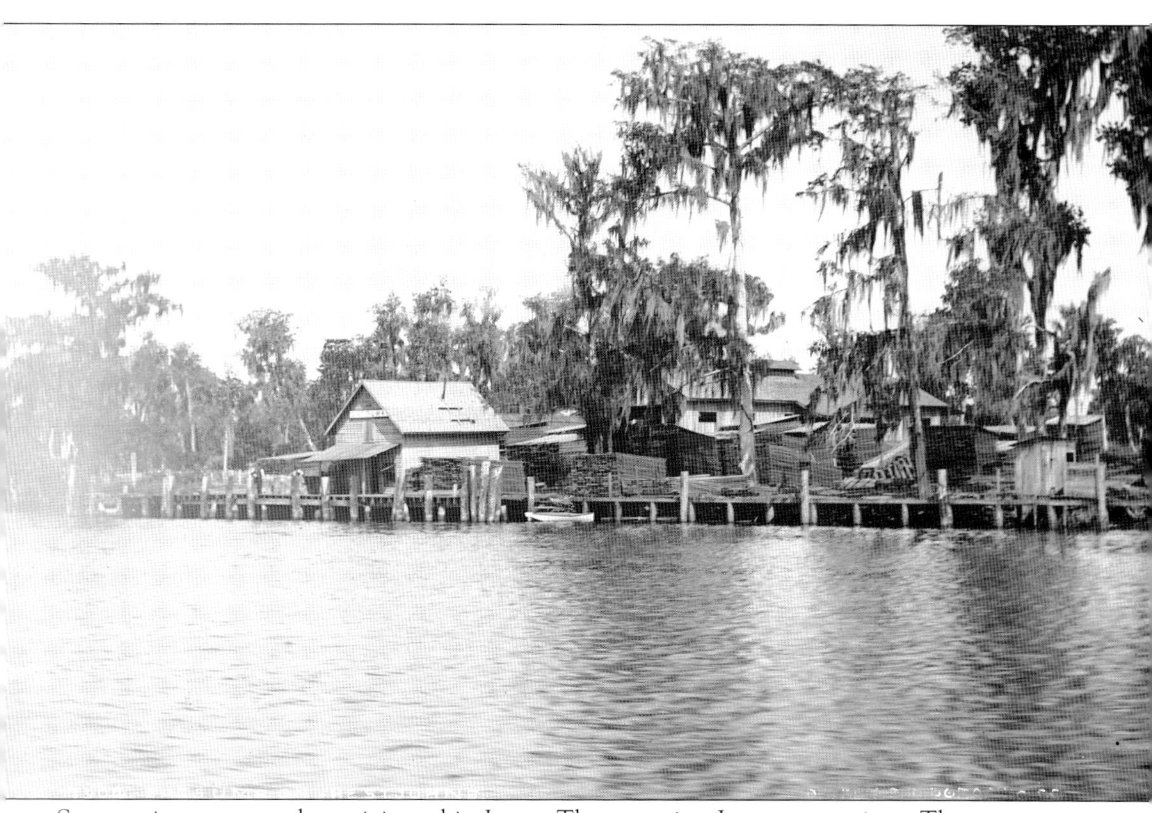

Satsuma is an orange that originated in Japan. The name is a Japanese province. The oranges were brought to the United States from Japan in 1878 by the wife of Van Valkenburgh, the US ambassador to Japan. They were renamed satsumas and planted in Florida, Alabama, Louisiana, and Texas. The town of Satsuma was founded near the St. Johns River and is named after the orange. This photograph shows Satsuma in 1880. (Library of Congress.)

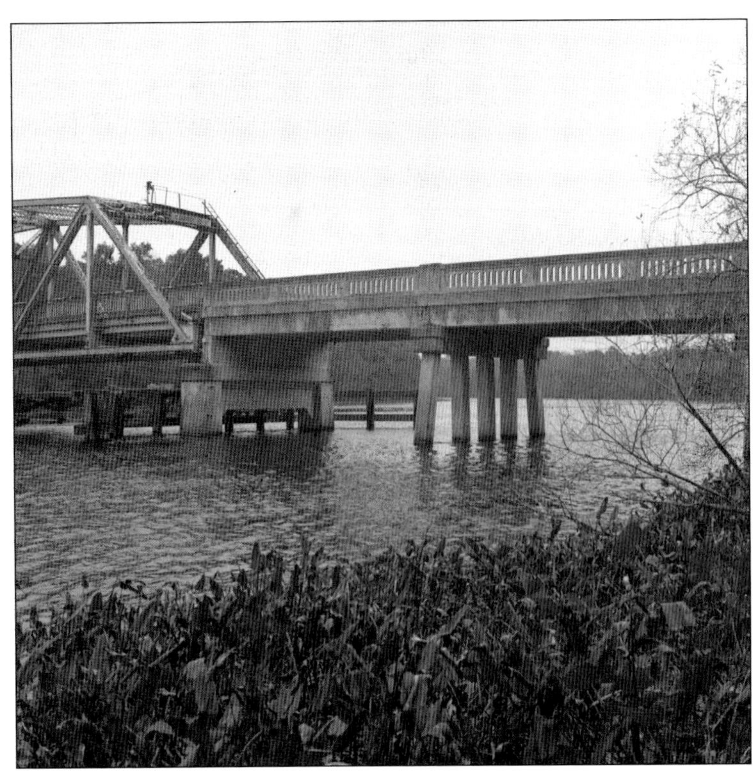

Dunn's Creek connects the St. Johns River with Crescent Lake. The creek is named after John Dunn, a lawyer and coffee planter who purchased land in this area in 1765. This photograph shows Dunn's Creek flowing under Dunn's Creek Bridge in 1981. The bridge connects San Mateo with Satsuma. (State Archives of Florida.)

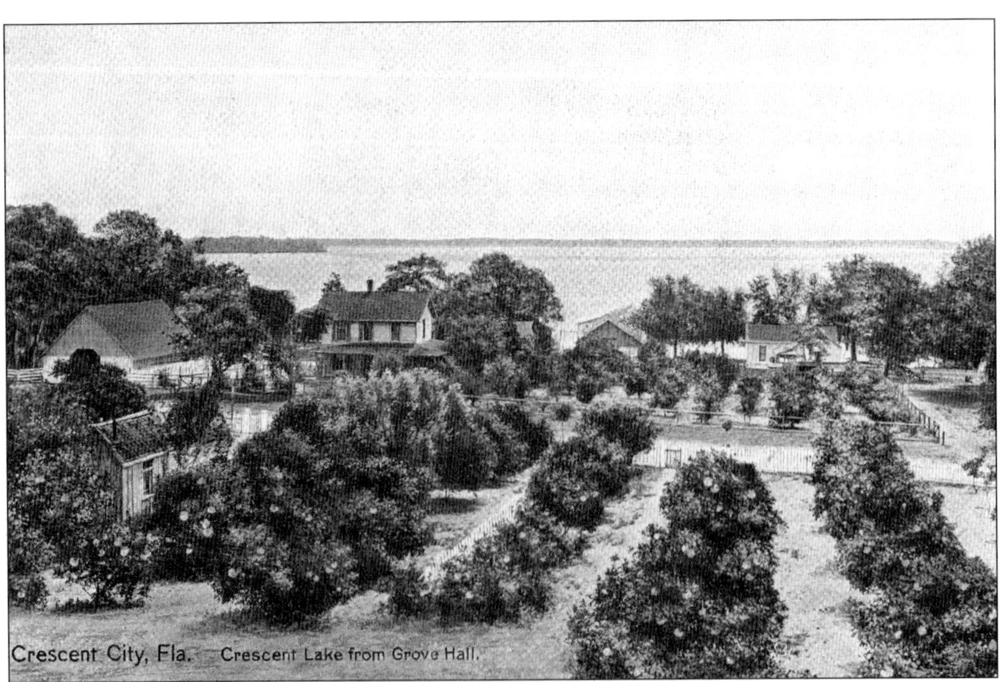

Crescent Lake is a two-mile-wide, 13-mile-long lake. It was once known as Dunn's Lake but became Crescent Lake due to its shape. This postcard shows Crescent Lake in the late 19th century.

The Ocklawaha River flows 74 miles north from Lake Griffin and enters the St. Johns River near Satsuma. The principal tributary of the Ocklawaha is the Silver River. In the 20th century, the Ocklawaha suffered from pollution, impoundments, and dredging. Construction of the Cross Florida Barge Canal was stopped in 1971 mainly due to conserving the Ocklawaha River. This photograph shows two people spearfishing on the Ocklawaha in 1902. (Library of Congress.)

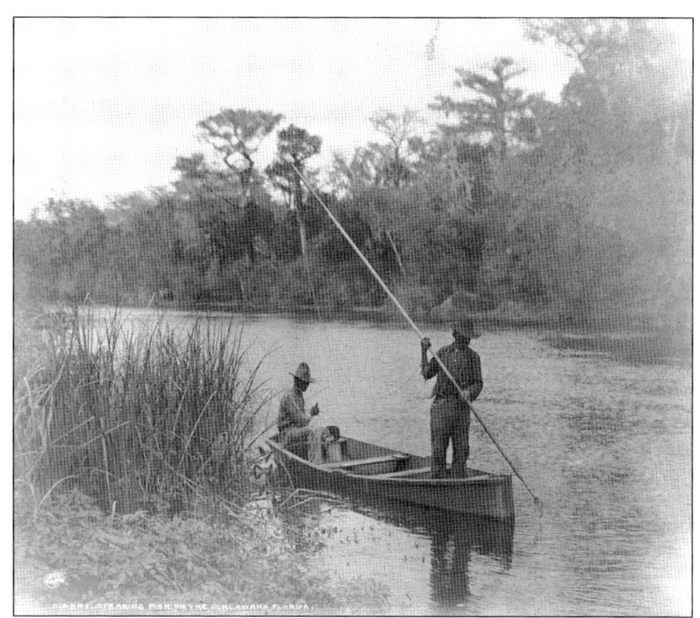

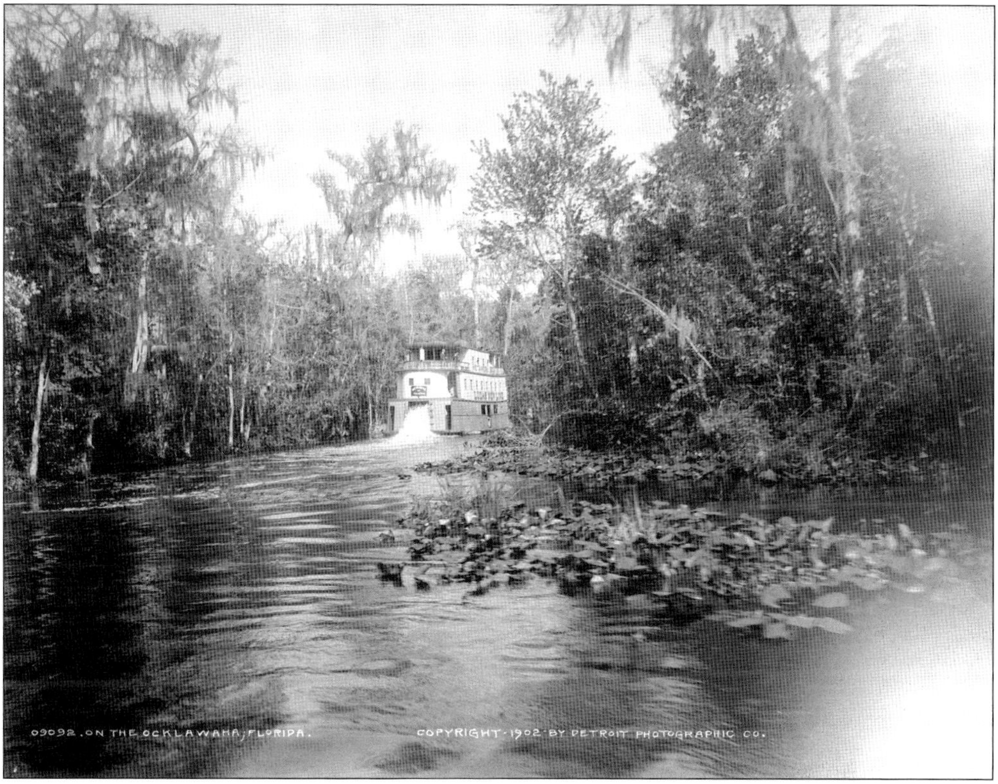

09092. ON THE OCKLAWAHA, FLORIDA. COPYRIGHT 1902 BY DETROIT PHOTOGRAPHIC CO.

The Ocklawaha River became well known for its steamship use in the late 19th century. Hart Line steamships were the most common on the Ocklawaha. In 1893, Ed Lucas wanted to take over the steamship monopoly of the Ocklawaha River and Silver Springs region. He had a large steamship built in Palatka called *Metamora*. This photograph shows the *Metamora* on the Ocklawaha, with Lucas New Line on the side. (Library of Congress.)

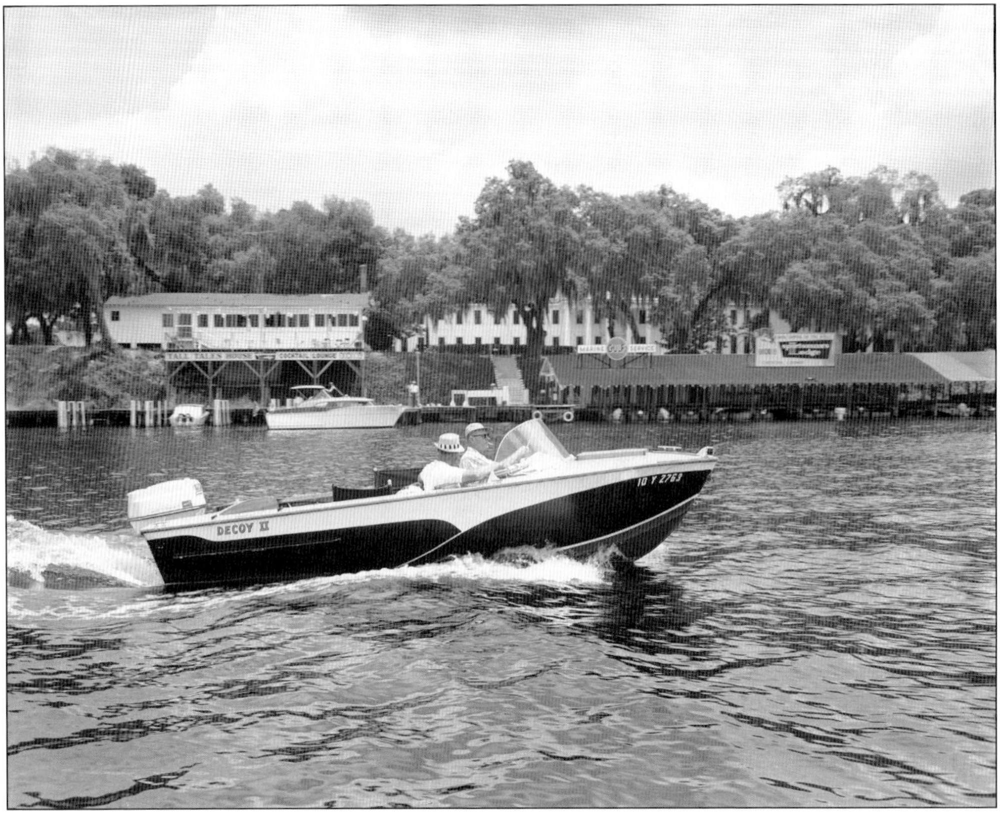

A settlement developed near the St. Johns River in present-day Welaka called Mount Tucker. It was named after John Tucker, a London merchant who had acquired 500 acres in the area. The settlement consisted of several orange and cotton plantations. In 1887, the town of Welaka was incorporated. The name is a Native American word meaning "river of lakes," which was used to refer to the St. Johns River. By the 1880s, Welaka became a tourist town. This photograph shows a boat with a Johnson outboard motor on the St. Johns River passing by Sportsman Lodge at Welaka in 1960. (State Archives of Florida.)

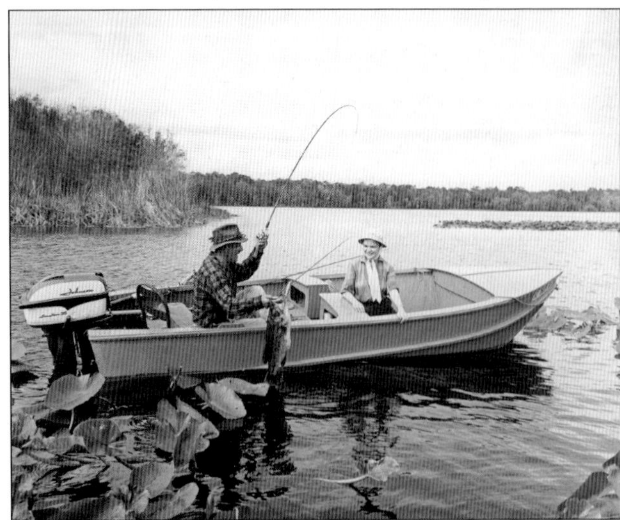

Largemouth bass are prevalent in the middle and upper St. Johns River, where it contains more freshwater than in the lower basin. In this photograph from 1960, a fisherman catches a largemouth bass in Little Lake George. Little Lake George is the last lake before traveling south to the larger Lake George. (State Archives of Florida.)

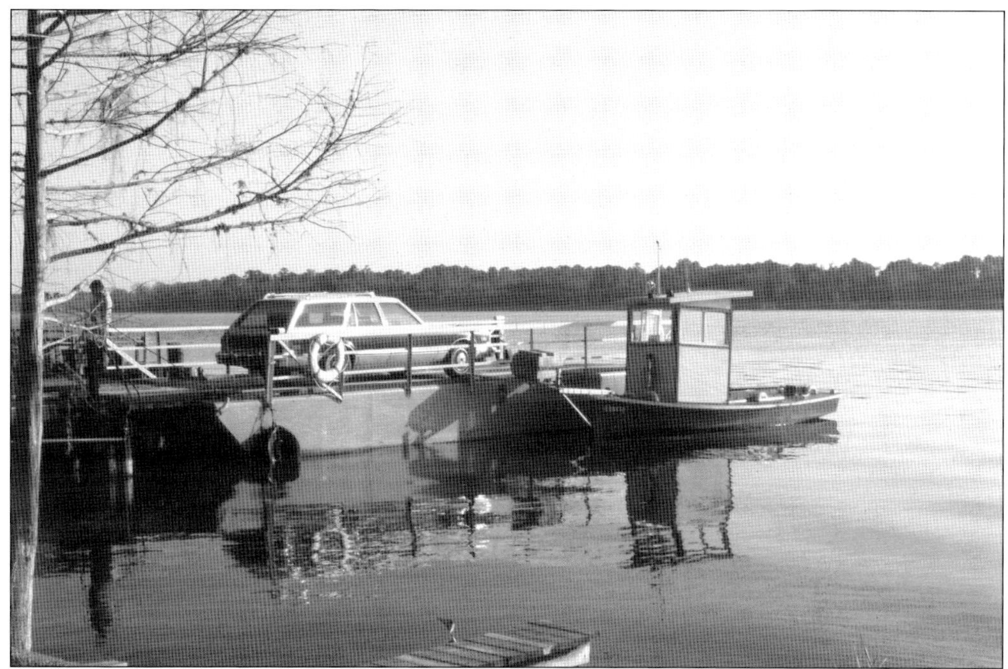

The Fort Gates Ferry was established in 1853 and is considered to be among the oldest ferry services still in operation in Florida. In 1914, a push boat and barge were added. The ferry is at the southern end of Welaka Forest. This photograph shows the push boat and barge with a passenger using the ferry in 1983. (State Archives of Florida.)

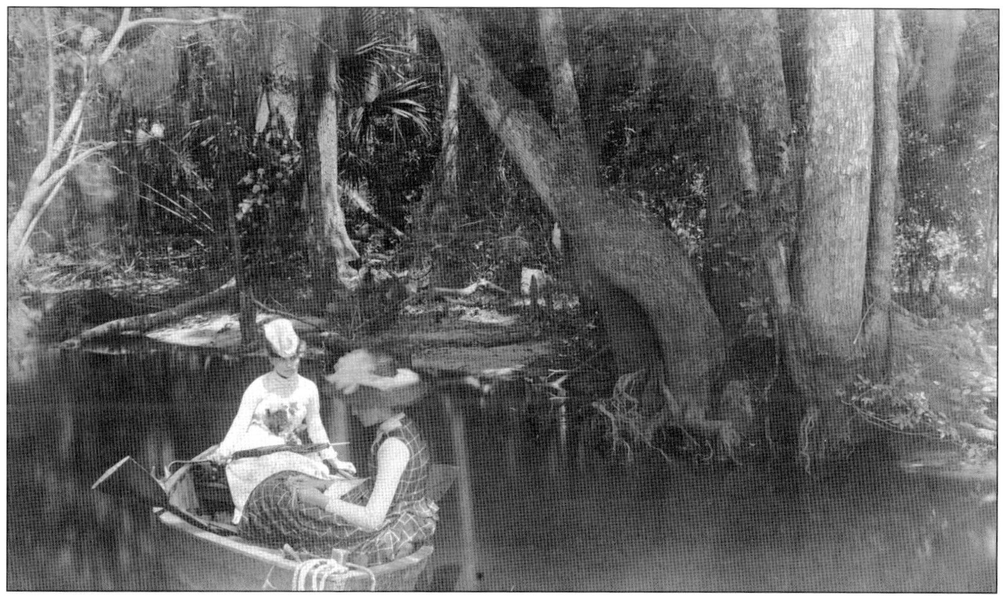

This photograph shows Florence Dakin and Eloise Bennett on the St. Johns River near Racimo Plantation in 1887. (State Archives of Florida.)

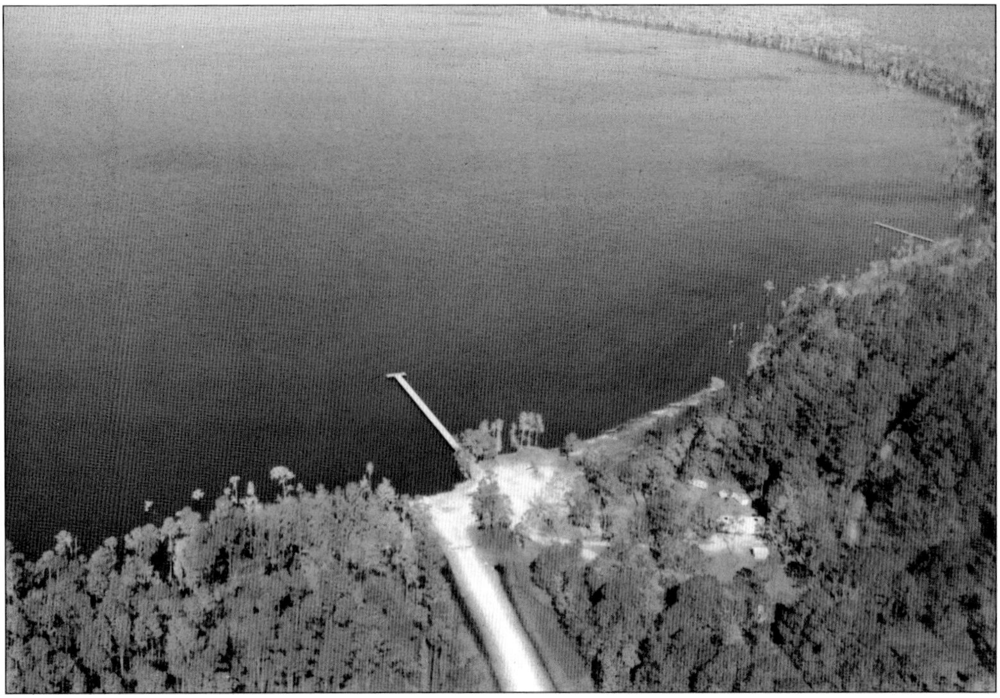

Lake George is the second-largest lake in Florida. It is roughly six miles wide and 11 miles in length, with an average depth of eight feet. John Bartram explored Lake George in 1765 and named it after King George III. This aerial photograph from 1965 shows only a small portion of the lake. (State Archives of Florida.)

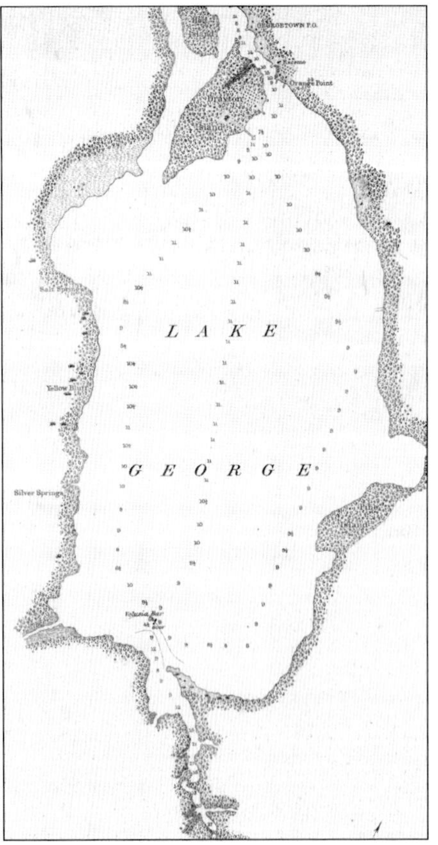

This map shows the St. Johns River flowing through Lake George. At the north end of the lake is Drayton Island. On the left is Ocala National Forest. (State Archives of Florida.)

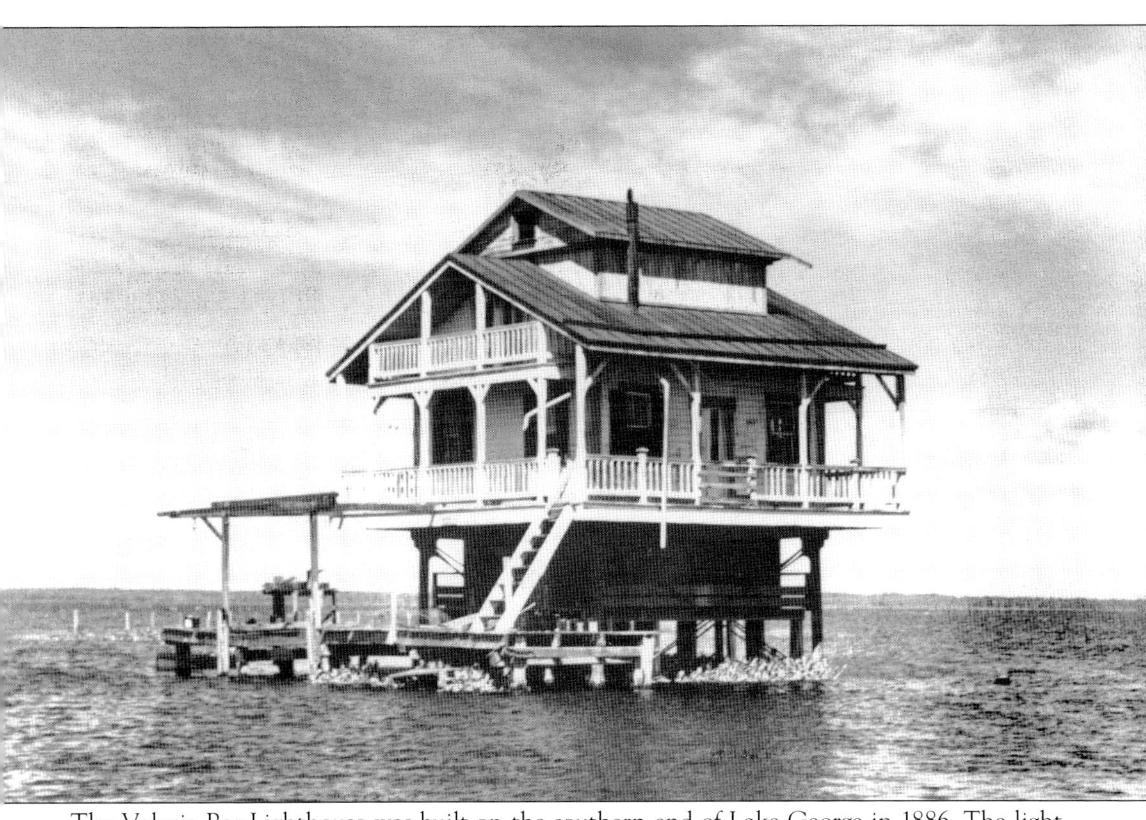

The Volusia Bar Lighthouse was built on the southern end of Lake George in 1886. The light at the top of the building was removed in 1913, leaving only the fog signal and minor lights in place. This photograph shows the lighthouse in the 1930s without its light. In winter 1938, local residents noticed that the lamps in the lighthouse were not being lit by the attendant. They went to investigate and found the body of attendant A.J. Anderson floating in the lake. Anderson was found to have been murdered and the lighthouse ransacked. The murder was never solved. The fog signal was later deactivated by the Coast Guard in 1943, and the lighthouse was abandoned. In 1974, it burned down, but the original pilings are still there with some minor lights to guide boaters. (State Archives of Florida.)

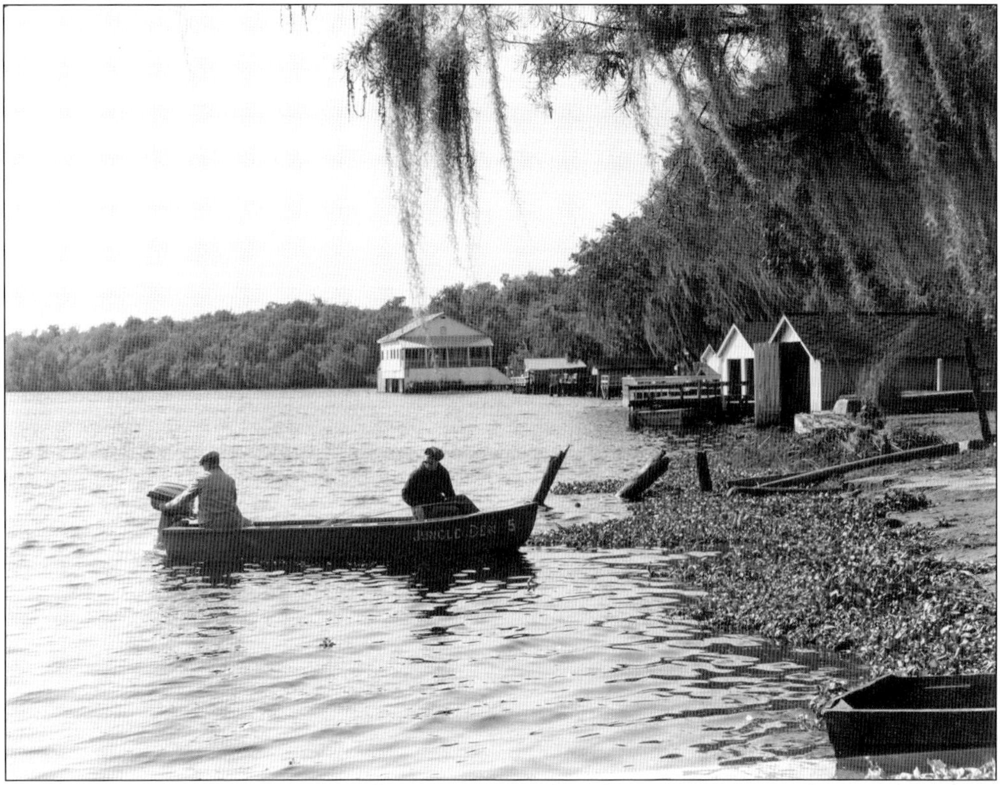

In 1874, American businessman William B. Astor Jr. bought 12,000 acres on the St. Johns River and named it Manhattan. He had a sawmill, hotel, church, and school built there. After he died in 1892, the residents renamed the town Astor. Astor's children inherited property there but had no interest in it and sold it. One of William's children, John Jacob Astor IV, had a net worth of $2.44 billion adjusted to 2021, which made him one of the wealthiest people in the world. He ended up perishing on April 15, 1912, aboard the *Titanic*. The town of Astor continues to thrive with its reliance on the St. Johns River. This photograph shows two men fishing near the shore of Astor in 1957. The outboard motor on the boat is an Evinrude. (State Archives of Florida.)

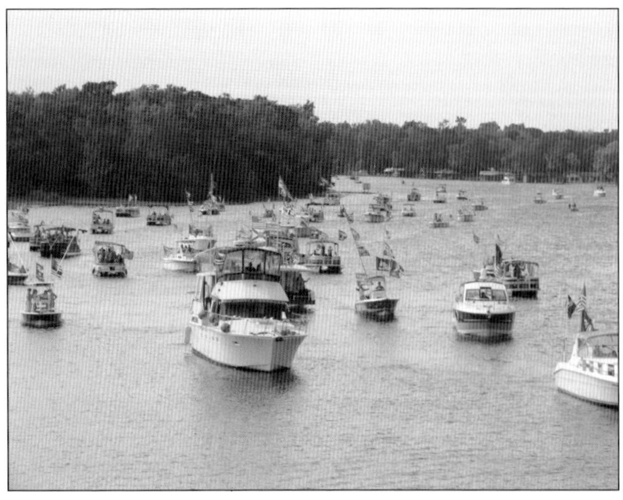

Boaters in Florida started holding boat parades on the St. Johns River in 2020 to show support for former president Donald Trump. This photograph shows a Trump boat parade in October 2020 on the St. Johns River in Astor. (Marlene Sparks.)

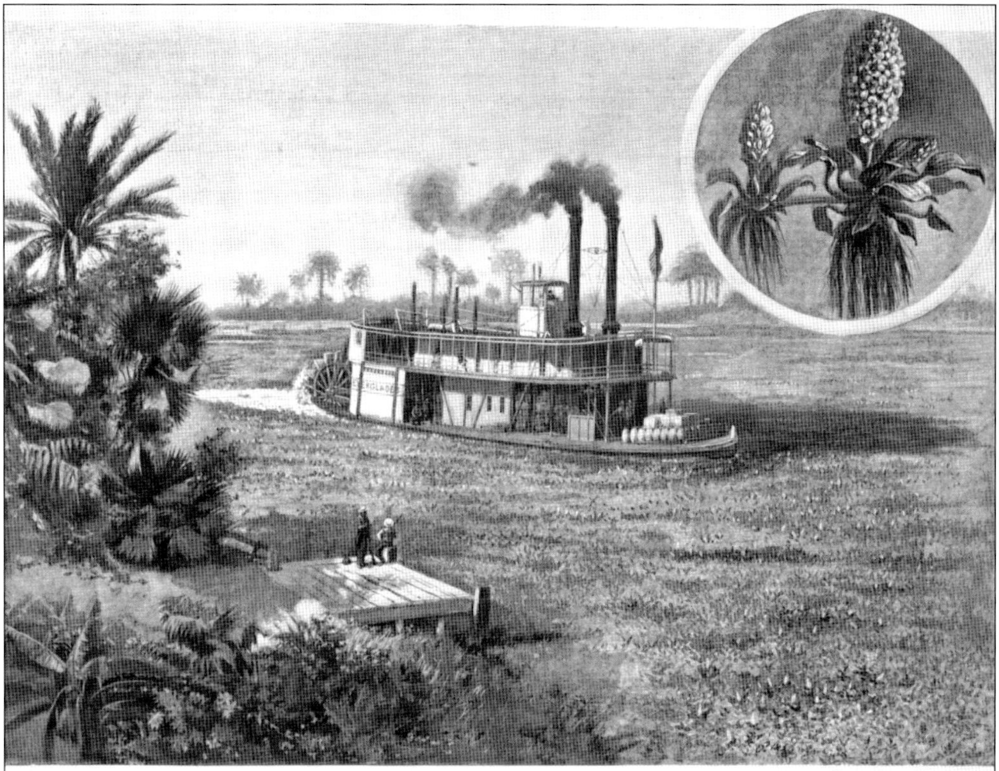

WATER-HYACINTHS IN THE ST. JOHNS RIVER, FLORIDA.

Water hyacinths originated from the Amazon in South America. They are perennial aquatic plants that float on the surface of a body of water, such as a river. The water hyacinths were introduced to the St. Johns River in the 1890s, apparently by someone who wanted to make it look more beautiful. That beauty turned into a nightmare, as the plant clogged the river due to its rapid reproduction, displacing species and blocking out sunlight for underwater plants. (State Archives of Florida.)

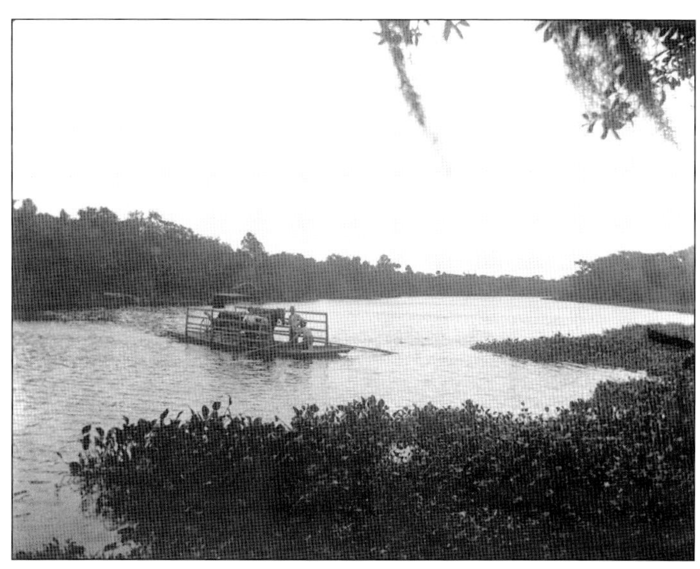

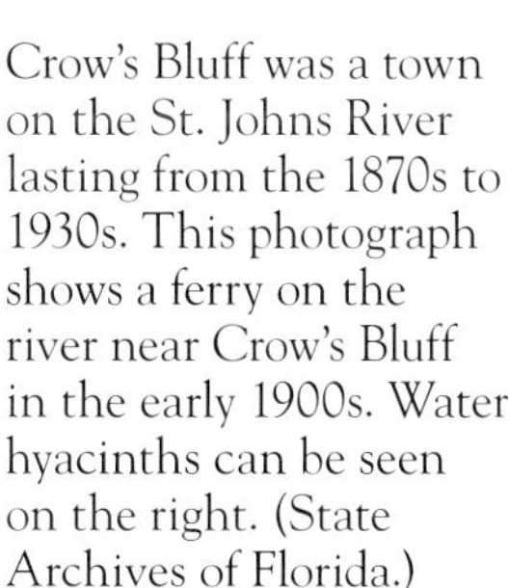

Crow's Bluff was a town on the St. Johns River lasting from the 1870s to 1930s. This photograph shows a ferry on the river near Crow's Bluff in the early 1900s. Water hyacinths can be seen on the right. (State Archives of Florida.)

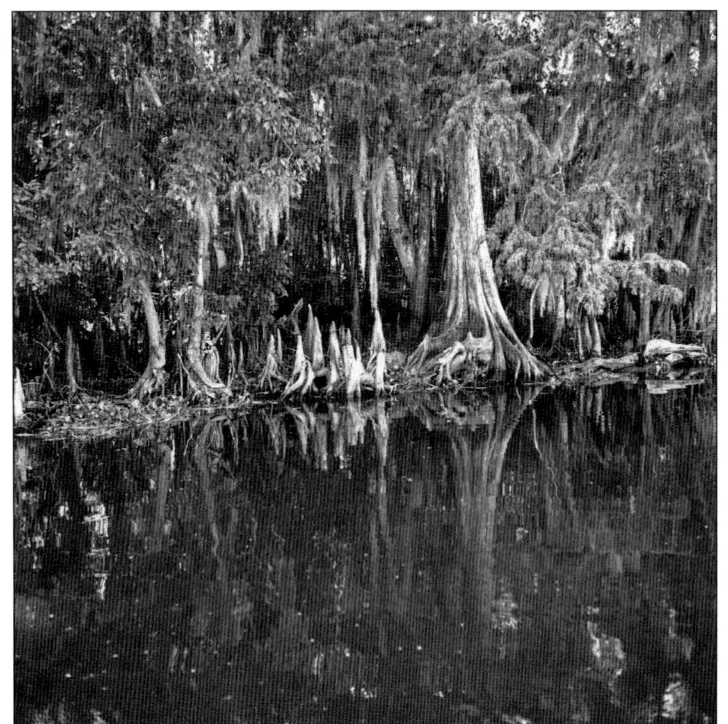

Hontoon Island is on the St. Johns River near Blue Springs. The Mayaca Native Americans were the first inhabitants of the island, possibly as far back as 12,000 years. This photograph shows cypress at Hontoon Island around 1970. (State Archives of Florida.)

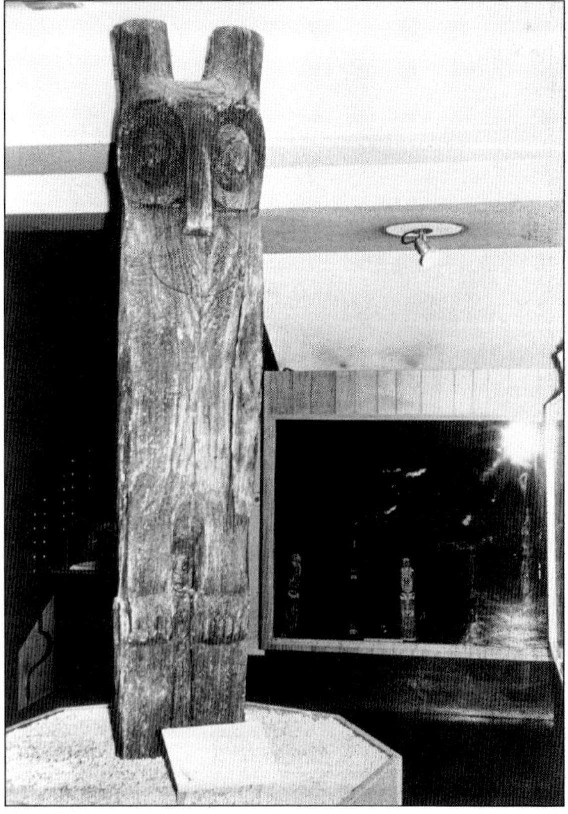

In 1955, a 10-foot owl totem pole was found in the St. Johns River near Hontoon Island. The totem pole was first believed to have been made by the Timucua Native Americans. However, the Mayaca are now believed to have made it. The totem pole was possibly made around 1350. This photograph from 1955 shows the totem pole on display at Fort Caroline National Memorial in Jacksonville. A replica is on display at Hontoon Island. (State Archives of Florida.)

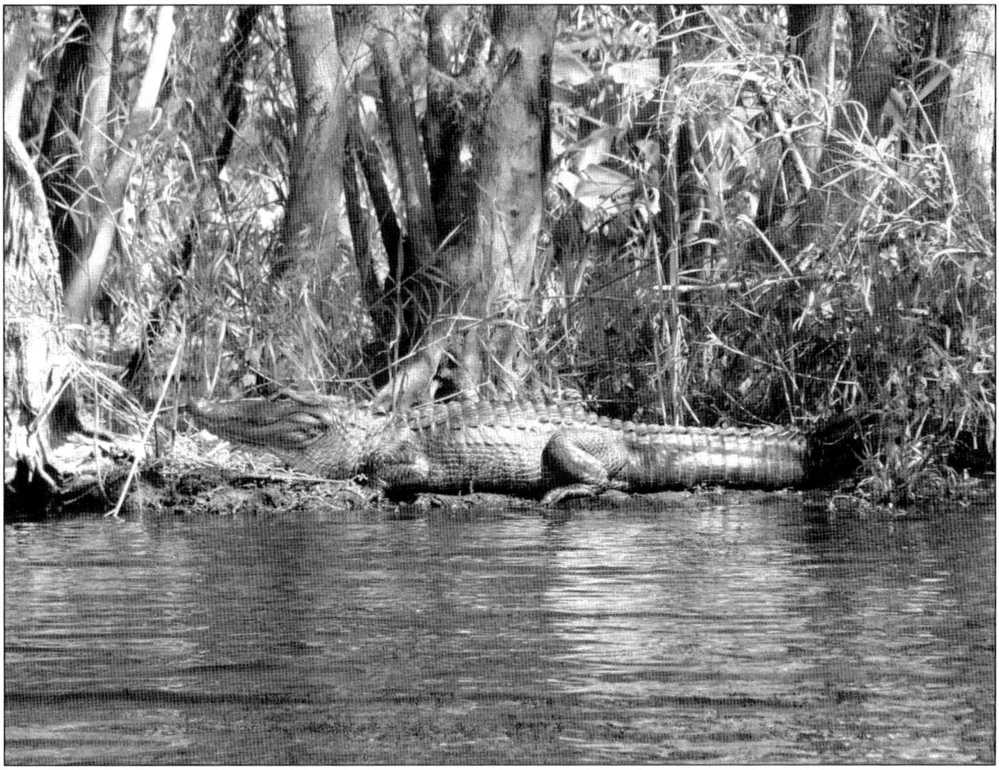

The American alligator can be found in the southeastern United States, mainly in Louisiana and Florida. They are estimated to have first appeared around 65 million years ago when dinosaurs roamed the earth. In the wild, they can live anywhere from 35 to 50 years old. With an average weight of around 1,000 pounds and a size of over 10 feet, they must be admired from afar. This photograph shows an alligator on the banks of the St. Johns River near Hontoon Island in 2016. (Alice Kiger.)

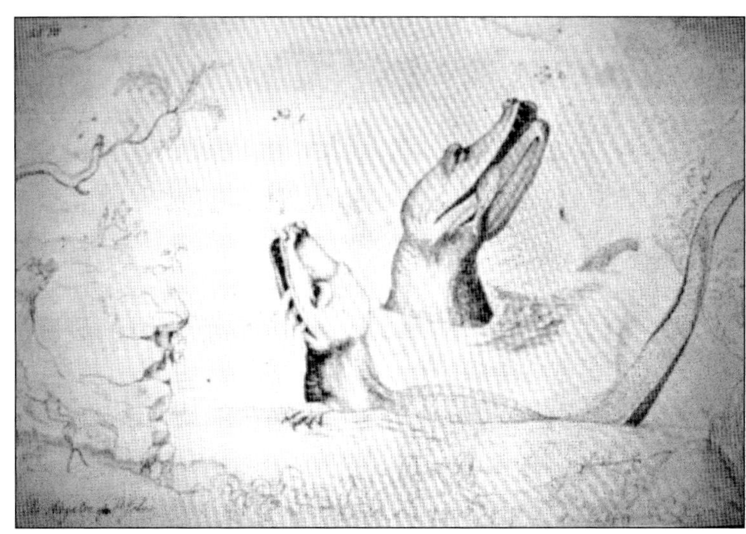

In spring 1774, William Bartram explored the St. Johns River in a dugout canoe. Bartram saw alligators near Lake Dexter and Lake George. He was attacked and almost killed while he was preparing his trout for dinner. Bartram made a sketch of the alligators he saw for his book *Travels*, published in 1791. (Library of Congress.)

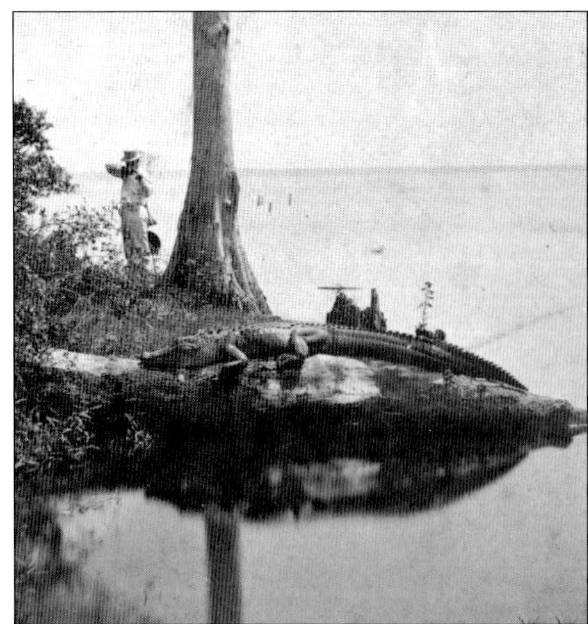

The American alligator was once on the brink of extinction. From the 1800s to the mid-1900s, it was hunted for its skin to make leather and poached for meat. This photograph shows a man pointing a rifle at an alligator on the St. Johns River in the 1880s. The Endangered Species Act of 1973 prohibited the hunting of alligators. By 1987, the alligator had recovered and was removed from the endangered species list. (Clay County Archives.)

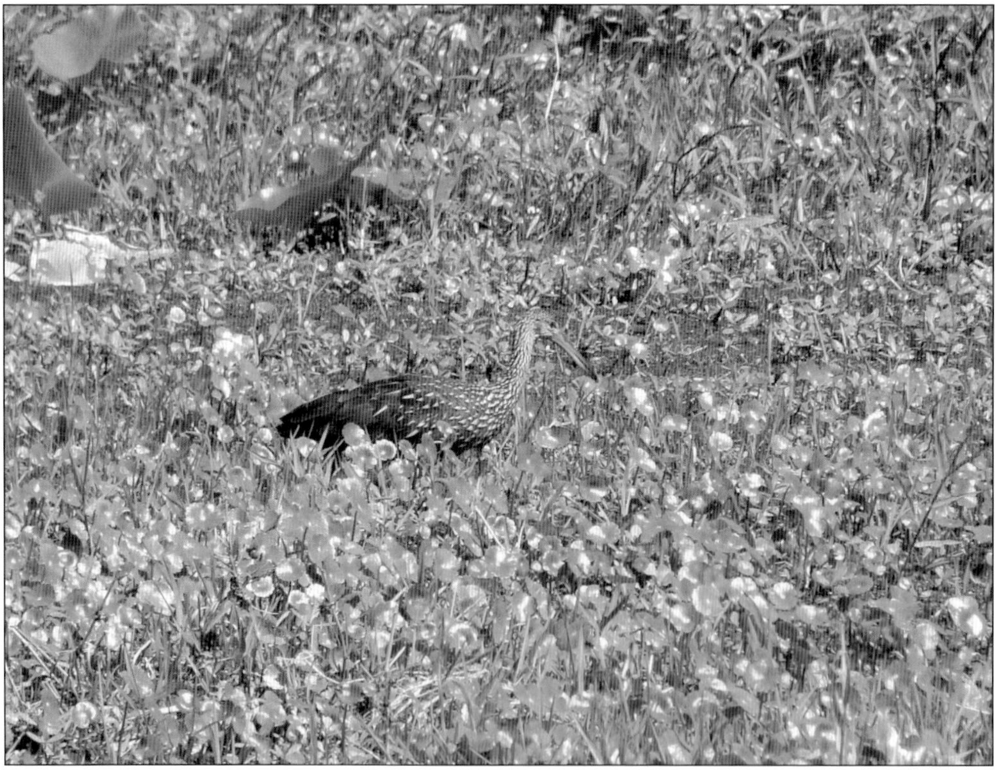

Limpkins can be found in South America, Central America, and the Caribbean. In the United States, the limpkin can only be found in Florida and southeastern Georgia. They were almost extinct in Florida in the early 20th century due to overhunting, but conservation efforts ensured their recovery. This photograph shows a limpkin wading through the St. Johns River near Hontoon Island in 2016. (Alice Kiger.)

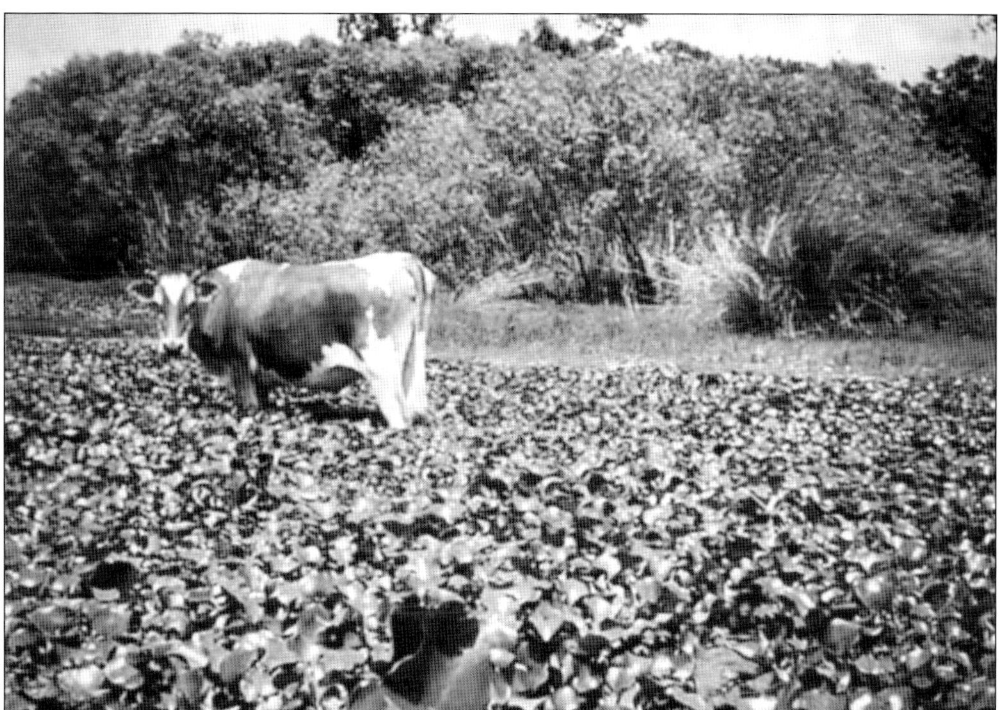

This photograph shows a cow among water hyacinths in the St. Johns River near Blue Springs in 1957. Despite the water hyacinth being an invasive plant, the cow has no concerns and continues strolling on the river. (Stetson University.)

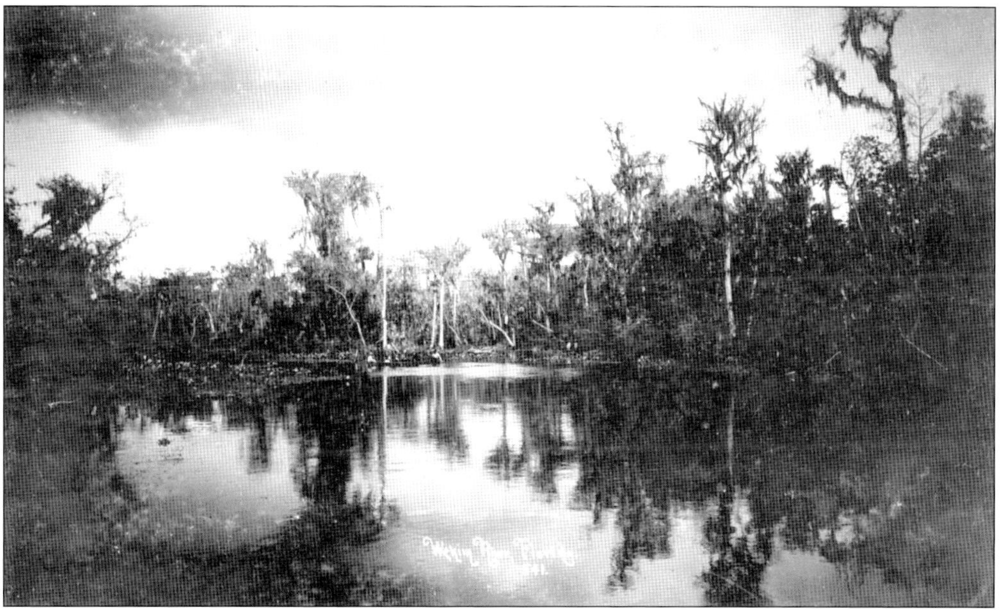

The 16-mile-long Wekiva River originates in Wekiva Springs east of Apopka. It flows north, joining the St. Johns River between Blue Springs and Lake Monroe. This photograph shows the Wekiva River in 1898. (University of South Florida.)

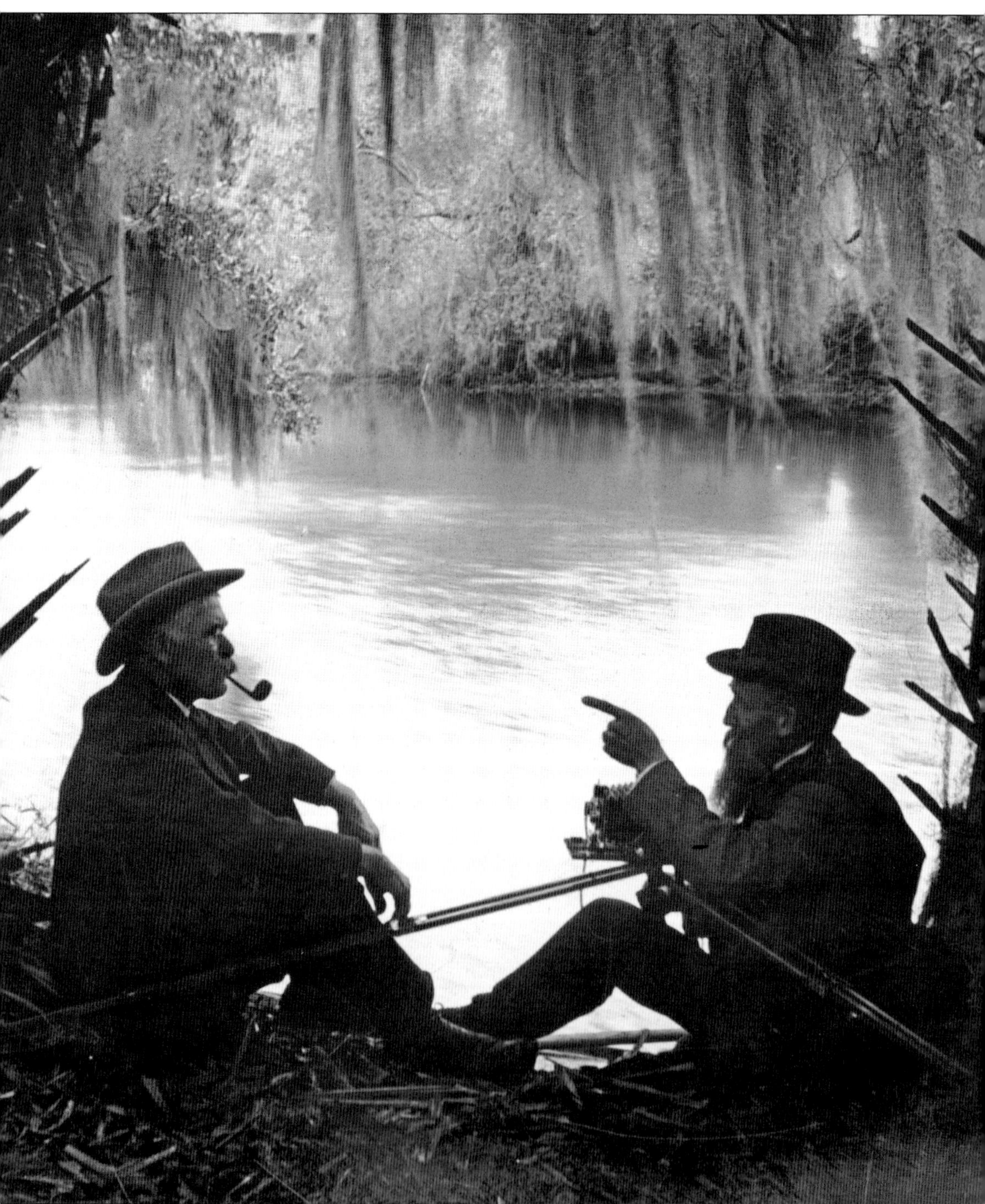

Blue Springs is connected to the St. Johns River near Orange City. The springs are the largest of the St. Johns and stay at a temperature of 72 degrees. John Bartram, father of William Bartram, visited Blue Springs in 1766 but was not too impressed with it. This photograph shows two men sitting under Spanish moss at Blue Springs in 1905. (Library of Congress.)

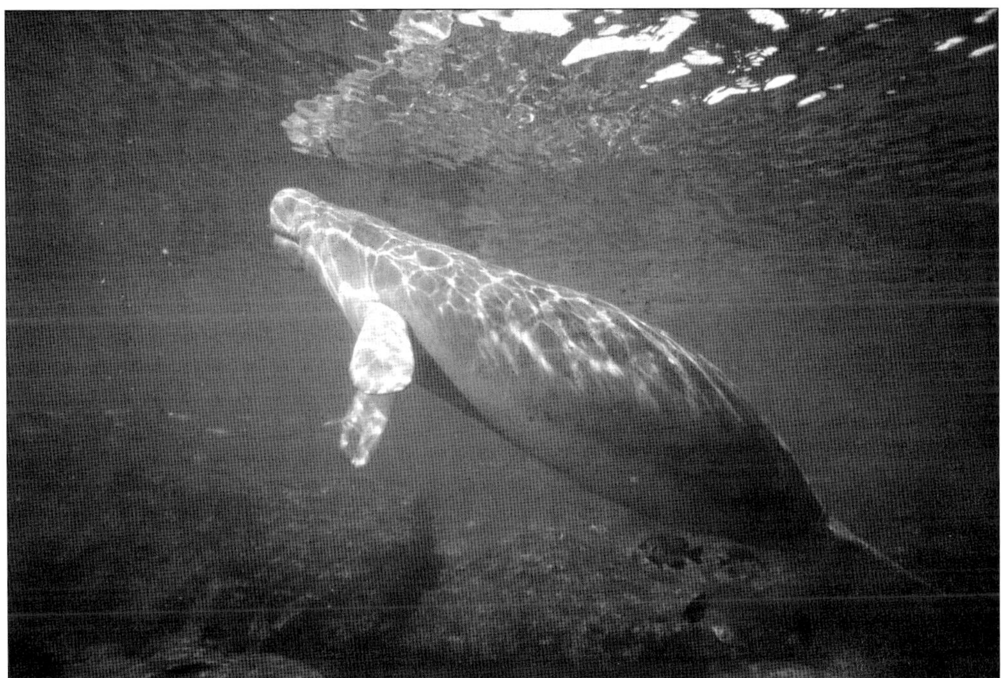

Blue Springs is notable for an abundance of manatees; it has been designated a manatee refuge as well as their winter home. An episode of *The Undersea World of Jacques Cousteau* called "The Forgotten Mermaids" was filmed at Blue Springs in 1971. The episode brought renewed attention to the manatee and Blue Springs, which influenced the State of Florida's decision to acquire the park. This photograph shows manatees at Blue Springs. (State Archives of Florida.)

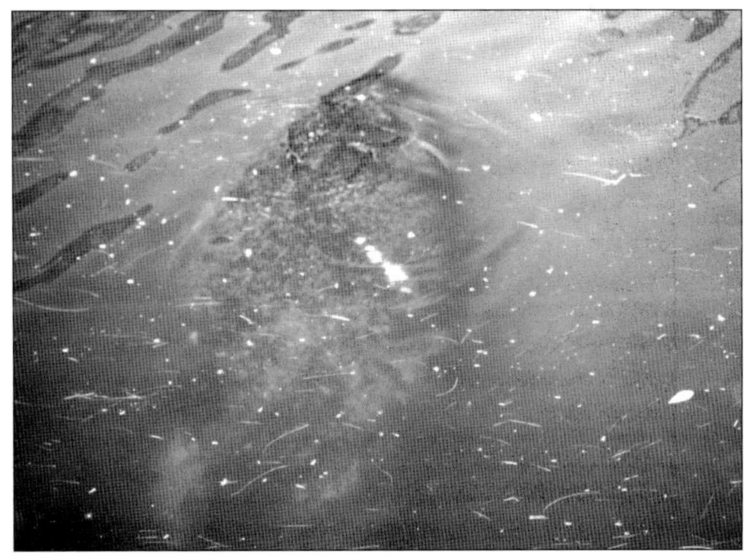

Manatees are large aquatic herbivorous mammals. The three subspecies are West Indian, West African, and Amazonian. The Florida manatee and Antillean manatee in the Caribbean are subspecies of the West African manatee. This photograph shows a Florida manatee at Blue Springs in 1986. (State Archives of Florida.)

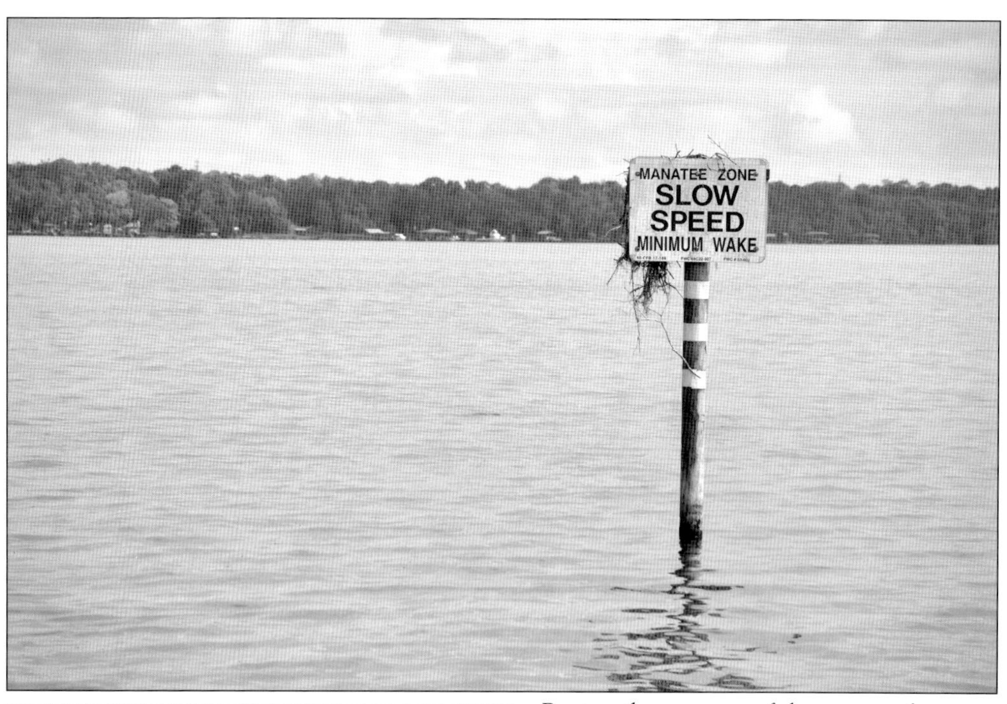

Boat strikes are one of the reasons for the decline in manatees. Many Florida manatees have been hit by boats. To reduce boat strikes, there are a number of boat speed zone signs on the St. Johns River. This photograph shows a manatee zone minimum wake sign at Doctors Lake. (Andrew R. Nicholas.)

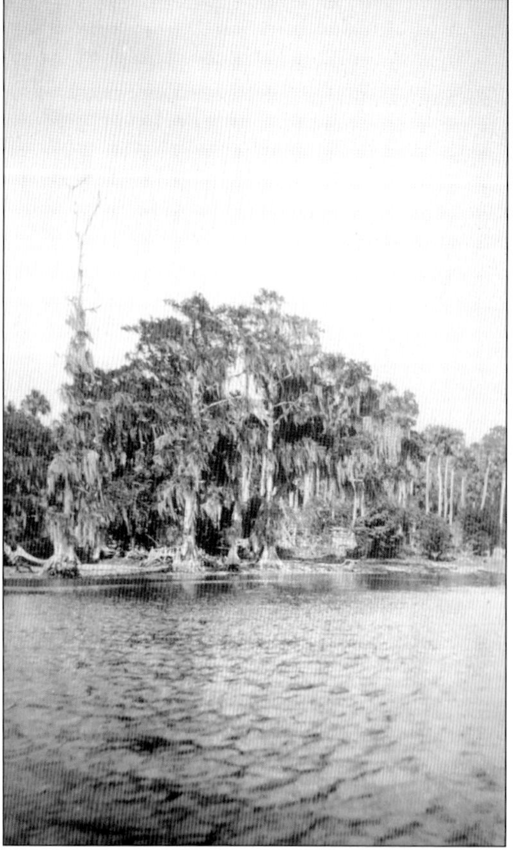

The St. Johns River traveling south past Lake Dexter becomes more snakelike as it twists left to right until reaching Lake Monroe. The river also stays roughly 400 feet wide until passing through the chain of lakes in central Florida. This photograph shows a tree on the St. Johns before entering Lake Monroe. (Stetson University.)

Six

Last of the Line

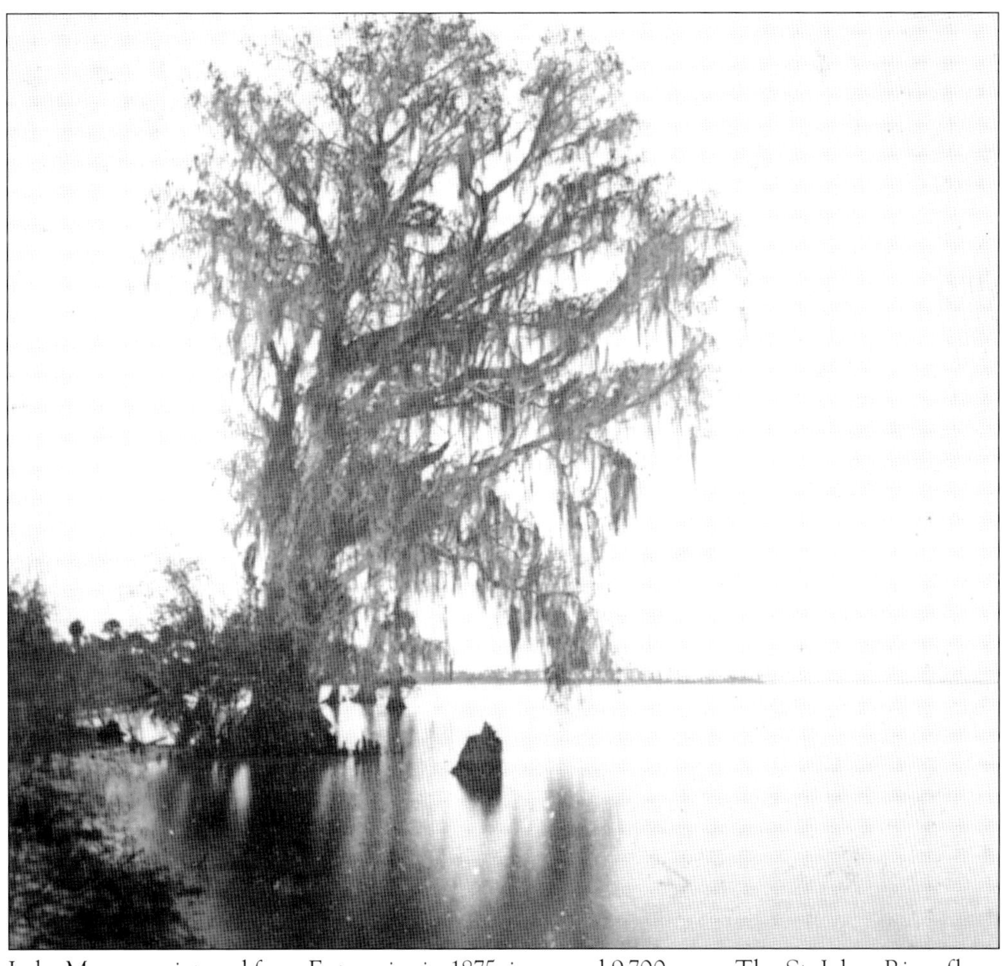

Lake Monroe, pictured from Enterprise in 1875, is around 9,700 acres. The St. Johns River flows into the lake from its eastern side and out through its western side. (New York Public Library.)

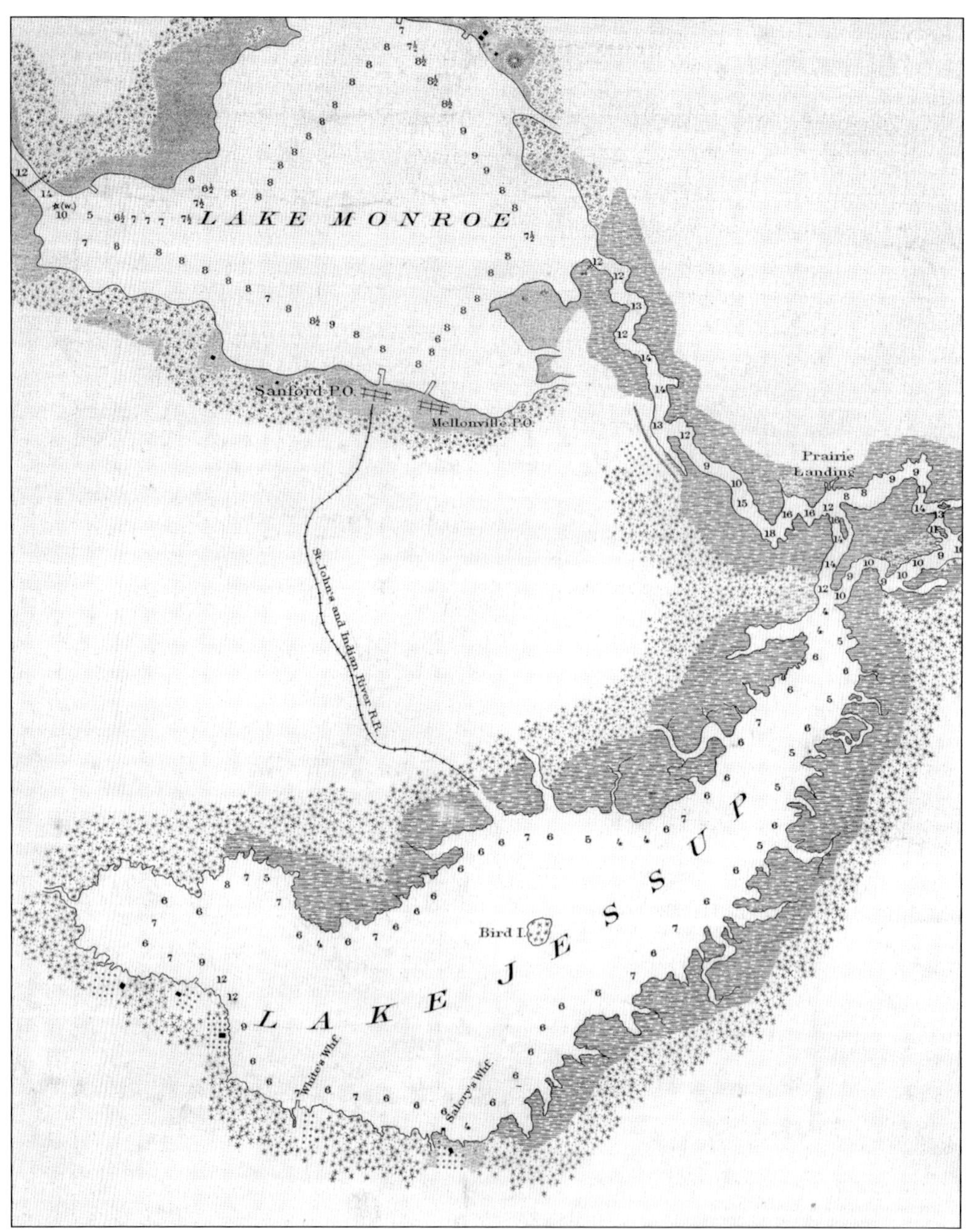

This map shows the St. Johns River flowing through Lake Jesup and Lake Monroe. Lake Monroe is named after Pres. James Monroe, and Lake Jesup is named after Brig. Gen. Thomas Jesup, who served in the Seminole War. (State Archives of Florida.)

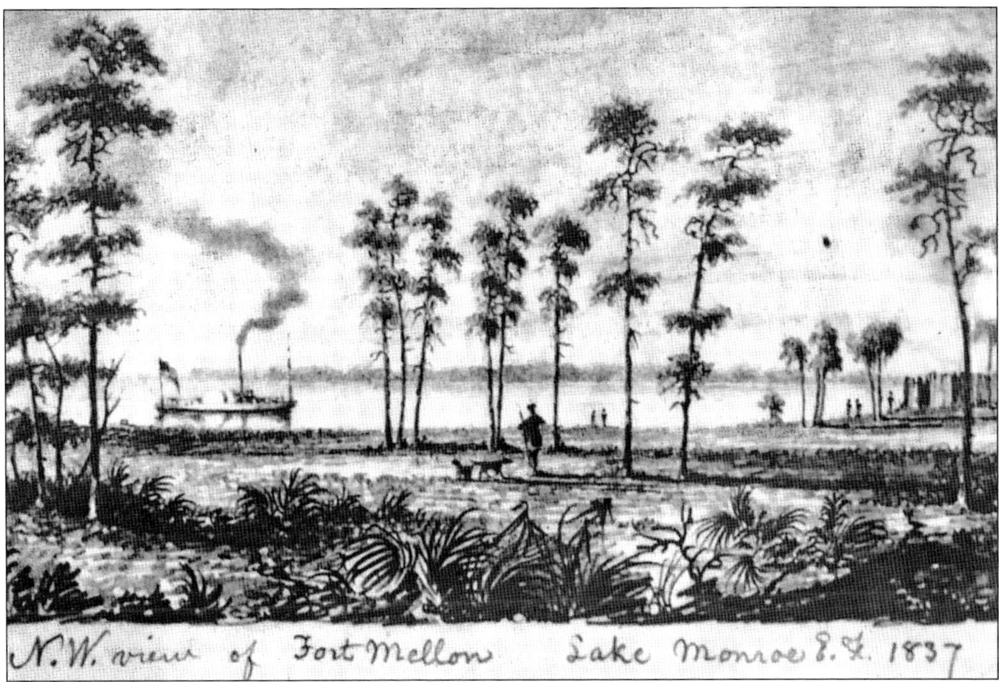

In 1836, Fort Monroe was established on the southern end of Lake Monroe during the Seminole War. On February 8, 1837, a force of Seminole warriors attacked the fort and killed Capt. Charles Melon. The next day, the fort was renamed Fort Melon in honor of him. This sketch shows Fort Mellon with a steamship on Lake Monroe in 1837. After the fort was abandoned, the area later became the town of Mellonville. (Library of Congress.)

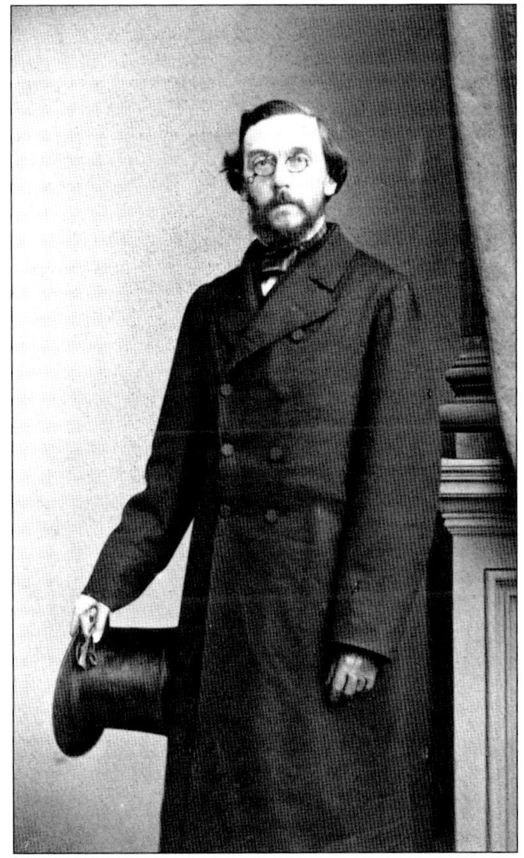

Henry Shelton Sanford was born on June 15, 1823, in Woodbury, Connecticut. In 1847, he began his diplomatic career as secretary of the American legation to Saint Petersburg, Russia, and then in Paris from 1849 to 1855. In 1861, Pres. Abraham Lincoln appointed Sanford US ambassador to Belgium, serving for eight years. In 1870, Sanford embarked on an ambitious project in central Florida by acquiring over 12,000 acres west of Mellonville on Lake Monroe. This photograph shows Sanford around 1865. (Library of Congress.)

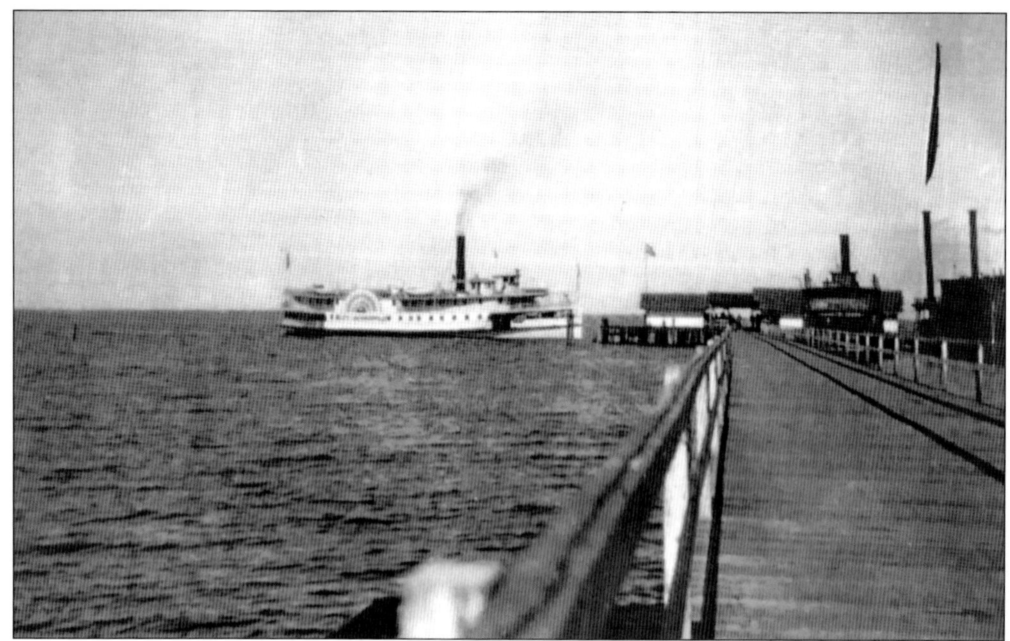

Steamships were popular on the St. Johns River in the 1870s and 1880s. The steamship lines that operated from Sanford to Jacksonville were Brock Line, Debary Line, Merchant Line, Debary-Baya Merchant Line, and Clyde St. John Line. This photograph shows a steamship at the wharf in Sanford. (West Volusia Historical Society.)

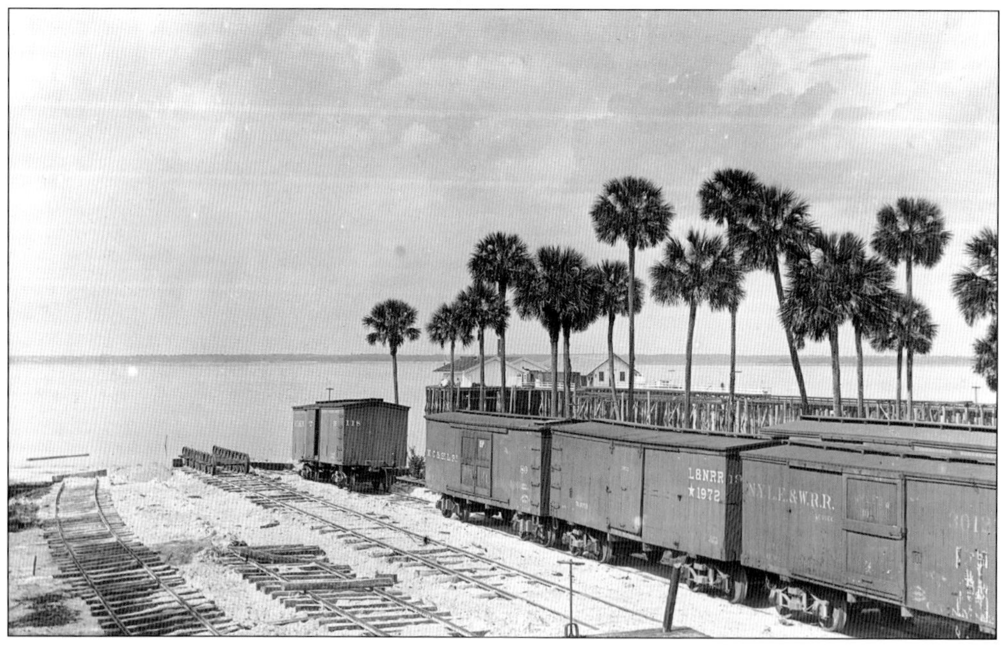

The South Florida Railroad connected Tampa with Sanford in the 1880s and later became the Jacksonville, Tampa, and Key West Railroad. The railroad gradually became the preferred method of transportation over the steamship. This photograph shows the South Florida Railroad depot on Lake Monroe at Sanford in 1883. (State Archives of Florida.)

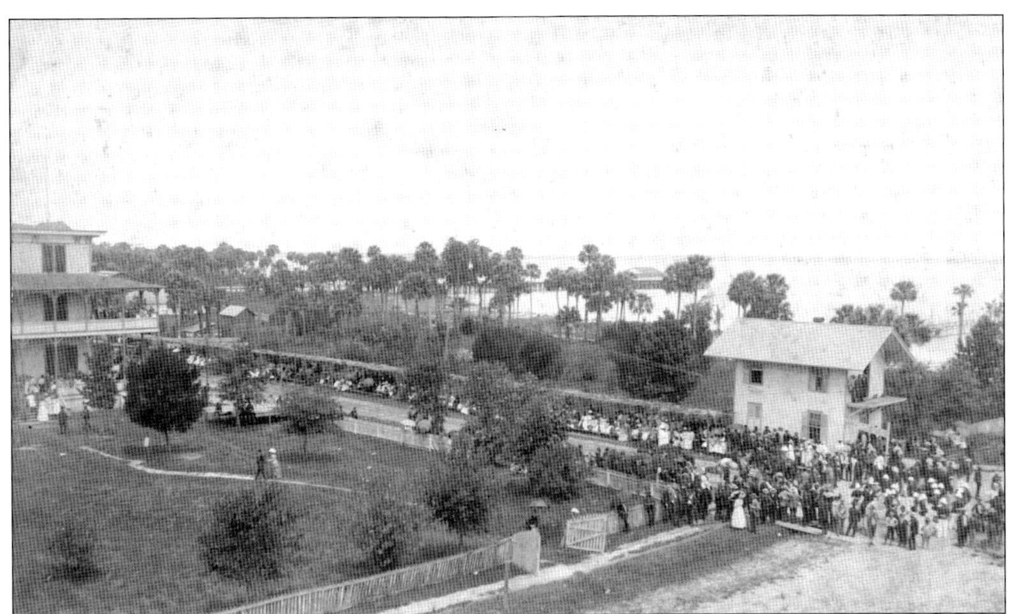

This photograph shows downtown Sanford with Lake Monroe in the distance in 1887. The people are celebrating the Fourth of July. (Florida Historical Society.)

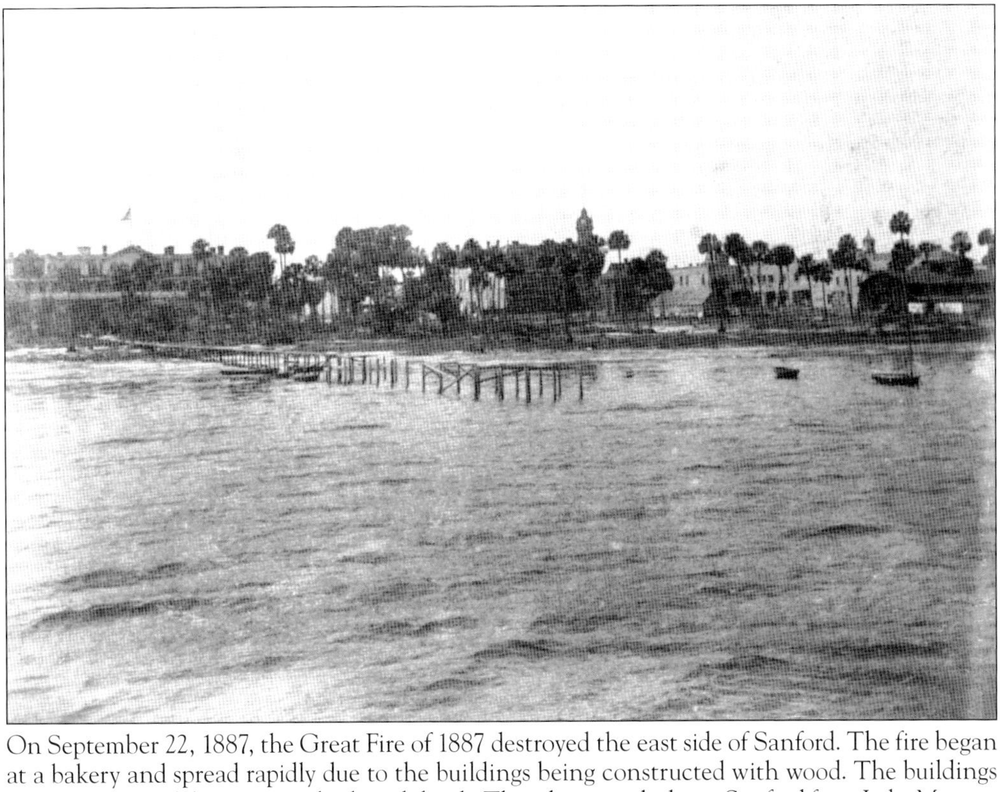

On September 22, 1887, the Great Fire of 1887 destroyed the east side of Sanford. The fire began at a bakery and spread rapidly due to the buildings being constructed with wood. The buildings that were burned down were rebuilt with brick. This photograph shows Sanford from Lake Monroe in 1892. (State Archives of Florida.)

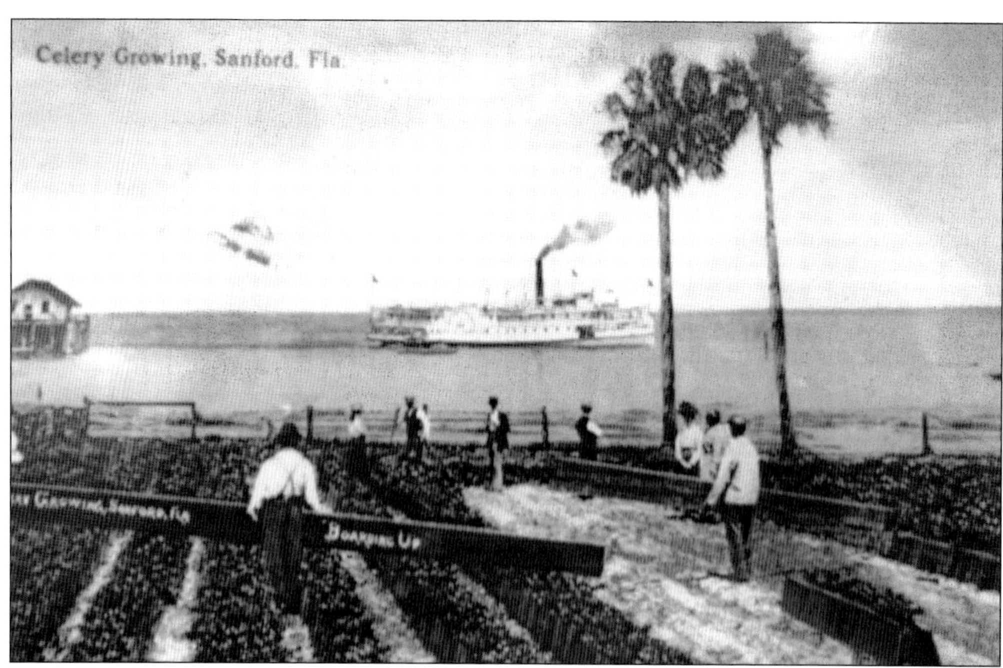

The Great Freeze of 1894–1895 severely hurt the citrus industry of Florida. Farmers in the area decided to diversify and began planting celery in 1896. This postcard of Sanford shows farmers growing celery by Lake Monroe in the early 20th century. (West Volusia Historical Society.)

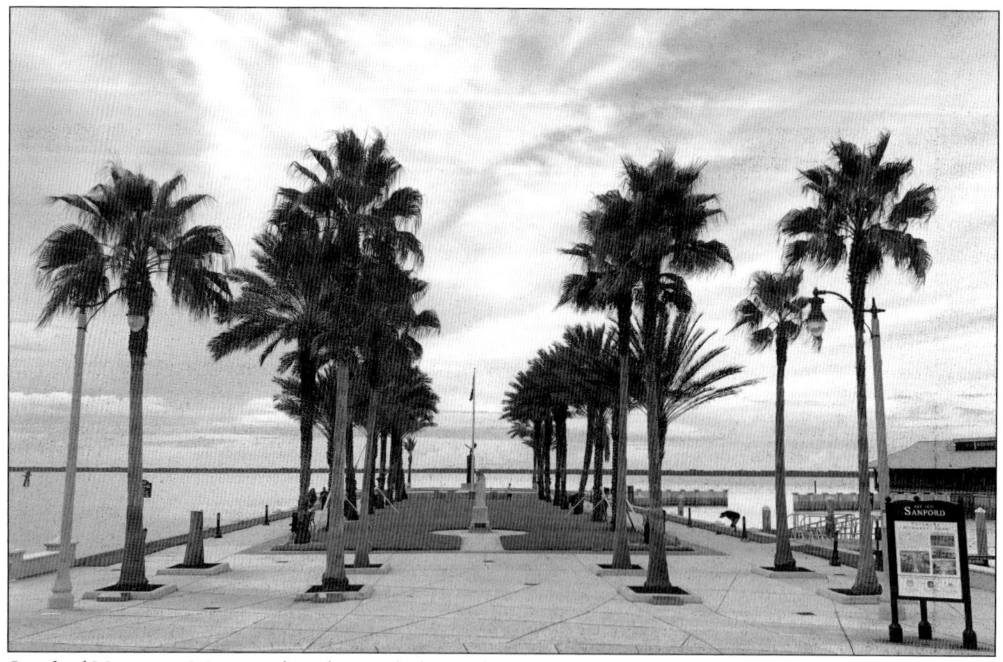

Sanford Veterans Memorial Park was dedicated in 1927. The park was first dedicated to the fallen veterans of World War I. In 1973 it was rededicated to all veterans. The park once had a concrete bandshell, but it was removed in the 1970s. The park was renovated in the 2000s and rededicated in 2006. (Sarah A. Nicholas.)

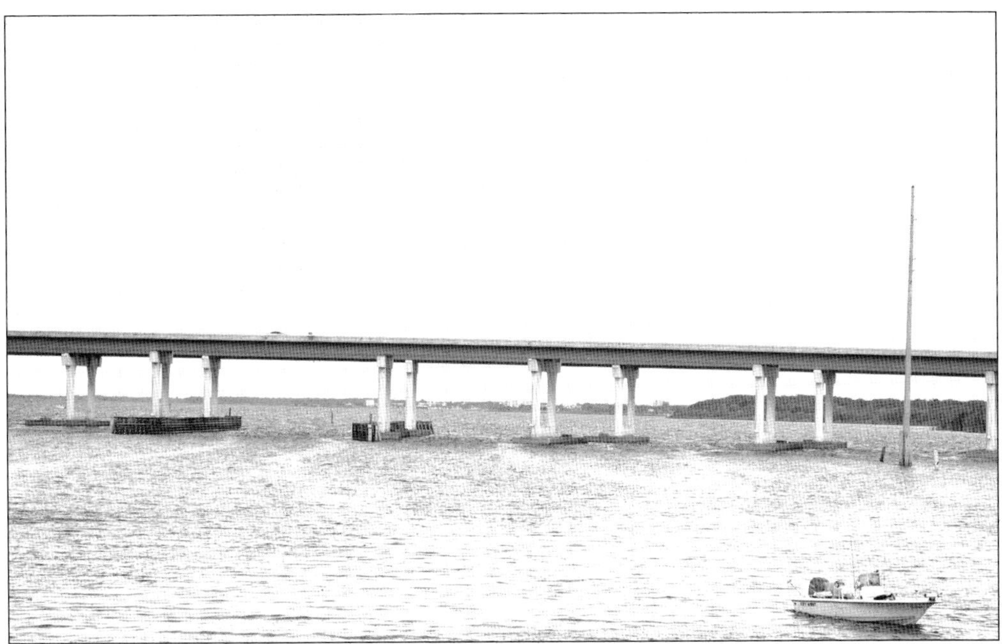

The St. Johns Veteran Memorial Bridge is two three-lane bridges carrying Interstate 4. This photograph shows the bridge going over the St. Johns River in 2022 with Sanford in the distance. (Sarah A. Nicholas.)

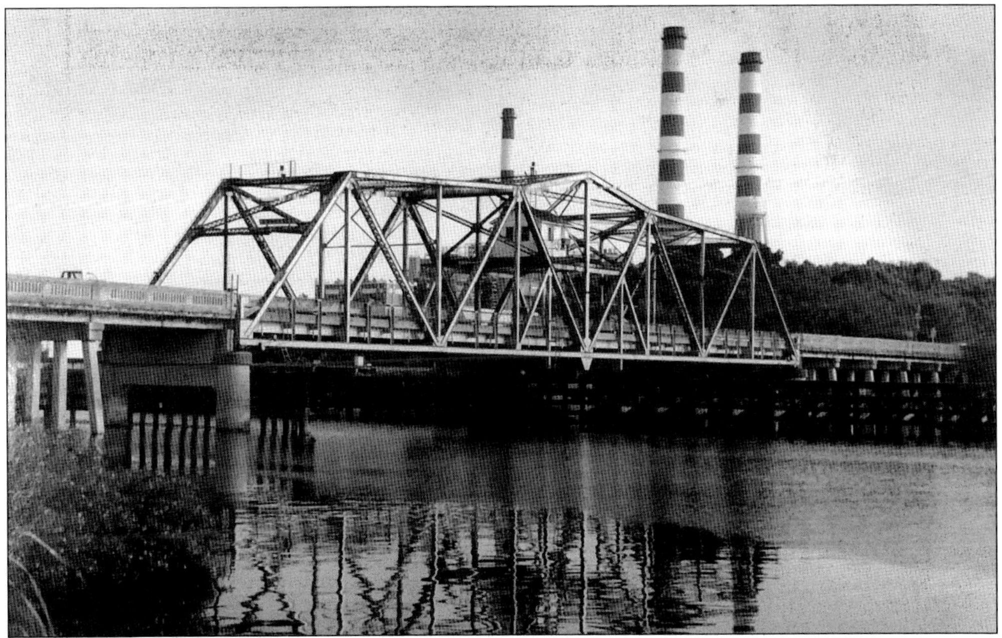

The Lake Monroe Bridge was a two-lane steel swing bridge built in 1934 for commuters to cross the St. Johns River on the western side of Lake Monroe. It is pictured in the 1960s. The bridge was later deemed inadequate to handle the number of commuters and closed in 1994. It was partially dismantled, leaving only a small portion still intact for use as a pier or lookout. In 2001, Kenny Chesney filmed a video for his song "Young" on the bridge. (West Volusia Historical Society.)

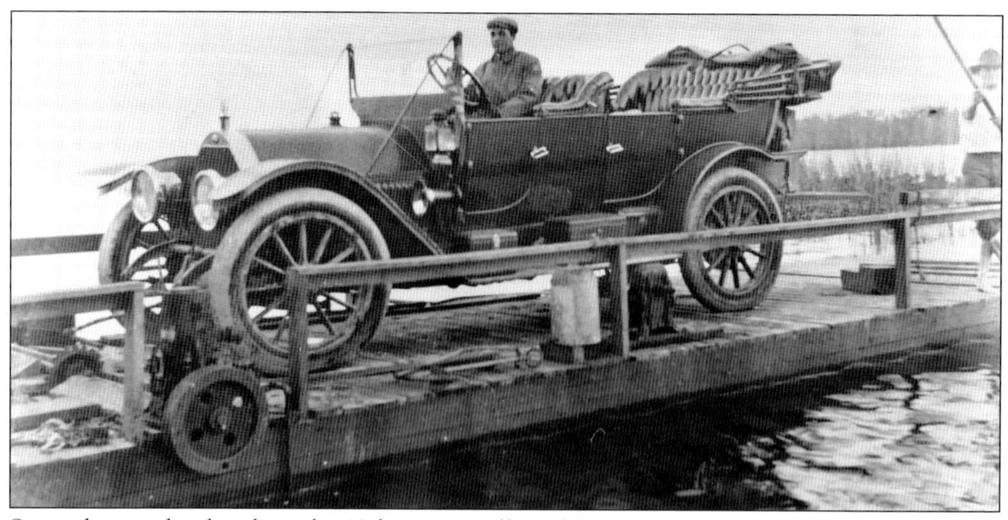

Steamships and railroads in the 19th century allowed for easier transportation into the interior of Florida. In the 20th century, the automobile gradually became the preferred way of travel, including at Sanford. Ferries that once carried only people and goods began to make room for the automobile. This photograph from 1912 shows a ferry at the mouth of Lake Monroe near Sanford with an automobile. (West Volusia Historical Society.)

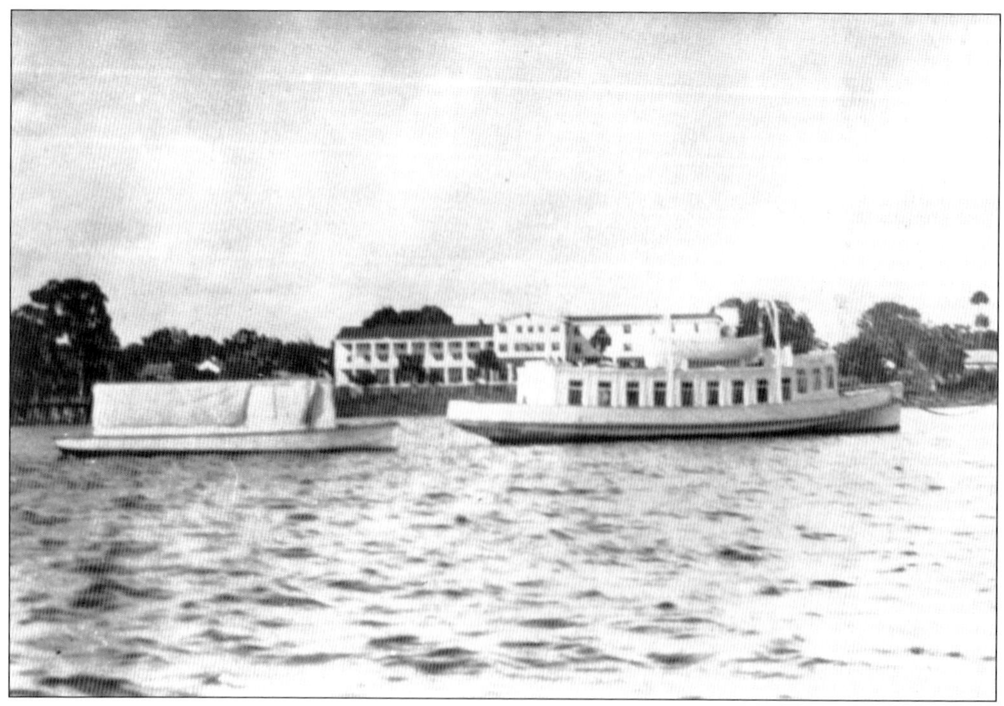

Enterprise is a small community on the north side of Lake Monroe. This photograph shows the ferries *Alma May* and *Nettie* docked at Enterprise. (State Archives of Florida.)

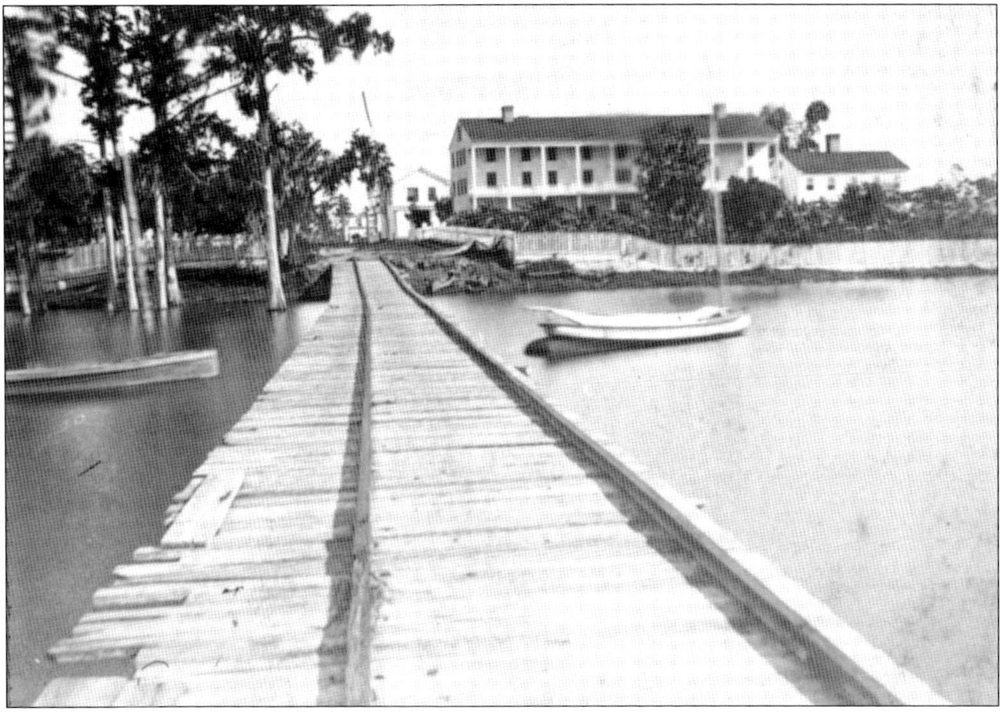

Capt. Jacob Brock began purchasing land in 1851 on Lake Monroe. In 1856, he completed building a 100-room hotel on the lake at Enterprise. His hotel was called the Brock House, and it made Enterprise a popular destination for steamboat travel. This photograph shows the Brock House on Lake Monroe in 1875. (New York Public Library.)

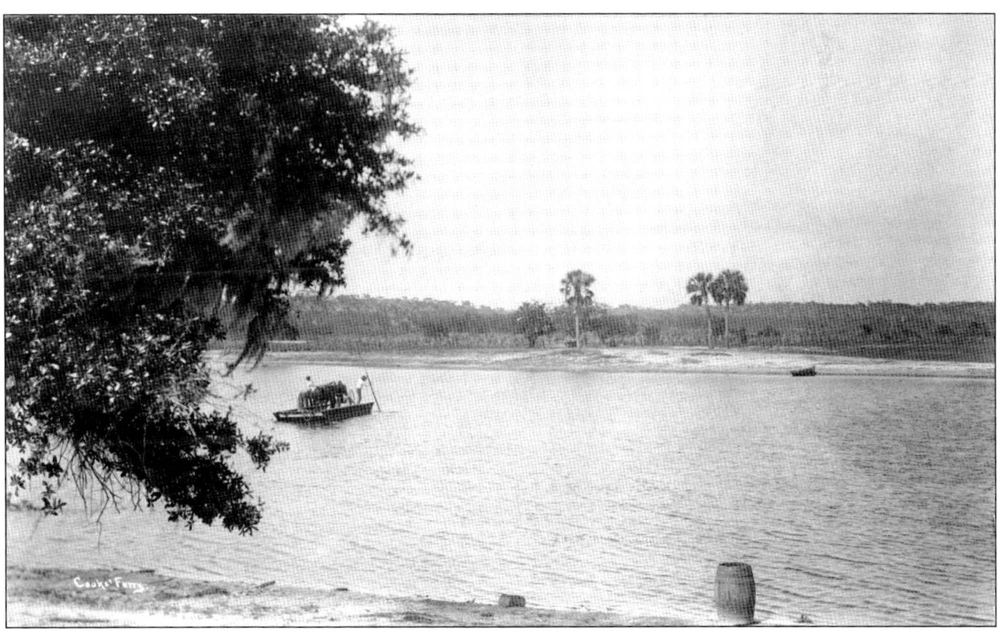

Around 1850, a man named Cook operated a ferry on the northern end of Lake Harney. The location later became known as Cook's Ferry, pictured here around 1870. (State Archives of Florida.)

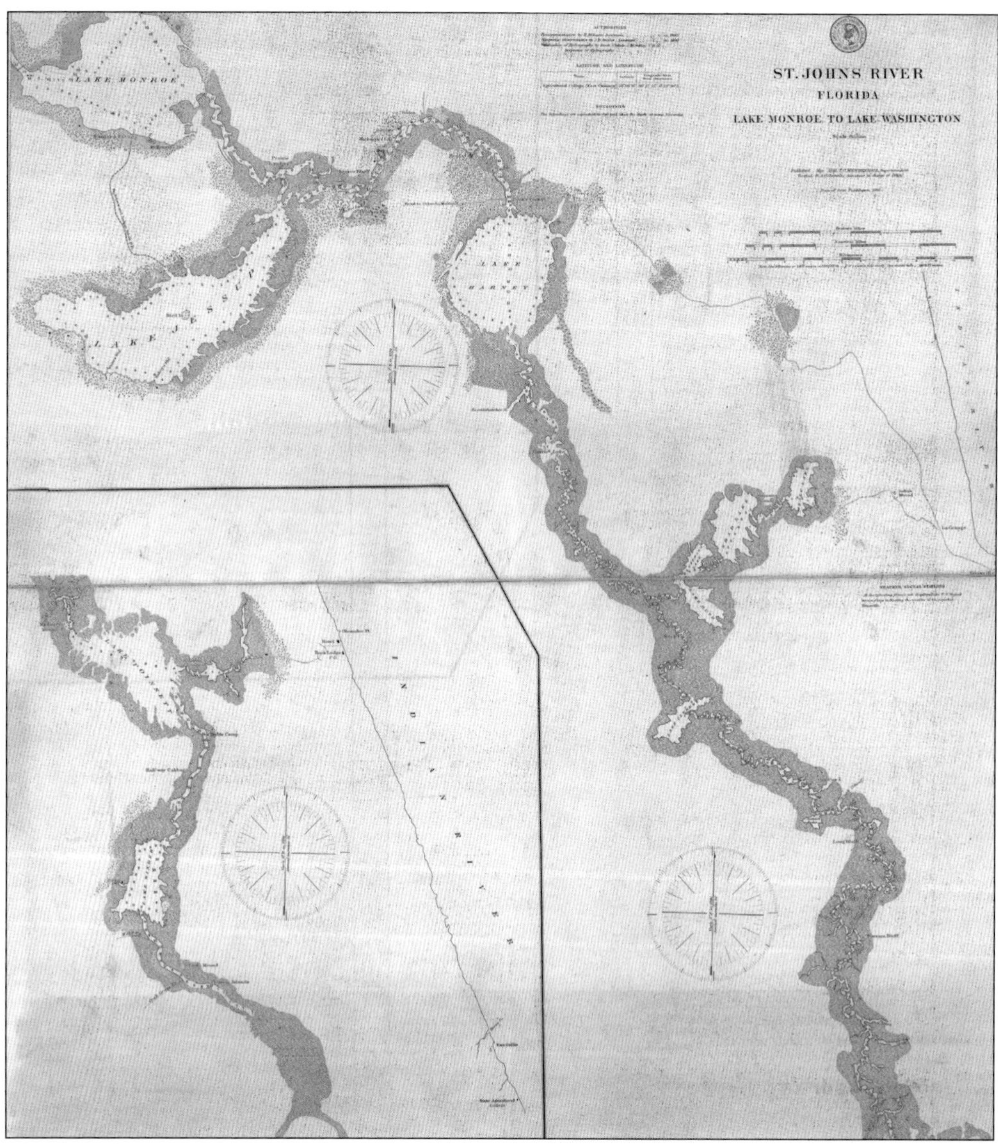

This map from 1891 shows the St. Johns River flowing north through Lake Washington, Lake Winder, Poinsett Lake, Lake Clement, Puzzle Lake, Lake Harney, Lake Jesup, and Lake Monroe. Lake Washington is barely visible at lower left. The Econlahatchee River can be seen flowing into the St. Johns between Puzzle Lake and Lake Harney. The Econlahatchee is a 54.5-mile blackwater tributary of the St. Johns. (State Archives of Florida.)

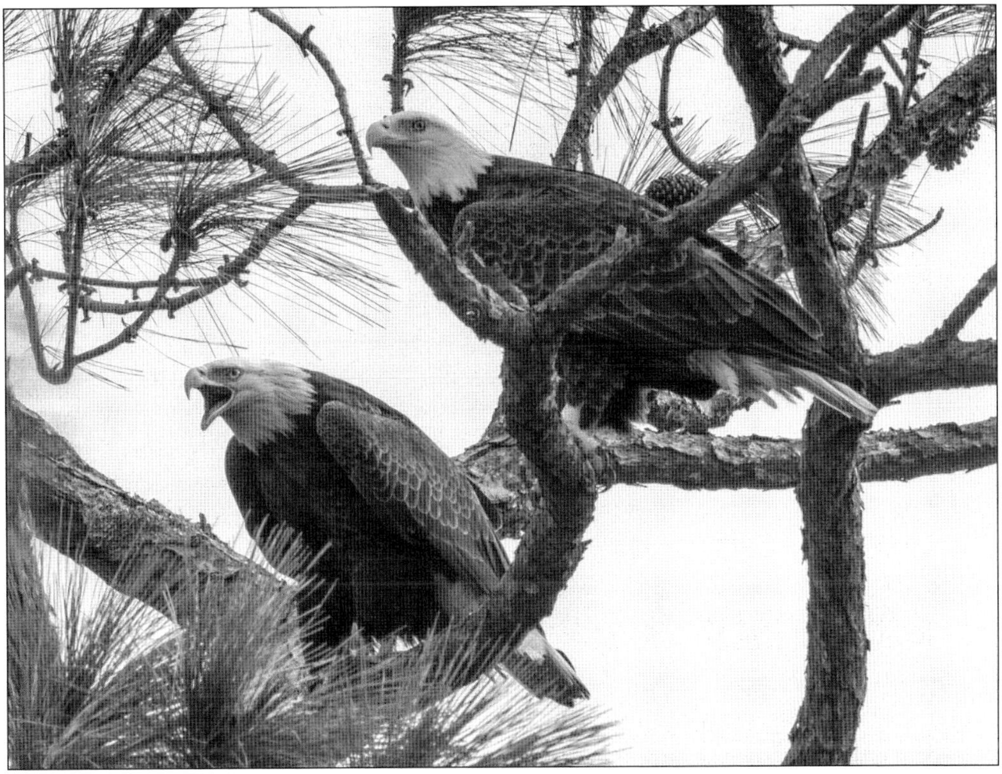

The bald eagle can be found throughout North America. According to the Florida Fish and Wildlife Conservation Commission, Florida has one of the densest concentrations of nesting bald eagles outside of Alaska. The estimated number of nesting pairs in Florida is around 1,500. This photograph shows two bald eagles in a tree at Lake Harney in 2017. (Thomas Lynch.)

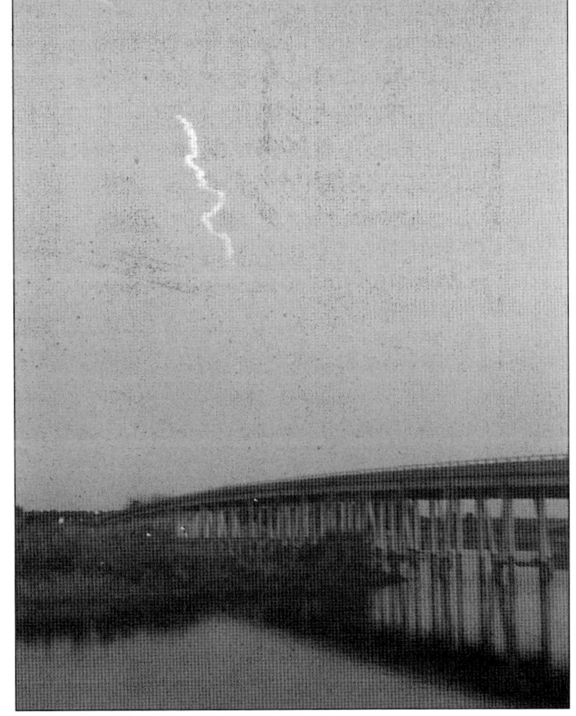

C.S. Lee Park is on the St. Johns River near the southern end of Lake Harney. County Road 46 can be seen in this photograph going over the river. The object in the sky is from a SpaceX launch at nearby Cape Canaveral in 2013. (Greg Pflug.)

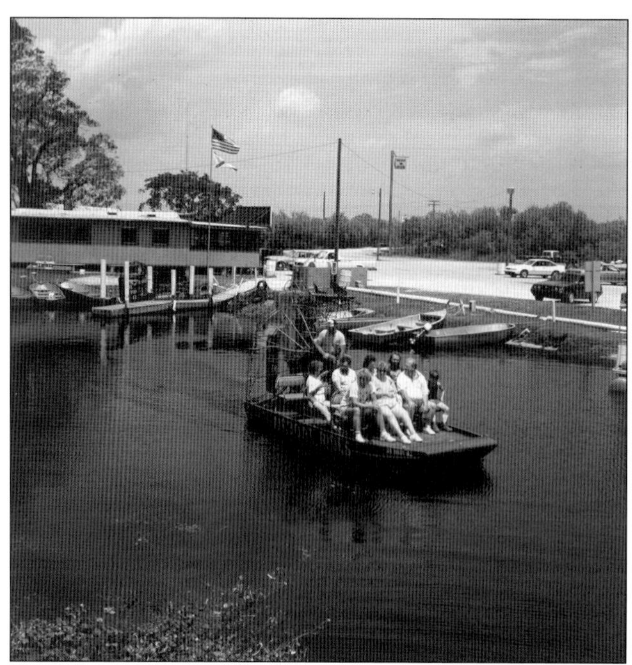

The Upper St. Johns River contains a vast amount of marshes, lakes, and a narrower river compared to the bigger area of the Lower St. Johns. The airboat allows easier access to these areas. Benny Rotgers was the first to build an airboat for use on the Upper St. Johns. Rotgers's airboat was a 16-foot tongue-and-groove cypress barge with a Ford Model A 45-horsepower engine. Today, there are a number of airboat businesses along the St. Johns for anyone wanting to take a tour of the river and get a close encounter with its wildlife. This photograph shows Camp Holly Airboat Rides in the 1980s. (State Archives of Florida.)

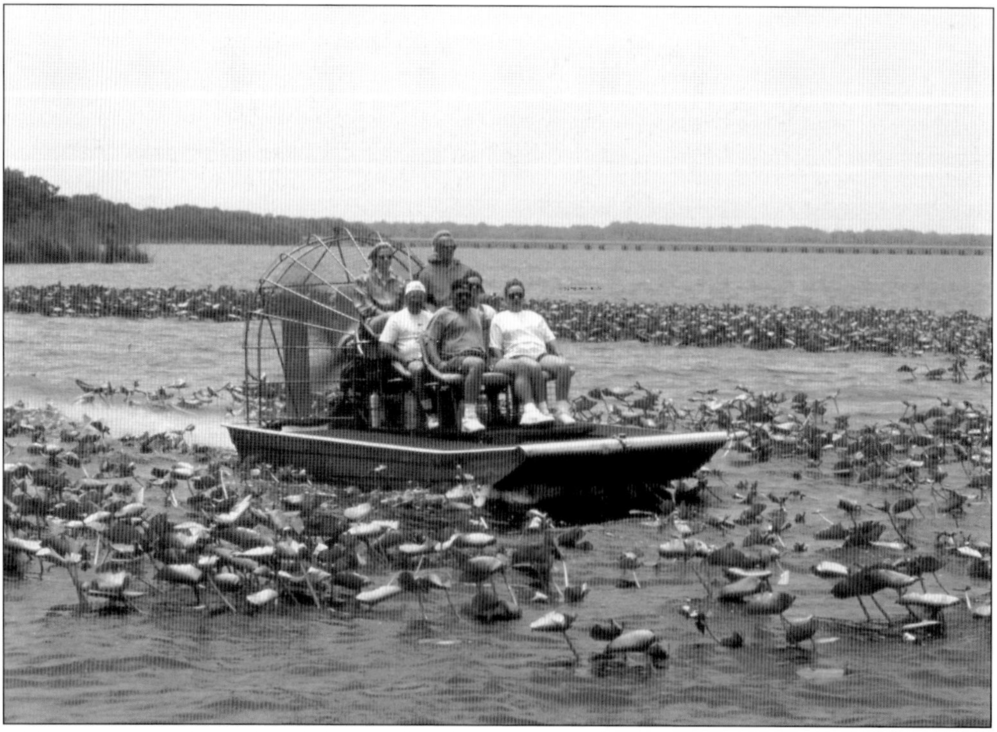

This photograph shows Black Hammock Orlando Airboat Rides on Lake Jesup in the 1980s. The bridge in the background is the Lake Jesup Bridge. (State Archives of Florida.)

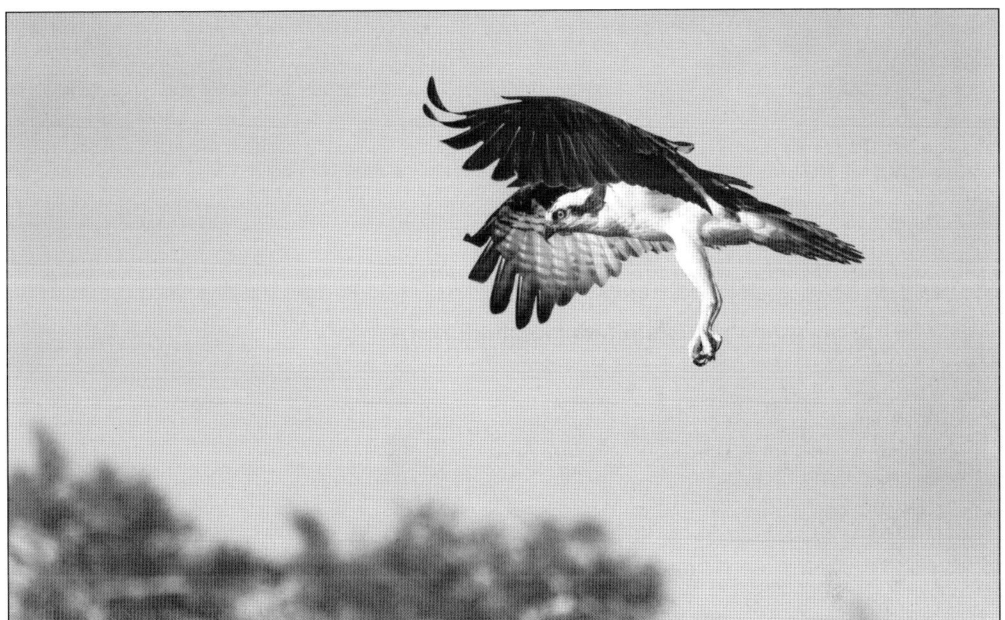

This photograph shows an osprey diving into Blue Cypress Lake in 2017. The mascot for the University of North Florida is the osprey. (Jennifer Lanam.)

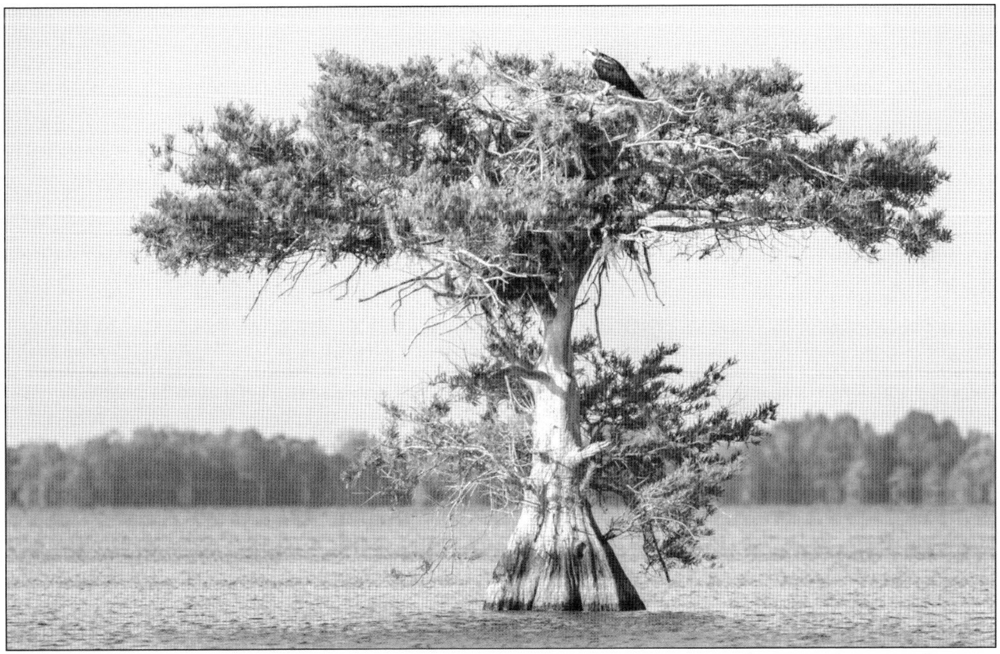

Blue Cypress Lake is the first lake where the St. Johns River begins to flow north. Once known as Lake Wilmington, it is 6,555 acres containing a number of cypress domes with a sawgrass marsh habitat on the eastern side. Blue Cypress Lake and the surrounding wetlands area are the headwaters of the St. Johns. Fort Drum Marsh Conservation Area is the southernmost wetlands of the river and is south of the lake. This photograph shows an osprey in a cypress tree dome on Blue Cypress Lake in 2016. (Jennifer Lanam.)